*Yale Linguistic Series*

# អក្សរសាស្ត្រខ្មែរ

# CAMBODIAN-ENGLISH GLOSSARY

*Franklin E. Huffman*

*and*

*Im Proum*

*New Haven and London, Yale University Press*

Designed by John O. C. McCrillis
and set in Baskerville type.

*Library of Congress Cataloging in Publication Data*

Huffman, Franklin E
Cambodian-English glossary.
(Yale linguistic series)

1. Khmer language—Dictionaries—English.
I. Proum, Im, joint author. II. Title. III. Series.
PL4326.H8 495.9'3'2321 76–50539
ISBN 0–300–02070–8

11 10 9 8 7 6 5 4 3 2

INTRODUCTION

This Glossary incorporates the some 4,000 vocabulary items introduced in the authors' <u>Cambodian Literary Reader</u> (Yale University Press, 1977) with the some 6,000 items contained in their two preceding volumes - <u>Intermediate Cambodian Reader</u> (Yale University Press, 1972) and <u>Cambodian System of Writing and Beginning Reader</u> (Yale University Press, 1970) - for a total of some 10,000 words. Words that are spelled irregularly or are likely to cause difficulty for the student are followed by their transcriptions.

Since this Glossary was prepared to accompany the authors' <u>Cambodian Literary Reader</u>, it cannot properly be considered a dictionary. However, in view of its rather comprehensive scope, and of the authors' attempt to provide both general and context-specific definitions, it was felt that the Cambodian-English Glossary might be independently useful as a reference work.

Cambodian dictionaries differ slightly in the order in which words are listed. The order used in this Glossary is based on that of the official two-volume <u>Cambodian Dictionary</u> of the Buddhist Institute. Words are listed <u>primarily</u> by initial consonant symbol, <u>secondarily</u> by vowel symbol, and <u>tertiarily</u> by final consonant symbol. The order of consonant symbols is as follows:

ក, ខ, គ, ឃ, ង, ច, ឆ, ជ, ឈ, ញ, ដ, ឋ, ឌ, ឍ, ណ, ត,
ថ, ទ, ធ, ន, ប, ផ, ព, ភ, ម, យ, រ, ល, វ, ស, ហ, ឡ, អ.

The order of vowel symbols is as follows:

-ា, -ិ, -ិះ, -ី, -ឹ, -ឹះ, -ឺ, -ុ, -ុះ, -ូ, -ួ, -ើ, -ឿ, -ៀ,
-េ, -េះ, -ែ, -ៃ, -ោ, -ោះ, -ៅ, -ុំ, -ំ, -ាំ, -ះ.

The order of independent vowel symbols is as follows:

ឥ, ឦ, ឧ, ឩ, ឪ, ឫ, ឬ, ឭ, ឮ, ឯ, ឰ, ឱ, ឲ, ឳ.

The following additional rules apply:

a) Words spelled with final /bɑntɑq/ ( -់ ) follow identically spelled words without a /bɑntɑq/.

b) Words spelled with a converted initial consonant symbol ( -៉ or -៊ ) follow identically spelled words without a converter.

c) Words spelled with initial ប៉ follow all words spelled with initial ប and precede all words spelled with initial ប plus a subscript.

d) Words spelled with initial ឫ and ឬ follow all words spelled with initial រ , and words spelled with initial ឭ and ឮ follow all words spelled with initial ល .

e) Words spelled with the remaining initial independent vowel symbols follow words spelled with initial អ plus the equivalent vowel symbol.

f) Words spelled with initial consonant plus subscript follow all words spelled with the same initial without a subscript.

The following abbreviations are used in the Glossary; when immediately enclosed in parentheses no periods are used.

| | | | |
|---|---|---|---|
| abbr. | Abbreviation | Lit. | Literary |
| av. | Adjectival Verb | masc. | Masculine |
| adj. | Adjective | mv. | Modal Verb |
| adv. | Adverb | n. | Noun |
| Arch. | Archaic | P. | Pali |
| Coll. | Colloquial | Pej. | Pejorative |
| conj. | Conjunction | pers.n. | Personal Name |
| Eleg. | Elegant | pl.n. | Place Name |
| Euph. | Euphemism | pl. | Plural |
| Excl. | Exclamation | Pol. | Polite |
| fem. | Feminine | p.r.p. | Polite Response Particle |
| Fig. | Figurative | pron. | Pronoun |
| Fr. | French | Roy. | Royal Vocabulary |
| Imit. | Imitative | Skt. | Sanskrit |
| Interj. | Interjection | sing. | Singular |
| iv. | Intransitive Verb | sp. | Specifier |
| lit: | Literally | tv. | Transitive Verb |

In addition, the following conventions are used:

... Omitted material not translated (discontinuous construction).

--- Omitted material translated (more frequent in Part One).

( ) Explanatory material, or words present in the Cambodian but not essential to the English translation.

[ ] Words not present in the Cambodian but necessary to the English translation.

# CAMBODIAN-ENGLISH GLOSSARY

ក /kαα/ throat, neck, collar

កដៃ wrist

ក៏ /kαα, kα-/ so, then, accordingly

...ក៏...ក៏ both...and

ក៏ដោយ to whatever extent, even though

ក៏ស៊ីបានដែរ can live on, can get along with

កក frozen, congealed

កកកុញ crowded, congested, dense

កក់ to shampoo

កកាយ to dig out, scrape out; to scratch about

កកូរ to stir, beat

កក្កដា /kaqkədaa/ July

កក្រើក to shake, jar, cause to rumble

កក្អែ babbling over and over

កខ្លេះកខ្លោញ to bubble with enthusiasm

កង military division, unit, force

កង load, roaring

កងខេមរភូមិន្ទ /kααŋ-khaemməreə̆q-phuumɨn/ Royal Cambodian Forces

កងទ័ព /kααŋ-toə̆p/ troops, army

កងរាជតម្រួត /kααŋ-riəc-dαmruət/ Royal Police Force

កងរំពង tumultuous(ly), noisily

កងអាសាស្ម័គ្រ /kααŋ-qaasaasmaq/ volunteer military unit

កងឯកភាព personal guard unit

កង់ wheel; bicycle

កង្ហញ kinky, curly, coiled

កង្កែប frog

កង្គន to be enraged, furious

កង្វល់ trouble, bother; to worry, be anxious

កង្ហារ fanwheel, gyroscope

កង្ហែកកង្ហល់ restless, impatient

កញ្ចក់ mirror

កញ្ចប់ package, wrapped parcel

កញ្ចាស់ old thing, old person; old, pathetic (Pej)

កញ្ឆក់ to snatch; with a jerk, by jerks and starts

កញ្ឆែត an edible aquatic plant

កញ្ជើ a tightly-woven basket

កញ្ជ្រោង fox

កញ្ជ្រោល to rear up, buck, jump (of a horse, etc.)

កញ្ញា /kaññaa/ girl, young lady; Miss

កណ្ឌ /kan/ episode, part, section; fascicle (of a palm-leaf manuscript)

កណ្ឌកុមារបព៌ one of the 13 sections of the Maha Vessantara Jataka

កណ្ដាប់ grasp, handful

កណ្ដាប់ដៃ grasp, clutches

កណ្ដាល center; in the center of

កណ្ដាលជំនុំ in the midst of the assembly

កណ្ដាលថ្ងៃ in the open, right in the sun

កណ្ដុរ /kαndao, kαndol/ rat, mouse

កណ្ដៀរ termite

កណ្ដែងកណ្ដោច (=កណ្ដោចកណ្ដែង) lonely, desolate

កណ្ដោចកណ្ដែង lonely, desolate

កណ្ដោលហ្មាត a kind of small plant

កតញ្ញូ /kattaññuu/ gratitude

កតញ្ញូតា /kattaññuutaa/ gratitude, recognition of service done

កតវេទី /kətaqweetii/ gratitude

កត់ to put down, jot down, record

កត់ចិត្តចងចាំ devoted (to), irrevocably attached (to)

កត់ត្រា to register, write down, record

កត្តា /kattaa/ factor

កត្តិក /katdək, kədək/ October-November (lunar system)

កឋិន /kathən/ presentation of gifts to the monks
កនិដ្ឋា /kɑnnitthaa/ youngest sibling (Lit)
កន្តើយ indifferent

កន្ត្រាក់ /kɑntraq/ to jerk (tv)

កន្ត្រៃ /kɑntray/ scissors

កន្ត្រោន drawn up, contracted

កន្ទក់កន្ទេញ to whine, plead, beseech

កន្ទុយ tail

កន្ទេល woven mat

កន្ទ្រឹស /kɑntrɨh/ stingy, miserly

កន្តែក spread apart, spraddled

កន្លង to pass, elapse (of time); exceedingly, surpassingly
កន្លង់ a small perch-like fish

កន្លង់ a large black flying beetle, woodborer
កន្លៀត nook, corner

កន្លេង agitated

កន្លែង place, position, office; seat

កន្លោង supreme one; supremely

កន្លោងអស់ស្រី above all other women

កន្លះ /kɑnlah/ half

កន្សែង cloth, napkin, handkerchief, towel
កន្សែង to weep, cry (Roy)

កប to be, be in essence, be endowed with; efficacious
កប៉ាល់ /kəpal/ ship, steamer

កប៉ាល់ហោះ /kəpal-hɑh/ airplane

កប្បាស /kapbaah, kəbaah/ cotton

កម្ជិល sloth, laziness; lazy person, good-for-nothing
កម្ពល /kɑmpŭəl/ woolen cloth

កម្ពុជបុត្រ /kampuccəbot/ Cambodian children (lit: Cambodian sons)
កម្ពុជរដ្ឋ /kampuccərŏət/ Cambodia

កម្ពុជា /kampucciə/ Cambodia

កម្ម /kam/ karma, fate (usually bad)

កម្មករ /kamməkɑɑ/ workers, coolies

កម្មគ្រោះ /kam-kruəh/ misfortune, (negative) karma
កម្មនិយម /kamməniyum/ natural laws of existence; effects of karma

កម្មអើយ what fate!

កម្មវិធី /kam-withii/ program, system

កម្មវិធីសិក្សា curriculum

កម្មិកលេខាធិការ /kammikaq-leekhaathikaa/ recording secretary
កម្រ /kɑmrɑɑ/ difficult (to); rarely
កម្រង garland, braid

កម្រាល cover, spread, blanket, sheet
កម្រិត mark, level, degree; to fix, decree; to allot
កម្រើក to move, budge (iv)

កម្រៃ interest, profit

កម្រោល brutish, crude, volatile

កម្លា to threaten

កម្លុង in, within; interval (Arch)

កម្លោះ single (of a man), bachelor

កម្លាំង strength, power

កម្លាំងទាន extent of one's charity

កម្លាំងមនុស្ស manpower

ករ hand (Lit)

ករណីយ /kaqrənəy/ duty

ករណីយកិច្ច /kaqrənəyyəkəc/ duty

ករុណា /kaqrunaa, kənaa/ to have pity on, have mercy on; please...
កល /kɑl/ trick, ruse, strategy

កល /kɑl/ like, as if

កលកិច្ច (=កិច្ចកល ) trick, ruse, strategy

កល់ to block, chock (e.g. the wheel of a vehicle)

កល់ intensifier: very much, very many
កល្ប /kal/ an age, long period of time
កល្បជល់តែលនហើយ for ages, for an extremely long time
កល្យាណ /kalləyaan/ good, beautiful, virtuous
កល្យាណស្ត្រី /kalləyaan-sətrəy/ virtuous woman
កល្យាណី /kalyaanəy/ beautiful woman

កវី /kawəy/ poet

កវីវង្សា /kawəy-wŭəŋsaa/ a clerical title
កសាង /kaa-saaŋ/ to build, erect

កសិកម្ម /kaqsekam/ agriculture

កសិករ /kaqsekaa/ farmer (Eleg)

កា to address (a letter), inscribe

កាក leavings, refuse

កាកសំបុត្រ discarded letters

កាកគតិ /kaaqkəteq/ a style of verse (lit: crow's gait)
កាកបាទ kaaqkəbaat/ the symbol +

កាកី /kaakəy/ Kakei, name and principal character of a well-known epic
កាកែស a plant with fragrant flowers
កាង to extend, stretch out, spread

កាច bad, wicked, malicious

កាច់ to break off, break in two (tv); to kill
កាច់រែក to twist and turn, posture, make exaggerated and slightly affected movements

កាច់ចង្កូត to guide, pilot

កាច់រាង to perform or utter with affected elegance
កាញ់ to be thrifty, frugal (with)

កាណ៌ /kaa/ ears (Roy, Lit)

កាណិកា a kind of yellow flower

កាណូត motorboat

កាត់ to cut, to sever; to cross; to ward off, bar, defend against; to cut off, alienate

កាត់ to be of mixed ethnic origin; to be a half-breed

កាត់ក្តី to settle an issue, settle a case
កាត់ខ្មាស to swallow one's pride

កាត់ខ្វាត់ខ្វែង to crisscross

កាត់ទោស to condemn, to sentence

កាត់យល់ to realize

កាត់អាល័យ to stop loving, to betray love
កាតាប /kataap/ briefcase, satchel

កាតូលិក /kaatoulik/ Catholic

កាន់ to hold, believe in, insist on

កាន់ toward

កាន់កាប់ to administer, be in charge

កាន់ការ to take charge

កាន់គតិតទៀវត្រិមត្រូវ be on your good behavior, mind your p's and q's
កាន់ចិត្ត maintain, insist on; stubborn, unyielding
កាន់តែ increasingly, the more

កាន់ទុក្ខ to mourn

កាប់ to cut, hack (with an axe or cleaver); to kill, execute (with a knife)

កាប់មិនមុត won't pierce, impervious to weapons, invulnerable
កាប់របើកសាច់ឈើ lay open the flesh of the tree
កាប់សំឡាប់ to kill with a hacking motion (e.g. with an axe)
កាប៉ូរាល់ (Fr. caporal) chief, commander
កាព្យ /kaap/ poetry, verse

កាព្យឃ្លោង /kaap-klooŋ/ verse, poetry

កាព្យសាស្ត្រ /kaapəsaah/ prosody, versification, composition of verse
កាម Kāma, god of love; sex, sexual desire, lust
កាមលោក /kaaməlook/ the intangible world, world of the senses
កាមា (=កាម) sex, sexual desire, lust
កាមាវចរ /kaamaawəcaa/ intangible or supernatural beings

កាយ body (Lit)

កាយវិការ /kaayeə̆qwikaa/ act, deed

ការ /kaa/ work, affairs, activity; nominalizing element before verbs

ការ /kaa/ wedding; to marry

ការ (= ការពារ) to prevent, to defend against

ការកសាង formation, development

ការការ work, the work that one does

ការកេរ្តិ៍អាករ្តិ៍ /kaa-kei-qaat/ personal honor, self-respect

ការកំសាន្ត pastime, sport

ការក្រាបថ្វាយបង្គំ greeting, homage, salutation

ការខុសត្រូវ responsibility

ការខ្វះខាត lack, shortage

ការគួរ item of business, some business or other

ការងារ task, duty, function

ការចិញ្ចឹមសត្វ raising livestock

ការចាំបាច់ necessity, necessary action

ការជប់លៀងភ្ញៀវ banquet, feast, entertainment

ការឈប់សម្រាក holiday, vacation

ការដឹកនាំ leadership, direction

ការដឹងយល់ understanding

ការដែល the fact that, the matter of (nominalizes following verb phrase)

ការទទួលភ្ញៀវ receiving guests

ការទម្លាប់ habit, customary action

ការធ្វើឆ្នាំង pottery-making

ការនឿយហត់ hard work, tiring work

ការនេសាទត្រី fishing, the fishing industry

ការនាំចូល importation

ការបើកឥណទាន establishing credit

ការប្រញាណ defend oneself

ការផ្ទះ housework

ការពារ /kaa-piə/ to protect, defend

ការពិសោធន៍ experience; experiment

ការយល់ព្រម consent, approval

ការយាមប្រចាំការ guard duty

ការរចនា decoration

ការរស់នៅ life, living conditions

ការរៀនសូត្រ studying; studies

ការរំជួលចិត្ត emotion, sentiment

ការសន្ទនា conversation

ការសិក្សា education

ការសុខ peace

ការស្អាតស្អំ cleanliness; honesty

ការហត្ថកម្ម /kaa-hattəkam/ manual labor

ការណ៍ /kaa/ affair, case, story, situation, event

ការិយាល័យ /kaariyaalay/ office, bureau

កាល time; when (conj)

កាលជាខាងក្រោយ recently

កាលដែល while, when

កាលណា when?; whenever

កាលណាបើ if, whenever

កាលបើ if, when, whenever

កាលពីព្រេងនាយ once upon a time

កាលៈទេសៈ /kaalaq-teesaq/ circumstances

កាហោ a kind of fish

កាហ្វេ /kaafei/ coffee

កាទ្សា to change form, transform oneself by magic

កាទ្សាខ្លួន to transform oneself magically, change one's form by magic

កិច្ច /kəc/ affair, matter (usually in compounds)

កិច្ចកាព្យ poem, poetry, verse

កិច្ចការ work, business

កិច្ចក្នុងក្រៅ internal and external matters

កិច្ចចាត់ចែង direction, supervision

កិច្ចដែលបម្រើលោក serving the priests

[illegible] conclusion, finale

rd

ment,

(of)

over,

old

d-

vior

th a



កុញ្ជរ /koñcɔɔ/ elephant (Lit); excellent, praiseworthy

កុដិ /kot/ monks' quarters

កុន movie, film

កុមសូមុលសូវីយេក /komsoumαl souwiyeek/ Soviet Komsomol (Russian Communist Youth Organization)

កុមារ /komaa/ boy; in compounds: children in general (Eleg)

កុមារា-កុមារី /komaaraa-komaarəy/ boys and girls, children (Eleg, Lit)

កុម្ភន្ធ (= កុម្ភណ្ឌ) /komphŏən/ ogre, giant (Lit)

កុម្ភៈ /kumphĕəq/ February

កុម្ភណ្ឌ /komphŏən/ ogre, giant (Lit)

កុម្មុនិស្ត /kommunih/ communist

កុម៉ៃ /kommay/ (Jean) Commaille, first Conservator of Angkor

កុលបុត្រ /kolləbot/ children of good families

កុវេរ /koqweerĕəq/ Kubera (god of wealth)

កុសល /kosαl/ merit, good deeds

កុសលផល /kosαl-phαl/ accumulated merit

កុហក /kohαq, kəhαq/ to lie, prevaricate

កុះករ in great numbers

កូក here!, here I am!

កូន offspring of either sex, child

កូន I (child to parent); you (parent to child)

កូនកន្សែង handkerchief

កូនក្រមុំគេ a certain maiden

កូនខ្ចី baby, newborn infant

កូនចៅ children, offspring

កូនឈើ sapling, bush, small tree

កូនត្នោត Sugarpalm Sapling (pl. n.)

កូនទូ small cabinet, small dresser

កូនបង្កើត one's own child

កូនប្រុស son

កូនប្រុសស្រី son(s) and daughter(s)

កូនពៅ youngest child

កូនភ្នំ hill, foothill

កូនលោក children of important men

កូនសិស្ស /koun-səh/ pupil, student

កូនសិស្សលោក temple-boy

កូនសំបុត្រ small letter, note

កូនស្រី daughter

កូនស្រុក inhabitants of the area

កូនឥតពូជ illbred person

កូប elephant howdah

កូរ to stir, agitate

កូលេស /koleh/ (Fr. collège) high school (grades 7 to 10)
កូលេសស៊ីសុវត្ថិ Collège Sisowath
កូវ /kəw/ empty poetic particle
កុឡា /koulaa, kolaa/ Cambodian of Burmese origin
កុលាប rose
កួច to swirl, twist, revolve, whirl
កួច to occur to one's mind, be engendered; to long for, desire
កួយ Kuy (name of a tribal group in Cambodia)
កួរ /kuə/ ear, pod
កើត to be born, come into existence
កើត to prosper, be successful; after a verb: to be able, possible
កើតក្ដីនឹងគ្នា to have a disagreement
កើតជាអស្ចារ្យ something extraordinary happened, a marvelous thing happened
កើតទុក្ខ to grieve, have troubles
កើតទោស trouble arises, problems arise, have problems (with someone)
កើតទោសនឹងគេ get into trouble with others
កើតមក to be born, come into existence
កើតមាន to develop, arise
កើតឡើង to arise, come about, happen
កើតអ្វី what's wrong?, what's the matter?
កើតអ្វីបានជា why is it that...?, how did it happen that...?
កើន to multiply, increase (iv)
កើយ to rest the head, support the head
កើយ stile for mounting an elephant or chariot
កើល to run aground (of a boat)
កៀក to hold or embrace with one arm
កៀកកើយ to embrace intimately
កៀង (= គៀង) to herd, round up
កៀន next to, up against
កៀប to squeeze, to pressure
កៀរ to round up, herd together
កៀវ to straddle, wrap the legs around
កេងកាង swing the arms, put the hands on the hips, swagger (symbolic of arrogance)
កេណ្ឌ /kaen/ to conscript, draft; commandeer, requisition
កេតុជម្ពូ /keetoq-cumphuu/ a kingdom in the Himalayas
កេរ្តិ៍ /kei/ heritage, legacy, reputation; honor, glory
កេរ្តិ៍កោះ honor, reputation; heritage, legacy, inheritance
កេរ្តិ៍ខ្មាស sexual organs (Euph)
កេរ្តិ៍ឈ្មោះ reputation, fame, honor
កេស /keh, keisaq/ hair; head (Roy, Clergy)
កេសរ /keisαα/ hair; head (Roy, Clergy); pollen (Lit)
កេសររាជសីហ៍ male lion (i.e. lion with hair)
កេសា head; hair (Lit, Roy)
កេសី (= កេសា) head; hair (Roy, Clergy)
កែ to repair, correct
កែខៃ to reflect, deliberate, resolve (a problem)
កែប្រែ to revise
កែសម្រួល to smooth, to correct
កែប Kep (a resort area)
កែម to cover, encrust, decorate
កែមកាល់ to decorate around the edge, embellish with a border; ornate
កែវ a glass, a cup; glass, crystal, precious stone
កែវ common personal name (lit: crystal, precious [one])
កែវកញ្ញា precious girl
កែវកាកី the fair Kakey
កែវចរណៃ term of endearment (Precious One)
កែវភ្នែក cornea of the eye
កែស a kind of small fish
កែះ /keh/ to scratch, nudge with one finger (a gesture characteristically used to get a friend's attention)

កៃលាស name of a Himalayan mountain

កោង curved, bent; arrogant, rude, blatant

កោដិ /kaot/ ten-million

កោណ្ឌិន្យ /kaondɨn/ Kaundinya (legendary founder of Funan)

កោត to be amazed at, impressed by, awed by

កោតគោរព to respect, honor

កោតញញើត to respect, be awed by

កោតថា amazed that, incredulous that

កោរ /kao/ to shave

កោរទាំងសក់ក្បាល have the head completely shaven

កោរសក់ to shave the head

កោរសក់ឱ្យ to shave his head for (him)

កោលាហល /kaolaahαl/ disorder, panic, consternation

កោស /kaoh/ to scratch out, dig out; to scrape (the skin) with a coin or other instrument (thought to have therapeutic value)

កោសិយ /kaosəy/ Indra

កោសៃយ្យ /kaosay/ silk cloth

កោះ /kαh/ island

កោះ to call, summon

កោះ to pull (a bowstring to shoot an arrow)

កោះកុង Koh Kong (Province)

កោះថ្មី New Island (pl. n.)

កោះត្រឡាច Koh Tralach (an island in the South China Sea where the French kept criminals and political prisoners)

កៅទណ្ឌ /kaw-toə̆n/ bow, arc (Lit)

កៅរវៈ /kawrərēə̆q/ the Kuravas

កៅសិប ninety

កៅស៊ូ /kawsuu/ (Fr. caoutchouc) rubber

កៅអី chair, seat

កៅអីវែង bench

កុំ negative imperative auxiliary: don't...

កុំគិតសង្ស័យ have no doubt (about it)

កុំឃើញ on seeing..., don't...(Idiom)

កុំ...ដែលដែរ don't...either

កុំថាតែ not only

កុំធ្វើ don't be

កុំបាច់ it's not necessary to, don't insist on

កុំបី so as not to, in order not to; don't

កុំបីឱ្យ so as not to have...

កុំព្រួយប្រសាសន៍ don't worry

កុំភ័យអី don't be afraid, don't worry about a thing

កុំស្បីបន្តិច whatever comes up

កុំអាល don't...yet, don't be in a hurry to

កុំអី otherwise, else

កុំ...អី discontinuous negative imperative: don't

កុំអីទៀយ otherwise

កុំឱ្យ in order not to, so that... won't

កុំឱ្យតែ just so it's not, so long as one doesn't

កុំ...ឱ្យសោះ strong negative imperative: never...; don't...at all

កុំឱ្យស្រាក relentlessly

កំចាត់ to expel, chase out, exorcise; to reject, shun

កំជិល laziness; to be lazy

កំដរ to accompany, assist in, contribute to

កំដរដៃ to occupy the hands

កំជឹង debt

កំដៅ heat; to heat, to warm

កំណត់ record, note, inscription; appointment, fixed period; decision, prescription; to fix, decide, set, record, keep

កំណត់ជន្ម predetermine [the length of] one's life, predetermine one's death

កំណត់ទៅតាមស្លាស្លា recorded faithfully, recorded accurately

កំណត់ព្រះចិន្តា to decide, conclude (Roy)

កំណប់ cache, treasure

កំណល់ a block, chock

កំណាច wicked; wickedness

កំណាញ់ stingy, miserly

កំណាត់ piece, section

កំណាន់ principle, precept, faith (cf. /kan/ to hold to, adhere to, believe in)

កំណាន់ close, intimate, favorite

កំណាព្យ poetry, verse

កំណើត origin, birth, beginning; nature, innate character; full-blooded (of kinship)

កំណែន conscription, forced labor, corvée

កំសាត់ a Chinese game of chance

កំទេច debris, bits, remains

កំបុត truncated

កំបុតក decapitated

កំបាំង to bar, block, shield

កំបាំងភ្នែក to block the vision; to glance away

កំប៉ោក swollen, bloated, rotund; Fig: haughty, self-important

កំប្លង់ ៗ very beautiful

កំប្លែង (=កំផ្លែង ) comical, humorous

កំផែង wall, enclosure, rampart

កំពង់ port, river bank, river town

កំពង់ខ្សាច់ស White Sand Port (pl. n.)

កំពង់ចម្លង ferry landing (lit: port [for] putting across)

កំពង់ចាម Kompong Cham (city, province)

កំពង់ឆ្នាំង Kompong Chhnang (city, province)

កំពង់លែង Kompong Leng (pl. n.)

កំពង់សោម Kompong Som (city, former province)

កំពង់ស្វាយ Kompong Svay (district in Kompong Thom Province)

កំពង់ហ្លួង Kompong Luong (town on the Tonlé Sap River)

កំពត Kampot (city, province)

កំពស់ height

កំពស់កំព height, size (Coll)

កំពឹងពួយ an aquatic plant used as a vegetable

កំពុង in the process of, -ing

កំពូល summit, peak

កំពែង wall, enclosure, rampart

កំព្រា to be an orphan, be orphaned (lacking one or both parents)

កំព្រីកំព្រា to be orphaned

កំភួន calf of the leg, muscle of the forearm

កំភ្លក់ a kind of fish

កំភ្លាញ a kind of small fish

កំភ្លឹង amaryllis

កំភ្លៀង the side of the face

កំរិត fixed level, mark, limit; to set, decree, prescribe, limit

កំរើក to move, budge (iv)

កំរើករិទ្ធិ bursting with power

កំរោល violent, uncontrolled, tempestuous

កំលៀង to glance sidelong

កំសត់ sad, pathetic, destitute, miserable

កំសាក coward

កំសាន្ត /kαmsaan/ to relax, amuse oneself, enjoy oneself

កំហល់ anger; one who is angry

កំហឹង anger; one who is angry

កំហឹងចូលមកដល់ [one] becomes angry

កំហុស fault, wrong

កំហែង to threaten, intimidate

កំឡា to threaten; to encourage; to take courage

កំឡុង in, during; period, interval (Arch)

កំឡាំងខាង good at

កំអែល dirt, filth

កាំ step (of stairs)

កាំបិត knife

កាំបិតស្នៀត hunting knife

កាំបិតស្លា folding knife

កាំងគីណា quinine (plant)

ក្ងក់ crooked, hooked, twisted

ក្ងោក peacock

ក្ដាត a tuber with edible stems

ក្ដាស់ extremely (Lit)

ក្ដាន់ deer

ក្ដាប់ to grasp, hold in the fist; handful

ក្ដាម crab

ក្ដារ /kdaa/ board, plank

ក្ដាឈ្នួន writing slate; blackboard

ក្ដារបន្ទះ plywood

ក្ដារទ័បន shelf, bench, flat step or stool

ក្ដិច to pinch, pinch off

ក្ដី /kdəy/ affair, situation, case; court action, suit

ក្ដី even though; to whatever extent

ក្ដី monastery, monk's quarters

ក្ដី...ក្ដី whether...or

ក្ដីកំសត់កម្រ adversity, struggle, difficulty

ក្ដីច្បាប់ education, savoir-faire, law

ក្ដីដូង Coconut Affair (pl. n.)

ក្ដីទុក្ខសោក misery, things which cause suffering (i.e. sin)

ក្ដីទុជ៌ន misfortune, bad results

ក្ដីទោសៈ ក្ដៅ misery and strife

ក្ដីបារម្ភ worry, concern, sense of responsibility

ក្ដុក imitative of the sound of a falling object: with a thump

ក្ដុកក្នុងចិត្ត heavy-hearted, sorrowful

ក្ដួច manioc, cassava (from which tapioca is made)

ក្ដួល to be in a torment, heart-sick

ក្ដែងៗ clamorously, insistently

ក្ដោង sail (of a boat)

ក្ដោចក្ដែង to cry, wail, lament

ក្ដៅ to be hot

ក្ដៅខ្លួន to run a temperature, have a fever

ក្ដៅចិត្ត furious, burning with anger, incensed

ក្ដៅទ៏រា agitated, suffused with emotion

ក្ដាំងងា a kind of flower

ក្ទម្ព tree of paradise

ក្នក់ a raised representation, a relief carving

ក្នង់ក្នក់ bas-relief carving

ក្នាញ់ exasperated

ក្នាញ់ indignant, incensed, disgusted

ក្នុង in, inside

ក្នុងខាងក្រោយនេះ below, following (in a text)

ក្នុងចំណោម among

ក្នុងពេលដំណាលគ្នានោះ at that same time, concurrently

ក្បត់ to betray, deceive

ក្បត់ជាតិ to betray one's country, commit treason

ក្បាច់ artistic design, embellishment

ក្បាច់បន្លាក់រាក់ៗ ស្ដើងៗ light relief, shallow relief

ក្បាច់រចនា /kbac-raccənaa/ carving, sculpture; art

ក្បាច់រំលេច bas-relief

ក្បាល head; bow (of a boat); volume (of books)

ក្បាលជង្គង់ knee(s)

ក្បាលជណ្ដើរ head of the balustrade

ក្បាលមួយ only one, alone

ក្បិន a roll of cloth; a typically Cambodian way of wearing a sarong

ក្បូន raft

ក្បួនក្បាច់ (= ក្បាច់) artistic technique

ក្បួន procession, parade, train; manual, textbook

ក្បឿង tile

ក្បៀស comma; to make a stroke

ក្បែរ beside, alongside

ក្បោះក្បាយ eloquent; in detail

ក្បុំ round and firm

ក្មួយ niece or nephew; affectionate term for young people of one's children's generation

ក្មួយបង្កើត full niece or nephew

ក្មេង child, children; to be young

ក្មេងជំនាន់ក្រោយ later generation, the younger generation

ក្មេងស្រីៗ /kmeiŋ srəy-srəy/ young girls

ក្រ to be poor; rare, scarce; difficult; to be poor at, slow to

ក្រងាយ /krαα-ŋiəy/ emergency, difficulty, eventuality (usu. bad)

ក្របើគិតណាស់ difficult to resolve

ក្រមាន rare(ly)

ក្រយប់ថ្ងៃ eventualities (i.e. difficulties [which can arise] night or day)

ក្រលំបាក to be poor, in difficult circumstances

ក្រអី there's no problem (about); that's no problem

ក្រកច្ឆេទ /krαqkəchaet/ Krakaccheda (hell for gluttons)

ក្រខុប large tree with edible fruit

ក្រខ្វក់ dirty, filthy; morally bad

ក្រងួរ nasal, muffled, indistinct

ក្រចក fingernail(s)

ក្រជឹង a fixed oar attached to the gunwales of a boat

ក្រញង់ stiff, rigid

ក្រញាង pointing in all directions

ក្រញី to scratch, mangle, shred (with teeth or claws)

ក្រញឹង extremely, violently (angry)

ក្រញុះ sad, dejected, morose (of facial expression)

ក្រញូវ to frown, scowl

ក្រញេងក្រញាង pointing in all directions; descriptive of sudden violent gestures

ក្រញោន drawn up, huddled up

ក្រញាំ claw

ក្រដាស paper

ក្រដាសប្រាក់ bill, paper money

ក្រទា to crouch aggressively

ក្រប casing, binding, cover, support

ក្របី water buffalo

ក្របីឈ្លៀច white water buffalo

ក្របុី monkey (Lit)

ក្រឡៅ a kind of large tree

ក្រពត blowfish

ក្រពើ crocodile

ក្រពុំ unopened, still in the bud

ក្រពុំខ្ចី young, tender

ក្រម /krαm/ law, rule, decree

ក្រមការ /krαmməkaa/ palace officials

ក្រមក្រឹត្យ /krαm-krət/ law, decree

ក្រមា towel, cloth, scarf (worn around the neck, as a turban, or as a short sarong while working)

ក្រមាច់ to make comical faces

ក្រមិចក្រមើម /krαməc-krαməɨm/ clownish, comical

ក្រមួន wax

ក្រមួនស name of a former province (lit: White Wax)

ក្រមុំ /krαmom/ young unmarried girl; virgin

ក្រមុំល្មមនឹងមានប្ដី of marriageable age

ក្រយាសំពះ wedding gifts

ក្រលៀស to slip away, wiggle free, evade

ក្រវាញ cardamom

ក្រវាត់ to girdle, tie around (the waist)

ក្រវាន់ a kind of flowering tree

ក្រវើន /krɑwəən/ make an effort to, try hard (to), be diligent in
ក្រវៀច twisted
ក្រសាល to amuse oneself, enjoy oneself (Roy, Lit)
ក្រសួង department; function, duty
ក្រសួងមហាផ្ទៃ Ministry of the Interior
ក្រសួងមានសមត្ថកិច្ច the department concerned
ក្រសួងសម្ងាត់ secret service
ក្រសួងសាធារណសុខាភិបាលនិងសង្គមកិច្ច Ministry of Public Health and Welfare
ក្រសួងអប់រំជាតិ Ministry of National Education
ក្រសោប to enfold, embrace
ក្រសាំង a thorny tree with sour fruit
ក្រស្នា /krəhsnaa/ Krishna
ក្រហម red (the spectrum of color from yellow to red)
ក្រហមទំទង rich red
ក្រឡង់ perfectly round
ក្រឡា /krɑlaa, kəlaa/ square; surface (of earth); court, yard
ក្រឡា high, supreme
ក្រឡាឈើត្រង់ square, block, check
ក្រឡាបញ្ជី /krɑlaa-bañcii/ court clerk
ក្រឡាបន្ទំ sleeping quarters (Roy)
ក្រឡាប្រឹថពី surface of the earth
ក្រឡាហោម /krɑlaahaom/ Minister of the Navy and Water Transport
ក្រឡាញ់ a large tree with edible fruit
ក្រឡាប់ to turn over, roll, rotate
ក្រឡាប់ចែលងដោះដៃ change [my] mind [and] abandon [you]
ក្រឡាស់ to turn over, roll over
ក្រឡាស់ត្រឡប់ on the other hand, contrarily; have a turn of fate, have a change of fortune
ក្រឡឹង to lathe; encircling, around
ក្រឡេក to glance
ក្រឡេកទៅក្រឡេកមក look here and there

ក្រឡេវ wide-eyed
ក្រឡុះ to break away, free oneself
ក្រអាញ husky, stocky
ក្រអូប sweet-smelling, fragrant
ក្រអួន massive, stocky
ក្រអើត stick out, thrust forward (the head)
ក្រាញ់ a kind of small fish
ក្រាន (= ជើងក្រាន) a fireplace composed of three stones as a tripod for cooking
ក្រាប to bow, prostrate oneself
ក្រាបថ្វាយបង្គំ to prostrate oneself in homage
ក្រាបថ្វាយបង្គំលា to take leave (of royalty)
ក្រាបទូល to inform, to say respectfully (to royalty)
ក្រាបបង្គំគាល់ to have an audience with (royalty)
ក្រាបបង្គំទូល to inform, say respectfully (to royalty)
ក្រាបបាទ prostrate oneself at the feet of
ក្រាម gram
ក្រាយ a kind of tree
ក្រាយ a kind of fish
ក្រាយ serpent
ក្រាល to spread out, to lay out
ក្រាស់ thick, heavy, many, accumulated
ក្រាស់ក្រែល many, abundant
ក្រាស់ក្រែ thick, numerous, in great numbers
ក្រិត្យសង្ឃ /krət sɑŋ/ Code [of Conduct] of the Sangha (priesthood)
ក្រិមិនិចយ /kreqminiqcay/ Kriminicaya (hell for blasphemers)
ក្រិស្នា /krɨhsnaa/ Krishna
ក្រិស្នាដែលកើតពីវិស្ណុ Krishna, an incarnation of Vishnu
ក្រីក្រ poor
ក្រឹត្យ law, rule, precept, decree
ក្រុង to cage

ក្រុង city

ក្រុង King, prince, the great... (Lit)

ក្រុងកម្ពុជា Cambodia

ក្រុងកម្ពុជាធិបតី Kingdom of Cambodia

ក្រុងកៃលាសច័ក្រ the realm of Kailāsa

ក្រុងគ្រុឌ Garuda

ក្រុងទេព Krungthep (lit: city of the angels)

ក្រុងទេពបុរីស្រីអយុធ្យា Ayuthia

ក្រុងព្រះសីហនុ Sihanoukville

ក្រុងយក្ស King of the ogres

ក្រុងរាពណ៍ King Rāvana

ក្រុងសិង្គបុរី /kroŋ-səŋkəborəy/ Singapore

ក្រុងសុភមិត្រ /kroŋ-soppəmɨt/ King Subhamitra, hero of the epic of the same name

ក្រុងស្រីអយុធ្យា Ayuthia (capital of Thailand 1350-1767)

ក្រុងអសុភមិត្រ King Asubhamitra

ក្រុងឧដុង្គមានជ័យ /kroŋ qutdoŋ miən-cɨy/ Oudong (capital of Ca. 1620-1867)

ក្រុម group, circle, team; department, division (of a ministry)

ក្រុមការ /krommәkaa/ title (very low ranking officials)

ក្រុមញាតិ relatives, family, ancestors

ក្រុមប្រឹក្សាព្រះរាជអាណាចក្រ Council of the Kingdom

ក្រុមព្រះនគរបាល Department of Police

ក្រុមព្រះរាជទ្រព្យ /krom preə̆h-riəccə-troə̆p/ the royal orchestra

ក្រុមមេការ construction forces

ក្រុមរបាំព្រះរាជទ្រព្យ Royal Ballet Corps

ក្រុមល្ខោនជាតិ National Drama Corps

ក្រុមល្ខោនព្រះរាជទ្រព្យ Royal Drama Corps

ក្រុមសង្ឃការី /krom sɑŋkaarəy/ Council on Buddhism

ក្រុមហត្ថករ the group of workers

ក្រុមហ៊ុន company, business establishment

ក្រុស a perch-like fish

ក្រុះ (= ក្រុស) a perch-like fish

ក្រូច orange, citrus fruit

ក្រូចពោធិសាត់ /krouc-poosat/ orange(s)

ក្រួញក្រាញ (=ក្រាញ) to resist

ក្រួញក្រាប to crouch, draw oneself up (in an attitude of deference)

ក្រួស gravel, small rounded stones

ក្រៀម hard and dried; sad (of facial expression)

ក្រៀមក្រោះ dry, arid

ក្រៀមក្រំ sad, dejected (of facial expression)

ក្រេប to sip

ក្រេបជញ្ជាក់ to taste, get the flavor of (Fig: to enjoy, appreciate)

ក្រេវក្រោធ angry (Lit)

ក្រែង to fear, be afraid; for fear that, in the unlikely event that

ក្រែងចិត្ត to feel diffident toward, have consideration for the feelings of

ក្រែងឈឺចាប់យប់ថ្ងៃ might get sick at any time

ក្រែង...ទេឬ did [he] perhaps...?

ក្រែលក្រាស់ (=ក្រាស់ក្រែល) many

ក្រែវក្រោធ (=ក្រេវក្រោធ)

ក្រៃ extremely (usually in compounds)

ក្រៃពេក extremely, excessively

ក្រៃលែង extremely, without bounds; beyond, exceeding

ក្រោក to get up, rise up

ក្រោកឈរ to stand up

ក្រោកឡើង to get up

ក្រោធ to be angry (Roy, Lit)

ក្រោម under, below, beneath

ក្រោមទឹក downstream

ក្រោមល្អងធូលីព្រះបាទ most respectfully, very humbly (lit: under the dust of your feet)

ក្រោយ behind, after

ក្រោយបង្អស់ last, last of all

ក្រោយមក afterward

ក្រោល corral, pen (for animals)

ក្រោលគោ Kraol Ko (pl. n.; lit: ox corral)

ក្រៅ outside, outside of

ក្រៅតម្រា inordinately, excessively, unreasonably

ក្រៅពី besides

ក្រៅពីនោះ the rest

ក្រៅសុច្ចរិត excessive, extreme, abnormal

ក្រៅអពី besides

ក្រំ to hurt (of internal organs)

ក្លស់ ceremonial umbrella

ក្លាយ to change, alter; to be mixed, adulterated, changed, transformed

ក្លាហាន brave, bold

ក្លិង្គ /kləŋ/ (Asian) Indian

ក្លិង parasol

ក្លិន smell, odor

ក្លើ male friend (Arch)

ក្លៀវក្លា vigorous, dynamic, full of vitality

ក្លែង false, counterfeit; to falsify, impersonate, pretend, disguise

ក្លែងក្លាយ to falsify, adulterate, hedge

ក្លែបក្លាយ to change, shift (aspect or appearance)

ក្លោងទ្វារ portal, lintel

ក្សត្រ /ksat/ king

ក្សត្រិយ៍ (=ក្សត្រ) /ksat/ king

ក្សត្រក្សាន្ត peaceful king, gentle king

ក្សត្រា (=ក្សត្រ)

ក្សត្រាធិបតី /ksattraathɨppədəy/ supreme king

ក្ស័យ /ksay/ to die (Lit)

ក្ស័យជីវិត to die (Lit)

ក្សាច់ /ksac/ sand

ក្សាន្ត /ksaan/ peaceful, tranquil

ក្សិណ just then, thereupon

ក្សិណក្ស័យ /ksən-ksay/ to die (Lit)

ក្សិណនោះ at that time (Lit)

ក្សិណពុំលង់ទៀយ not long afterward

ក្សេត្របុរី /ksaet-borəy/ Kset Borey (pl.n.)

ក្សេមក្សាន្ត /ksaem-ksaan/ peaceful, tranquil

ក្អក to cough

ក្អម a water-pitcher

ក្អមឆ្នាំង pottery, earthenware

ក្អាកក្អាយ jovial, genial, vivacious; loudly, raucously, with a cackle

ក្អិត a small fish

ក្អី a long flat fish

ក្អុក a kind of small fish

ក្អួត to vomit

ក្អេងក្អាង to talk audaciously, brag, bluster, vituperate

ក្អែក crow

ក្អែក a kind of black fish

ក្អែកគោក a land crow

ក្អែកទឹក water crow

ក្អែរ to drool

ខ point, aspect, respect

ខ ៗ imitative of a gutteral hissing sound

ខសន្យា /khαα-sαnnəyaa/ contract, agreement; to contract, promise

ខណៈ moment, time

ខ័ណ្ឌ /khan/ to dictate, order imperiously

ខ័ណ្ឌ /khan/ to separate (tv)

ខត្សាវង្ស /khatsaawŭəŋ/ noble family, warrior family

ខន្តី /khantəy/ endurance, patience, restraint

ខន្ធ /khan/ (Skt. khandhā) factors conditioning the appearance of life (usually listed as 5: material form, feeling, perception, coefficients of consciousness [?], and consciousness)

ខបច៉ៃ considerate (Thai: grateful) (Lit) [?]

ខាង side, direction; in the field of, in the area of

ខាងកើត the east

ខាងក្នុង inside

ខាងក្រោម below, lower part

ខាងក្រោយ behind, the back

ខាងគ្នា close together

ខាងឆ្វេង the left side, on the left

ខាងជើង the north

ខាងត្បូង the south

ខាងផ្លូវនយោបាយ in the area of policy

ខាងមុខ front, in front

ខាងលិច the west

ខាងលើ above, upperside; northern

ខាងអាត្មា nearby, at one's side

ខាត to lose; to lose money, to lose time

ខាត់ to polish

ខាន to lack, to miss, to fail to

ខានពុំបាន to be essential, indispensable

ខានយូរ to delay, prevent for a long time

ខាន់ sword (Roy)

ខាន់ស្លា bride-price (sum paid by the groom's parents to the bride's parents)

ខារ bitter (taste)

ខាល់ to spin, twirl, whirl (of a fan or augur)

ខិត to move over, scoot over, slide over, to inch along

ខិតខំ to try hard (to), work assiduously (at)

ខឹង to be angry

ខឹងកើតខាត anger causes grief

ខឹងខេ (= ខេខឹង) angry

ខឹម pink, rose

ខឹមខាត់ elaborate gold belt encrusted with jewels

ខុន officer, commander (Arch)

ខុស to be different, wrong

ខុសក្រមក្រឹត្យ to be against the law, be a transgression

ខុសគំនិត to be mistaken, wrong-headed

ខុសគ្នា different from each other, to vary

ខុស ៗ គ្នា varied, different from one another

ខុសឆ្គង to make mistakes, to be wrong

ខុសទម្លាប់ against tradition

ខុសទំនង improper, incorrect

ខុសធ្លោយ make a mistake, do harm unintentionally

ខុសបែបបទ wrong, improper

ខុសពីធម្មតា exceptional, unusual

ខុសពីផ្លូវ out of the way, off the path

ខូង dented, sunken, concave

ខូច broken, ruined, spoiled

ខូចលក្ខណ៍ unprincipled, promiscuous

ខួប year of age (for children); anniversary

ខួរក្បាល brain

ខៀវ general term for the spectrum of colors from blue to green

ខេខឹង (= ខឹង )

ខេត្ត (= ខែត្រ , ខេត្រ , ខែត ) /khaet/ province; head-word in compound names of provinces

ខេត្តកំពង់ចាម Kampong Cham Province

ខេត្តកំពង់ឆ្នាំង Kampong Chhnang Province

ខេត្តក្រៅ outer provinces

ខេត្តត្បូងឃ្មុំ name of a former province

ខេត្តពារាំង name of a former province

ខេត្រកណ្ដាល Kandal Province

ខេមរភូមិន្ទ /khaemәreә̆q-phuumɨn/ Cambodia (Lit); name of a boulevard in Phnom Penh

ខេវខឹង (=ខេខឹង) angry

ខែ month; moon; head-word in names of months

ខែកក្កដា /khae-kaqkәdaa/ July

ខែកញ្ញា September

ខែកត្តិក /khae-katdәk/ October-November (lunar system)

ខែកុម្ភៈ /khae-kumphĕәq/ February

ខែក្រោយ next month, the following month

ខែក្រោយនេះឯង this very next month

ខែចេត្រ /khae-caet/ March-April (lunar system)

ខែជេស្ឋ /khae-ceeh/ May-June (lunar system)

ខែតុលា /khae-tolaa/ October

ខែធ្នូ December

ខែបុស្ស /khae-boh/ December-January (lunar system)

ខែប្រាំង the dry season (months)

ខែផល្គុន /khae-phɑlkun, -phәkun/ February-March (lunar system)

ខែពិសាខ /khae-pisaaq/ April-May (lunar system)

ខែភទ្របទ /khae-phɑttәbɑt/ August-September (lunar system)

ខែមករា /khae-meә̆qkәraa/ January

ខែមាឃ /khae-miәq/ January-February (lunar system)

ខែមិគសិរ /-mɨkkәsei/ November-December (lunar system)

ខែមិថុនា June

ខែមីនា March

ខែមេសា April

ខែវស្សា the rainy season (months)

ខែវិច្ឆិកា /khae-wɨccәkaa/ November

ខែសីហា August

ខែស្រាពណ៍ July-August (lunar system)

ខែអស្សុជ /khae-qasoc/ September-October (lunar system)

ខែអាសាឍ June-July (lunar system)

ខែឧសភា /khae-quhsәphiә/ May

ខែង strong, brave, bold

ខែត្រកំពង់ធំ Kampong Thom Province

ខែត្រកំពង់សៀម name of a former province

ខែត្រក្រចេះ Kratié Province

ខែត្រខ្សាច់កណ្ដាល name of a former province

ខែត្រទទឹងថ្ងៃ name of a former province

ខែត្របាភ្នំ name of a former province

ខែត្រព្រៃវែង Prey Veng Province

ខែត្រភ្នំពេញ name of former province

ខែត្ររំដួល name of a former province

ខែត្រលង្វែក name of a former province

ខែត្រល្វាឯម name of a former province

ខែត្រសំរោងទង name of a former province

ខែត្រស្វាយទាប name of a former province

ខែល shield (used for protection in battle)

ខោ trousers, pants

ខោអាវ clothing, suit of clothes

ខោក to rap, strike (with the knuckles)

ខំ to try hard, to devote oneself to

ខាំ to bite; to hold between the teeth

ខាំមាត់ to compress the lips (in anger)

ខាំង to block, obstruct

ខះ dried out, dried up, dehydrated

ខ្ចប់ to wrap, envelop

ខ្ចរខ្ចាយ to spread

ខ្ចាត់ to separate, leave

ខ្ចាត់ខ្ចាយ scattered, in disarray; to spatter, spread all over

ខ្ចាយ to scatter, spread; scattered

ខ្ចាយខ្ចាត់ (=ខ្ចាត់ខ្ចាយ)

ខ្ចី tender, green; of persons: inexperienced, naive

ខ្ចី to borrow

ខ្ចីគំនិត naive

ខ្ចៅ small water snail; parts (of motors, watches, etc.)

ខ្ជាក់ to spit out, emit

ខ្ជាក់ស្លាប្តូរគ្នា exchange chews of betel (a traditional way of pledging eternal love)

ខ្ជាប់ firm, tenacious

ខ្ជាប់ខ្ជួន tight, firm, tenacious

ខ្ជិល to be lazy; to be disinclined to

ខ្ជិប /kcɨp/ to contract, come together, bring together

ខ្ជះខ្ជាយ to be wasteful, extravagant

ខ្ញារ (=ខ្ញាល់) whirling madly

ខ្ញាល់ to be angry (Roy, Clergy)

ខ្ញី ginger

ខ្ញៀវខ្ញា shrill, piercing

ខ្ញុំ I, me, my

ខ្ញុំ servant, slave

ខ្ញុំករុណា /kñom-kaqrunaa, kñom-kənaa/ I (addressing a monk)

ខ្ញុំកំដរ servant, attendant

ខ្ញុំបាទ I (masculine, polite)

ខ្ញុំបារាំង French collaborators (lit: French slaves)

ខ្ញុំព្រះករុណា /kñom-prĕəh-kaqrunaa, kñom-kaqrunaa, kñom-kənaa/ I, me (layman to priest)

ខ្ញុំព្រះបាទ I (addressing one's superior or a high-ranking official)

ខ្ញុំព្រះបាទអម្ចាស់ I (to royalty)

ខ្ញុំរាជការ officials (of a royal government)

ខ្ញុំសូមចិត្តនាង I beg of you (to a girl)

ខ្ទង់ cross-beam; unit of vertical measure

ខ្ទប់ to stop up, cover; to corner, shut in

ខ្ទប់មុខ to cover the face

ខ្ទម hut, cabin

ខ្ទរ to vibrate, reverberate, resound

ខ្ទរខ្ទារ vibrant, resonant

ខ្ទាត to spread, scatter, diffuse

ខ្ទារខ្ទរ (=ខ្ទរខ្ទារ)

ខ្ទឹង a resinous tree

ខ្ទឹម onion, garlic

ខ្ទេច shattered, smashed

ខ្ទះ large round-bottomed skillet, wok

ខ្នង the back, dorsal ridge

ខ្នង specifier for buildings

ខ្នងសំបុត្រ the address side of an envelope (in Cambodian this is considered to be the 'back' of the envelope)

ខ្នល់ (nominalization of ទល់ ) a support, block, cushion

ខ្នាញ់ disgusted, irritated

ខ្នាត model; measuring rod, ruler

ខ្នាយ tusk, fang, spur

ខ្នើយ pillow

ខ្នើយអោប a long cylindrical pillow, Dutch-wife

ខ្នោះ handcuffs, shackles

ខ្ពង់ high, high up; top, peak

ខ្ពង់ខ្ពស់ high, lofty

ខ្ពស់ high, elevated

ខ្ពស់ទៅ ៗ /kpŭəh tɨw, kpŭəh tɨw/ higher and higher

ខ្ពើម be disgusted by, repelled by, (a sight, smell, etc.)

ខ្ពោក sound of falling; with a crash

ខ្មាញ់ churning, spinning rapidly, turbulent

ខ្មាញ់ខ្មៅ jet black

ខ្មាស embarrassed, ashamed; to lose face (to)

ខ្មាសកុំ one's shame (i.e. genitals)

ខ្មី quickly, immediately, soon; newly, recently (Lit)

ខ្មីឃ្មាត hurriedly, quickly, with all dispatch; to hurry to

ខ្វល់ខ្វាញ់ swirling, turbulent, churning

ខ្មែរ /kmae/ Cambodia; Cambodian; Cambodian people

ខ្មែរក្រហម Red Khmer, Khmer Rouge

ខ្មែរខៀវសេរី (Blue) Khmer Serey

ខ្មែរនគរវត្ត pure Khmer (lit: Khmer of Angkor Wat)

ខ្មែរព្រៃលើ Upland Khmer (i.e. hill tribes)

ខ្មែរលើ Upland Khmer (hill tribes in general)

ខ្មោច corpse; ghost, spirit

ខ្មោចទឹក water-spirit, water-ogre

ខ្មោចព្រៃ spirits

ខ្មោចសេដ្ឋី the late merchant

ខ្មៅ black

ខ្មៅប្រផេះ dark gray

ខ្មៅមុខស្អែ pale, blanched

ខ្មាំង enemy

ខ្យង bigger snail, water snail

ខ្យល់ /kyɑl,kcɑl/ wind, air, breath (in Cambodia the essence of life and health was tradition ally thought to reside in the breath, or wind of the body)

ខ្យល់កម្មជ្ជវាត /kyɑl kammaccəwiət/ life-force

ខ្យល់គ fainting spell, stroke

ខ្យល់គចាប់ to have a fainting spell, to faint, have a stroke

ខ្យល់ចាប់ to have a fainting spell

ខ្យល់ជំនោរ breeze, wind

ខ្យល់ព្យុះ a wind-storm, typhoon

ខ្យល់អាកាស air, weather

ខ្លា tiger

ខ្លាខ្លាំង strong, dynamic, energetic

ខ្លាច to fear, respect; for fear that, in case

ខ្លាចចិត្ត to respect, be deferential toward

ខ្លាញ់ oil, grease, fat

ខ្លី short

ខ្លឹម heart, core, essence

ខ្លឹមសារ meaning, depth, substance

ខ្លុះ to put a ring or rope through the nose of (a buffalo, ox, etc.)

ខ្លួន person, body, oneself

ខ្លួន you (familiar)

ខ្លួននេះ I myself

ខ្លួនអើយ alas!, woe is me!

ខ្លួនឯង oneself, himself, herself, etc.; sometimes used as familiar 2nd person pronoun

ខ្លោច to be burned, scorched, charred

ខ្លៅ stupid

ខ្លំ svelte; firm

ខ្លាំង strong; loud; severe

ខ្លះ some, to some extent

ខ្វល់ concerned, worried, preoccupied

ខ្វល់ខ្វាយ be concerned, worried, in a dither

ខ្វាក់ to be blind

ខ្វាត់ខ្វែង from all directions, criss-crossing

ខ្វាប់ with a whoosh, with a swish

ខ្វាយខ្វល់ (= ខ្វល់ខ្វាយ)

ខ្វិន to be lame, paralyzed

ខ្វៀក to write rapidly, dash off

ខ្វេះ to scratch or dig out with the fingers

ខ្វៃ roasted; to roast (pig, chicken, duck)

ខ្វះ to lack

ខ្សត់ weak, poor, destitute; to be without, lacking in

ខ្សត់ខ្សោយ poor, weak, lacking in wealth and status

ខ្សាច់ sand

ខ្សាវ ៗ in a murmur

ខ្សឹកខ្សួល to sob

ខ្សឹង a kind of flowering tree

ខ្សឹប to whisper

ខ្សែ string, thread, rope

ខ្សែក្រវាត់ a belt

ខ្សែធ្នូ the string of a bow

ខ្សែពេជ្រ diamond necklace

ខ្សែមាស gold necklace

ខ្សោយ weak

គ to be mute, dumb

គក់ to pound, beat (with closed fists)

គគាត vigorously, without further ceremony

គគីរ a kind of tall tree

គគឹកគគាក់ imitative of a rumbling, thunderous sound (such as the approach of a train)

គគ្រាត rough, scaly, coarse

គគ្រឹកគគ្រេង loud, tumultuous, boisterous

គគ្រុក stinking and full of worms

គគ្រេងគគ្រាំ (=គគ្រាំគគ្រេង) with a constant roar

គង gong

គង to cross (legs, sticks, etc.); to rest the legs (across something); put across

គងអន្ទាក់ខ្លា cross-legged

គង់ to sit on, to ride on; to stay, remain, reside (Clergy, Roy)

គង់ to remain, endure, persist, resist

គង់ surely, sure to, certain to

គង់ជីវិត to be still alive

គង់តែ surely, inevitably

គង់នៅ to survive, live on, still remain

គង់មានថ្ងៃណាមួយ one of these days...

គង់វង់ to exist, survive

គង្គា water (Lit)

គង្ឃិន to plan revenge, be vindictive

គជ /kuccĕəq/ elephant (Lit)

គជសារ /kuccəsaa/ elephant (Lit)

គជសីហ៍ /kuccəsəy/ mythological lion with an elephant's trunk

គជា /kucciə/ elephant (Lit)

គជេន្ទ្រ /kəceen/ elephant (Lit)

គជេន្ទ្រក្លាយ magically produced elephant

គជេន្ទ្រា /kuccentriə/ elephant (lit: Indra's elephant)

គ្រជា a kind of fish

គណ /kŭən/ party, group

គណៈ /kənaq/ party, group

គណៈកម្មការ /kənaq-kamməkaa/ commission, committee

គណៈកម្មាធិការ /kənaq-kammaathikaa/ committee

គណៈកម្មាធិការពង្រីកការសិក្សា Committee for the Development of Education

គណៈរដ្ឋមន្ត្រី /kənaq-rŏət-mŭəntrəy/ cabinet of ministers

គណន៍ /kun/ to estimate, calculate

គណនា /kunnəniə/ to estimate, calculate

គត់ exact; exactly

គតិ /kəteq/ path, way (i.e. of conduct, morality)

គតិធម៌ the path of Dharma

គតិយុត្តិធម៌ /kəteq-yuttəthɔə/ justice, fairness

គតិលោកថ្មីដែលកើតមានឡើង modern morality, the new morality

គន់ watch, observe

គន់គយ to watch, look at, observe

គន់គូរ to figure out, calculate (by writing)

គន់មើល to observe

គន្ធ /kŭən/ odor, aroma, fragrance

គន្ធា (=គន្ធ)

គន្លង path, furrow, tradition, way

គន្លាក់ notch, crease, depression

គប់ to throw (something) overhand at (tv)
គប្បី /koə̆pbəy/ auspicious, appropriate, proper
គភ៌ /kɔə/ pregnant

គមនាគមន៍ /kumməniəkum/ communication, transportation
គម្តែង /kummədaəŋ/ King, Master, Supreme Ruler
គម្ពីរ /kumpii/ the Scriptures, (Buddhist) Bible
គម្ភីរា (= គម្ពីរ) deep, profound, unfathomable (Lit)
គម្រាម to threaten

គម្រោងការ plan, project

គយ customs, duty tax

គយ to watch, to observe

គយគន់ to observe

គរ /kɔɔ/ to pile up

គរ /kɔɔ/ kapok

គរុកោសល្យ /kəruqkaosɑl/ pedagogy

គល់ log, trunk

គ.ស. (abbreviation for គ្រិស្តសករាជ /krɨhsaqkəraac/ Christian Era (A.D.)
គហស្ថ /kɔɔhŏəh/ layman

គាង tapered, tapering

គាងឃ្វាយ globular ornament, often resembling a flame, surmounting a monument (lit: buffalo chin)
គាត silk thread

គាត់ respectful 3rd person pronoun: he, she, they; him, her, them
គាត់ឯង you (Pej)

គាថា saying (esp. of the Buddha), proverb; incantation; magic formula; poetry, verse (Pali)

គាប to pinch

គាប់ (= ប្រសើរ, ល្អ) good, proper, appropriate
គាប់ coincidentally, by fortunate coincidence
គាប់ចិត្ត be pleasing to

គាប់ជួនជា it happened that, incidentally
គាប់បទអាល័យ in satisfaction of [their] desires, to [their] hearts' content
គារវភាព /kiərəwĕəq-phiəp/ salute, greeting
គាល់ to have an audience (with the king)
គាស់ to pry open; to dig out

គាស់ to turn a boat by paddling away from oneself
គិត to think, plan, intend; to realize, understand; to figure, charge for
គិតក្រែង to consider, take into account
គិតក្រោយ consider the consequences, think of the future
គិតគន់ consider, be judicious

គិតគូរ concern oneself with, pay attention to
គិតឃើញវែងឆ្ងាយ think deeply, consider all aspects
គិតងាយ to take lightly

គិតតែពី to think only of

គិតត្រូវគ្នាហើយ having agreed among themselves
គិតថា to think that, to think as follows
គិតទៅ having considered [it]

គិតទៅឆ្ងាយ to think deeply

គិតប្រមាណក្នុងចិត្ត to calculate privately

គិតមិនវែង short-sighted

គិតអ្វីមិនលេច unable to concentrate one's thoughts
គិម្ហ: hot (Lit)

គិរី mountain (Lit)

គិរីវង្គត /kiriiwŭəŋkɑt/ name of a mountain in the Himalayas
គិល imitative of the sound of a roar of anger or emotion: with a roar
គិលានដ្ឋាន /kiliənnəthaan/ infirmary

គិលានុបដ្ឋាក /kiliənuppəthaq/ male nurse
គិលានុបដ្ឋាយិកា /kiliənuppəthayikaa/ female nurse
គីង្កក់ toad

គីម - សំអុន Kim Samon, a contemporary poet

គីឡូម៉ែត្រ /kiloumaet/ kilometer

គីឡូម៉ែត្រក្រឡា square kilometer

គឹកកង boisterous

គឺ copulative relator: to be, to be as follows, to equal

គុណ /kun/ good deeds, merit, quality

គុណគ្រូ the value of teachers

គុណបុណ្យ goodness and power

គុណស្រ័យ reward, recompense, good deeds done in return

គុណានុភាព /kunaanuphiəp/ power of virtue, moral force

គុម្ព /kum/ clump, bush

គុម្ពោត bush, clump of bushes

គុយ a vine with edible fruit

គុយទាវ /kuy-tiəw/ a Chinese noodle dish

គុលិកា /kulikaa/ pill

គុហា /kuhiə/ cave, lair

គូ couple; pair; mate

គូកន friend

គូព្រេង predestined mate

គូវិវាទ /kuu-wiwiət/ protagonists, parties involved, contestants

គូសត្រូវ /kuu-satrəw/ adversaries, opponents

គូសាមីខ្លួន the couple themselves

គូទ buttocks, rear end

គូរ to draw

គូរវាស to draw, mark

គូលី coolie

គូលែន litchi (nut, tree)

គូស to strike (a match); draw (a line), make a mark

គួច to whirl, churn (of wind, water)

គួប joined together

គួយ Kuy, Kuoy (name of a tribal group in Cambodia)

គួរ /kuə/ proper, correct

គួរណាស់តែបាន... really should have...

គួរតែចង់ឱ្យមើលណាស់ very appealing, very interesting to look at

គួរទុកដូច should be considered as

គួរសម /kuə-sɑm/ reasonable, moderate, appropriate

គួរសវនា interesting (to hear)

គួរសម to pay respects

គួរឱ្យ worthy of (when /kuə-qaoy/ precedes a verb, its meaning is comparable to the suffix -able in English; e.g. likeable)

គួរឱ្យចាប់ចិត្ត likeable, appealing

គួរឱ្យចាប់អារម្មណ៍ captivating, interesting

គួរឱ្យណាយ one should eschew [it], be leery of [it]

គួរឱ្យស្តាយ regrettable

គួរឱ្យអនិច្ចា worthy of pity, one should pity

គួរឱ្យអាណិត too bad for..., unfortunate, one should pity

គួរនា (=ដូច, ដូចជា) /kuərəniə/ like, as if (Lit)

គៀង to drive (cattle), round up, herd together, head off

គេ indefinite 3rd person pronoun: he, she, they, one, someone

គេច sneak away; evade, shirk, avoid

គេចកែដោះសា to make excuses, extricate oneself

គេចកែបែរ to evade, elude, equivocate, hedge

គេចចេញ to wiggle free, get away, avoid

គេហដ្ឋាន /keehaqthaan/ residence (Formal)

គែ chicken's craw

គោ cow, ox, beef

គោក្របី oxen and buffalo, livestock

គោបាល cattle herdsman

គោមូត្រ /koomout/ the symbol ~~~

គោក land, by land; to be grounded, aground

គោកគាំង dried out, dried up, parched

គោកនួន name of a village

គោម paper lantern

គោរព to pay respects, to venerate

គោល aim, goal, mark

គោល ៗ main points, essential ideas

គោលការណ៍ principle, ideal

គោលគីឡូម៉ែត្រ kilometer marker

គោលបំណង purpose, intention, goal

គោះ to strike, beat

គុំ to plan revenge, resolve to retaliate, feel vindictive

គុំគួន be vindictive

គុំធ្វើគ្នាឲ្យសោះសូន្យ scheme to destroy each other

គំនរ pile, heap (n)

គំនាប់ to salute, greet

គំនាប់គំនួរ pleasing and proper, desirable

គំនិត thought

គំនិតមារយាទ conduct, behavior

គំនូរ drawing, picture

គំនុំ vindictiveness

គំរក់ filthy, wicked

គំរូ model, example

គំរោះ rude, crude, coarse

គាំទ្រ to support

គ្នា 1st, 2nd, or 3rd per. familiar pronoun; together, reciprocally

គ្នាន់គ្នាញ់ bothered, annoyed, irritated

គ្នាន់គ្នេរ figure, plan, calculate

គ្នីគ្នា acquaintances, partisans

គ្នេរ to figure, calculate, think

គ្មាន not have, not exist, there is/are no

គ្មានចិត្ត indifferent, callous; disinclined to, uninterested in

គ្មានឈប់ឈរ unceasingly

គ្មានទាស់អ្វីទេ [I] have no objections

គ្មានបុរសណាមួយ there is no man (who)

គ្មានប្រណី with abandon

គ្មានស្គាល់ទិសដំបន់អ្វី without knowing where to go, uncontrolled

គ្រង to watch over, take care of, protect

គ្រញ៉ៀង to shudder, have a chill of revulsion, creep (of flesh)

គ្រប to cover; a cover, lid

គ្របដណ្តប់ to cover over

គ្របទ្រប envelop, protect

គ្រប់ every, every one of

គ្រប់ imitative of the sound of a sudden fall

គ្រប់គ្រង to regulate, govern, administer

គ្រប់គ្រាន់ enough, plentiful

គ្រប់ចំនួន the full number

គ្រប់តែ every

គ្រប់តែមាតា every mother, all mothers

គ្រប់ទិសទី in all sectors

គ្រប់បែប of all kinds, of every variety

គ្រប់បែបយ៉ាង of all kinds

គ្រប់ប្រការ everything, every aspect

គ្រប់ផ្លូវ (in) every field

គ្រប់មាត់ (from) everyone (lit: every mouth)

គ្រប់មុខ all kinds, every kind

គ្រប់មួយសម្រាប់ a complete set

គ្រប់រូប each and every one

គ្រប់លក្ខណ៍ virtuous, exemplary (of a woman)

គ្រលីងគ្រលោង a grey bird

គ្រលុក hole, cavity

គ្រលែងគេក a kind of bird

គ្រវាត់ to toss away

គ្រវី to swirl, fling in a circle, shake with a circular motion

គ្រវែង to toss away, throw away (a long object)

គ្រហឹម to roar (of an animal); to produce a throaty sound of displeasure or disapproval

ក្រហែម /krɔhɛɛm/ to clear one's throat

គ្រា time, occasion

គ្រា to support in walking, help along

គ្រាណា when

គ្រានោះ at that time, once upon a time

គ្រាន់ enough; pretty good, good enough; enough to, just for; for the purpose of, to serve as

គ្រាន់តែ only, just

គ្រាន់តែជាលេង just as a game, just for sport

គ្រាន់តែមាត់ enough to eat, enough to live on

គ្រាន់នឹង just to

គ្រាន់បើ quite, sufficient, so-so; recovered, better (of patient)

គ្រាន់បើដែរ not bad; pretty good

គ្រាប់ specifier for matches, grains, pellets, pills, etc.

គ្រាប់ឈើគូស a match

គ្រិស្តសករាជ /krɨhsaqkəraac/ Christian Era

គ្រឹកគ្រេង thunderous, clamorous, tumultuous

គ្រឹប sound of knocking together

គ្រឹហា /krɨhhiə/ house (Lit)

គ្រឹះស្ថាន firm, company, place of business; residence, home

គ្រុឌ /krut/ Garuda

គ្រុឌា (=គ្រុឌ) /krutdiə/ Garuda

គ្រុនចាញ់ malaria; to have malaria

គ្រូ teacher, master; mediating spirit, folk-doctor, medicine-man

គ្រូបង្រៀន school teacher

គ្រូបឋមសិក្សា primary school teacher

គ្រូបាធ្យាយ /kruu-baatyiəy/ teachers, mentors

គ្រូអាចារ្យ /kruu-qaacaa/ teachers

គ្រួ family

គ្រួសារ family

គ្រឿង spices, ingredients, things, accessories; specifier for machines, motors, etc.

គ្រឿងប្រដាប់ things, accessories, equipment

គ្រឿងប្រដាប់សម្រាប់អាភរណ៍ clothing, jewelry

គ្រឿងមាសពេជ្រ jewelry

គ្រឿងសម្រាប់ពិធីយុទ្ធនា paraphernalia of battle

គ្រឿងអលង្ការ /-qalaŋkaa/ jewelry

គ្រឿងឧបភោគបរិភោគ /krɨəŋ-quppəphook-baariphook/ commodities (lit: things to use and to eat)

គ្រឿយគ្រឿន slowly, gradually

គ្រេងគ្រឹក (=គគ្រឹកគគ្រេង) thunderously, tumultuously

គ្រែ bed

គ្រោង to plan

គ្រោងការណ៍ plan (n)

គ្រោងទុក to envisage, plan for

គ្រោតគ្រាត rough, ugly, crude

គ្រោះ accident, misfortune, (bad) fate, danger; dangerous

គ្រោះថ្នាក់ accident, danger; dangerous

គ្រោះនាយ accident

គ្រំ a kind of shell fish

គ្រាំ to be damaged internally

គ្រាំគ្រា mauled, injured internally

គ្លាយ (=ក្តី) situation, case, affair (Thai)

## ឃ

ឃាត់ to prevent, to stop (tv)

ឃាត់ឃាំង to oppose, object

ឃាត់ឱ្យនៅក្នុងផ្ទះ required that [he] stay in the house

ឃាតកម្ម /khiəttəkam/ murder

ឃឹកៗ sound of giggling, chuckling

ឃុន next to the lowest title of nobility

ឃុប snapping sound

ឃើញ to see, perceive

ឃើញចំនេញ (=ឃើញចំណេញ) anticipate a profit

ឃោឃៅ cruel, harsh

ឃោរ ferocious

ឃោសៈ /khoosaq/ voiced; the 2nd series of Cambodian consonants

ឃុំ administrative unit composed of several villages

ឃុំ to put under guard, to imprison

ឃុំឃាំង to arrest, to detain, imprison

ឃុំថ្ម the khum of Thmâ

ឃុំពល to raise and command forces

ឃ្នង bar, pole (put across an opening)

ឃ្នង arrogant, wayward, wicked; savage, mean

ឃ្នាង pillory, stockade, device to hold a prisoner by the neck

ឃ្នាប pincers, press

ឃ្នើសចិត្ត to be displeased

ឃ្មាតខ្មី quickly, in a hurry

ឃ្មស gong

ឃ្លា space; sentence, phrase; one phrase or line bounded by space

ឃ្លាឃ្លៃ exhausted and dejected

ឃ្លាត to be separated from

ឃ្លាតឃ្លា be separated from

ឃ្លាតឃ្លៀង be separated from

ឃ្លាតឃ្លៃ (= ឃ្លាតឃ្លា )

ឃ្លាន to be hungry

ឃ្លានថ្ពុះខ្លាចផ្សា to have hunger pains, to suffer from hunger

ឃ្លៀងឃ្លាត to be absent, away from, separated from

ឃ្លៀងឃ្លាំ to watch, observe

ឃ្លេងឃ្លោង pitching and rolling (of a boat); tottering, staggering

ឃ្លោក gourd

ឃ្លោង to roll, pitch (of a boat)

ឃ្លាំ (=ឃ្លាំមើល) /klŏəm/ to watch, check on, watch secretly

ឃ្វាល to herd, guard

ង curved

ងក់ to nod, lower the head

ង៉ក់ abruptly, jerkily

ង៉ក់ៗ descriptive of jerky or staccato motion

ងងឹត dark, dim

ងងឹតងងល់ ignorant; blind, heedless, insensitive

ងងឹតមុខ to be dizzy, feel faint

ងងុយដេក to be sleepy

ងងុះ to wheedle, entreat

ងប់ a kind of small tree

ងា to gesture with the arm, move the hand in an arc

ងាក to turn one's head, look around, turn aside

ងាកចិត្ត to switch one's loyalty or devotion

ងាប់ to die, be dead (Pej, or of animals)

ងាយ easy, simple (to do)

ងារ work, function, status, title

ងាវ a kind of clam

ង៉ាវ noise-maker

ងិល imitative of the sound of a roar of displeasure

ងីងី lolling, nodding

ងុយដេក to be sleepy

ងូងៗ sound of a beetle

ងូត to bathe (iv)

ងូតទឹក to bathe (iv)

ងើប to get up; to raise oneself up a bit; to lift (one's head, chin, etc.)

ងៀត dried and salted

ងេះ /ŋeh/ Ngeh (personal name)

ងោក to nod; to roll, rock

ងោកងាស to nod forward and back, rock back and forth
ង៉ោឌិនយៀម /ŋao-dɨn-yiəm/ Ngo Dinh Diem
ង៉ោះ /ŋɑh/ Ngah (personal name)

## ច

ចក្ខុ /caqkhoq/ eye (Lit)

ច័ក្រ /caq/ a magical flying disc with jagged teeth

ចក្រពត្តិ /caqkrəpŏət/ royal, imperial; empire, kingdom

ចក្រវាឡ /caqkrəwaal/ the mountains surrounding the Universe; limitless space

ចក្រវិត (= ចក្កវិត្តិ, ចក្រពត្តិ) king, emperor

ចក្រី /cɑkrəy/ king, prince

ចក្រី /cakrəy/ Minister of War and Land Transport

ចង to tie; be tied; to ensnare, catch up with, devolve on

ចង to compile, collect

ចងក្រង to compile, collect

ចងចិត្ត to be in love with, enamored of

ចងចាំ to retain, remember, hold on to

ចងជាឧបមា create a simile

ចងដៃ ceremonial binding of couple's wrists; give a wedding gift

ចងទោស to contemplate violence, plan villainy (thereby incurring guilt)

ចងបេតី have a love affair

ចងពន្ធ to connect, tie together

ចងមេត្រី to establish (friendly) relations; to make love

ចង់ to want (to)

ចង់បើ even if

ចង់ស្រី to desire, court, seduce a woman

ចង្កា chin

ចង្កឹះ chopsticks

ចង្កុលណី /cɑŋkollənəy/ an aquatic plant (same family as lotus, water lily)

ចង្កូត tiller, rudder, steering wheel

ចង្កូម long canine tooth, fang

ចង្កៀង lamp, lantern

ចង្កៀងប្រេងកាត kerosene lamp

ចង្កេះ the waist, hips

ចង្រៀក a kind of tree

ចង្រៃ harmful, detrimental; bothersome, annoying

ចង្វាភ្លៀង tiny minnow-like fish

ចង្វាឫស្សី a kind of small fish

ចង្វាក់ rhythm, gait

ចង្ហាន់ food (of clergy)

ចង្ហូរ ditch, gully, small channel of water

ចង្អុល to point out

ចង្អូរ small ditch, channel, canal

ចង្អូរត្នាត a kind of tree

ចង្អៀត narrow, crowded

ចង្អេរ a wide flat basket

ចចក wolf

ចចិក to peck at repeatedly

ចចេស /cɑceh/ to persist (in), insist (on)

ចត to park, moor

ចតុ /cattoq-/ four (usually in compounds)

ចតុប្បាទ /cattobaat/ quadruped

ចតុមុខ /cattoq-muk/ Cattomuk (the site of the confluence of four rivers in Phnom-Penh; lit: the four faces)

ចតុរាបាយ /cattoraabaay/ the four levels (of hell)

ចន្ទន៍ /can/ sandalwood; a sweet-smelling fruit

ចន្ទបុរ (= ចាន់តាប៊ុន) Chantaburi (Thailand)

ចន្ទ្រា /cantriə/ moon (Lit)

ចន្លុះ torch (made of bark treated with resin)

ចន្លោះ intervening space; between

ចប blade, hoe

ចបកាប់ a hoe

ចប់ to finish, come to the end of; completion (of an action)

ចម summit, peak; highest, supreme

ចមទិន្ត្រ appellation for a king

ចមពង្ស appellation for a king

ចម្ការ /camkaa/ garden, plantation (other than rice)

ចម្ងាយ distance; to be distant (from)

ចម្ប៉ា fragrant red or white flower

ចម្បាំង war, battle

ចម្រឹង bar, slat, column, colonnade

ចម្រឹងជើងទៀន bars (shaped like) candle-holders

ចម្រុះ mixed

ចម្រូង a spike, sharpened stake

ចម្រើន to increase, prosper, progress; progress, success

ចម្រើនផ្លូវព្រះរាជមេត្រីក standard form of written salutation between kings: to (lit: [with] growing royal friendship to)

ចម្រើនព្រះបរិត្ត /-preăh-barət/ to bless, hold a ceremony of benediction

ចម្រៀង song

ចម្រៀងប្រជាប្រិយ folk songs

ចម្លង take across, put across

ចម្លាក់ sculpture, frieze

ចម្លែក special, different

ចរ /caa/ to go (Lit)

ចរចា to negotiate; to converse, talk (Lit, Formal)

ចរចេញយាត្រា to go out (Lit)

ចរចេរ go, walk (Lit)

ចរចៅរ៉ៅ /caa caw-raw/ be kind, be gentle, be affable

ចរណៃ /caarənay/ cut glass, crystal

ចរិយាសម្បត្តិ /caqriyaa-sambat/ personality, manner

ចលនា /callənaa/ movement (political, literary, etc.)

ចលនាខ្លាំង violent action

ចលាចល /cəlaacal/ unrest, uprising, trouble

ច.ស. /colləsaqkəraac/ an era beginning 638 A.D.

ចា to inscribe

ចាក to leave, abandon

ចាកចេញ to leave, depart

ចាកចោល to leave, abandon

ចាកសិក្ខាបទ leave the priesthood

ចាកស្ថាន /caaq-thaan/ to die (Eleg)

ចាក់ to stab, insert, inject; to deposit; to pour; to crochet; to lock or unlock

ចាក់ពូន to pile up, make a mound or hillock

ចាក់រុក to sow discord, instigate trouble

ចាក់ឫស to take root, penetrate

ចាក់សាប to fence off

ចាគៈ /caakĕəq/ liberality, generosity, munificence

ចាគៈសម្បទា the possession of generosity

ចាងហ្វាង /caaŋ-waaŋ/ director, manager

ចាញ់ to lose (to), be defeated (by); be inferior to

ចាញ់កល to be deceived, fooled by a trick

ចាញ់ to be [easily] affected by (heat, diseases...)

ចាញ់កំដៅ to suffer from heat

ចាញ់ដាច់ to lose repeatedly

ចាត់ to organize; to employ, deploy, assign; undertake to

ចាត់ការ to prepare to

ចាត់ចែង to organize, plan, order, arrange

ចាត់ទុកជា to consider as

ចាត់សំបុត្រ to send a message or letter

ចាន plate, dish

ចានក្បាន dishes

ចាន់ sandalwood tree

ចាប sparrow

ចាប់ to get hold of, catch; begin, start

ចាប់ខ្យល់ to pinch the skin at various points (thought to have therapeutic value)

ចាប់ចិត្ត to like, be interested in

ចាប់ចុងចួន to make rhymes (in Cambodian sense); establish poetic relations between words

ចាប់ដើមកំណើត to originate, to come into existence

ចាប់ដើមតាំងពី beginning from, starting with

ចាប់ដៃគ្នាជាប្ដីប្រពន្ធ to take one another as husband and wife

ចាប់ផ្ដើម to commence, to begin

ចាប់ព្រះរាជហឫទ័យ to like, be attracted by (Roy)

ចាប់យាម to predict, foretell

ចាប់អារម្មណ៍ to be interested, intrigued

ចាប៉ី a stringed musical instrument

ចាម Cham (n, adj)

ចាយ to spend, disperse

ចាយវាយ to spend (Coll)

ចារ to put in stakes, branches (as a fence or barrier)

ចារ a kind of tree

ចារចែង say (Lit)

ចារឹក inscription; to inscribe

ចាលចិត្ត to learn (one's lesson), be reformed

ចាវ-តា-កួន Chou Ta-Kuan, a 13th century Chinese visitor to Angkor

ចាស់ old, second-hand, former

ចាស់ៗ elders, old people

ចាស់ជរា old and decrepit

ចាស់ទុំ elders; old

ចាស់ព្រឹទ្ធាចារ្យ /cah-prɨtthiəcaa/ old age, elders

ចាស់ព្រះវស្សា elderly, senior (Clergy)

ចា៎ះ /caah/ polite response particle used by women

ចិក Uncle (polite term of address to an older Chinese man)

ចិញ្ចឹម to care for, raise

ចិញ្ចើម eyebrow

ចិញ្ចើមថ្នល់ curb (of a street or road)

ចិញ្ចែង /cəñcaeŋ/ bright, gleaming

ចិញ្ច្រាំ to hack up in little pieces

ចិញ្ចៀន /cəñciən/ finger-ring

ចិត to slice, to cut up

ចិតសិប seventy

ចិត្ត /cət/ heart, mind, disposition

ចិត្តខ្មាំង malicious, characterized by enmity or ill-will

ចិត្តជា good-natured, patient

ចិត្តជ្រះថ្លា sincere, pure, unreserved

ចិត្តត្រង់ honest, faithful

ចិត្តត្រង់នឹង to be faithful to

ចិត្តថ្លើម disposition

ចិត្តទន់ tender-hearted

ចិត្តធំ to be bold, presumptuous

ចិត្តមុត daring, stout-hearted, resolute

ចិត្តលាមក dirty, crooked, vile-hearted

ចិត្តល្អ kind-hearted

ចិត្តស្នេហា love, affection

ចិត្រគុប្ត /cəttrəkup/ Citragupta

ចិន China; Chinese (n, adj)

ចិន្តា /cəndaa/ thoughts, thinking processes

ចីពរ /cəypɔɔ,cəpɔɔ/ monk's outer garment

ចីរកាល /ceirəkaal/ permanence, duration, long time

ចឹក to peck (of a bird), bite (of a snake)

ចុក to have a pain, a cramp

ចុក to fill, stuff into

ចុង end, point

ចុងចួន rhyme, rhyming

ចុងជើង at the foot

ចុងដង place name (lit: end of the handle)
ចុតហ្មាយ letter, message (Roy)

ចុះ to descend; to put down, work out, formalize; dated...
ចុះ hortatory final particle

ចុះកាសែត to put or to publish in the newspaper
ចុះចូល to surrender, submit, concede

ចុះញ៉ម to back down, surrender, give way
ចុះដី to go down (from the house)

ចុះបើ but if

ចុះប្រេង to rut; go wild, run amuck (Idiom)
ចុះហត្ថលេខា to sign

ចុះរបៀប to fit in, conform, adapt (to prevailing conventions)
ចុះឡើង go back and forth

ចុះឡើង ៗ back and forth

ចូក to shovel

ចូរ hortatory auxiliary: let us, go ahead and (Lit)
ចូល to enter

ចូលគ្នា to combine

ចូលចិត្ត to like (to); to understand (that), interpret (as)
ចូលឆ្នាំ the New Year (lit: enter year)
ចូលដៃ to side with, collaborate with
ចូលដំណេក to go to sleep

ចូលត្រណម follow a prescribed ritual

ចូលទូក to dock a boat

ចូលបុណ្យ to contribute (money) to a religious ceremony
ចូលមិនចុះ unable to approach

ចូលរៀន to begin studies, go back to school
ចួន euphony, poetic relationship between words
ចួនអក្សរដើមព្យាង្គ alliteration

ចួបចួន to meet

ចើក wanton, sensuous

ចើស bulging, rotund; in an advanced stage (of pregnancy)
ចៀម sheep

ចៀវ name of a famous monk-politician
ចៀស to avoid; to pass by

ចៀសមិនរួច to be unable to avoid

ចេក banana

ចេកទេស a kind of flower (canna lily?)
ចេញ /cəñ/ to go out, exit; to come out for, take responsibility for, speak out
ចេញចូល to go out and in

ចេញដំណើរ departure; to depart, leave on a trip
ចេញថ្លៃ to pay

ចេញទូក to push off, embark

ចេញមុខ to dare, defy, stand up

ចេញរួច to be able to get out

ចេញលេង take a break (between classes, etc.)
ចេញស្តី to speak

ចេតនា /caettənaa/ to like, desire

ចេតិយ /caetdəy/ reliquary monument, stupa
ចេស្តា authority, power (Lit)

ចេស្តាធិការនុភាព /ceisdaathikaarĕəq-nuphiəp/ great power
ចេះ to know how to, to be able to; to be learned
ចេះគិតគូរ to be wise, to know right from wrong
ចេះដឹង be learned, educated

ចេះតែ always, characteristically

ចែក to divide

ចែកចាយ to give out, distribute

ចែង to shine; to set out, inscribe, write, tell; to clarify
ចែងចង to compose

ចែងចងជានិទាន to compose in [the form of] discourse
ចែចង់ to court (a woman)

ចែចូវ to approach the parents of a

prospective bride (by a go-between)

ចែត្រ March-April (lunar system)

ចែវ to row (standing up) with a single oar fixed to the stern of a boat

ចៃ louse

ចៃដន្យ /cay-dɑn/ circumstance, chance

ចោត steep

ចោទ to warn, accuse; to raise an issue, pose a question

ចោទប្រកាន់ to accuse

ចោម to surround, crowd around

ចោមរោម to surround

ចោរ thief

ចោរកម្ម /caorəkam/ thievery

ចោល to throw away, abandon, give up; to throw something (at something)

ចោលកន្ទុយភ្នែក glance at, catch a glimpse of

ចោលទទេ uselessly, to no purpose

ចោលភ្នែកមើល glance at, look at

ចោលម្សៀត indigent, irresponsible

ចោលស្រុក to be exiled (lit: abandon the country)

ចៅ grandchild; general term for children of one's grandchildren's generation

ចៅ Young Mister..., Master...

ចៅ chief, head

ចៅក្រម /caw-krɑm/ judge, magistrate

ចៅក្រសួង department head

ចៅក្រុងយក្ស King of the ogres

ចៅប្រសា grandchild-in-law

ចៅពញា Chau Ponhea (a title meaning roughly 'Prince')

ចៅពញាចក្រី /caw-pəñiə-cəkrəy/ title (Arch)

ចៅពញាមហាទេព title (Arch)

ចៅពញារាជដេជះ /caw-pəñiə-riəccə-daeccəəh/ title (Arch)

ចៅពញារាជាមេត្រី title (Arch)

ចៅពញាសេនាស្រ្គាម archaic military title (general?)

ចៅពញាស្រែសន្សេនាឫទ្ធិ title (Arch)

ចៅមហា male go-between in a marriage negotiation

ចៅសង្កាត់ chief of a (municipal) division

ចៅហ្វាទឡ្ហៈ /cawwaatəlaq/ Prime Minister (Arch)

ចៅហ្វាយ /cawwaay/ owner, master, headman

ចៅហ្វាយខេត្ត provincial governor

ចៅហ្វាយនាយ superior, owner, master, headman

ចៅហ្វាយស្រុក district-chief

ចៅអធិការ /caw-qathikaa/ abbot, head monk

ចំ right, exact; coincide with

ចំជា certainly, really, precisely

ចំមុខ just opposite, right in front of

ចំការ garden, plantation (other than rice)

ចំការកៅស៊ូ rubber plantation

ចំការមន Chamcar Mon (a section of Phnom Penh)

ចំការលើ Chamcar Leu (district)

ចំកួត idiot, crazy person; crazed, out of one's mind

ចំកោង to bend, arch (iv)

ចំងាយ distance

ចំណង knot, binding

ចំណត station, parking place

ចំណតអយស្ម័យយាន train station

ចំណតអាកាសយាន airport

ចំណាន good at, skilled in; special, of best quality

ចំណាន ៗ of the very best quality, outstanding

ចំណាប់ special, excellent; exceedingly, the most, in the extreme

ចំណាប់ (=ការចាប់) seizure, arrest

ចំណាយ to spend, expend, disburse

ចំណាយមាត់គេ be talked about, be the subject of rumors

ចំណារ inscription, character, marking; stake, marker
ចំណាស់ elderly, rather old; age

ចំណី dessert, sweets; food (Lit)

ចំណីចំណុក food, knick-knacks

ចំណីអាហារ various kinds of food

ចំណុច to stipple; a dot; point (of an argument)
ចំណុះ vassal, dependant; to be under the suzerainty of
ចំណុះ load, capacity

ចំណូល profit, revenue

ចំណេញ profit, proceeds

ចំណេរ future; afterward, henceforth
ចំណេរទៅលង់ in the future, later on

ចំណេះ knowledge

ចំណេះចេះតែឯង you're always right, you know everything
ចំណេះវិជ្ជា learning, education, knowledge
ចំណែក section, part; as for, on the part of
ចំណែកខាង as for

ចំណែក...វិញ as for...on the other hand
ចំណែកឯង as for

ចំណោទ question, problem

ចំណោម group, totality; encirclement
ចំណាំ to remember, keep in mind, keep account of; memory, recollection; used to, accustomed to
ចំនួន number, total

ចំបែង to brood, agonize, worry

ចំបាំងរាំងជល់ war, battle, confrontation
ចំប៉ី frangipani

ចំប្រប់ to shiver, tremble, shake

ចំពុះ beak, bill

ចំពូក category, kind, variety; chapter
ចំពើប newly encountered, just met

ចំពោះ toward, especially for

ចំពោះព្រះភក្ត្រ before the very eyes of, right in front of (Vessantara)
ចំរិត following closely behind [?]

ចំរើន to advance, increase, prosper

ចំរើនកើន to increase

ចំរៀក strip, lengthwise piece

ចំហាយ steam

ចំឡែក extraordinary, special, different
ចំអក to taunt, mock, make fun of

ចំអិន to cook (until done)

ចំអើត to stretch up on the toes

ចំអៀក to dawdle, be a laggard, be sluggish
ចំអែត to fill, satisfy, satiate; a meal
ចាំ to wait for; to remember, recognize; to guard; just wait until I..., just let me...
ចាំ have to, be necessary to

ចាំចេះ to know, be informed

ចាំជម្ងឺ to minister to a sick person

ចាំនៅ remain with

ចាំបាច់ to be necessary, imperative (that)
ចាំបាច់...អ្វី why is it necessary to...?
ចាំអ្វីទៀត come on, what are we waiting for?
ចាំង to shine on, reflect, sparkle, refract light
ច្នេះ (=ស៊ូច្នេះ)

ច្នោះ (=ស៊ូច្នោះ)

ច្បង eldest

ច្បា an odorless flower

ច្បាប់ law; custom

ច្បាប់ issue, version, copy; specifier for stories, books, newspapers, etc.
ច្បាប់ក្រម /cbap krɑm/ 'Code of Conventions'
ច្បាប់ព្លុសច្បាប់ក្ដាមច្បាប់ស្វា the law of the jungle

ច្បាប់ទម្លាប់ customs, law

ច្បាប់សាណា prescribed law

ច្បាប់ស្រី feminine code (customary law for women)

ច្បារ garden, plot

ច្បារអំពៅ place name (lit: sugar cane field)

ច្បាស់ clear, plain, sharp (of sounds, images, speech, writing, but not of liquids or weather)

ច្បាស់ច្បង appellation for a king

ច្បាស់ជា surely, clearly

ច្បាស់លាស់ clearly, precisely

ច្យុត fall from heaven (both morally and physically)

ច្រក to force into, stuff into

ច្រកែង a kind of small fish

ច្រកែងទួយ a kind of tree

ច្រងាប់ច្រងិល falling and rolling, higgledy-piggledy

ច្រងូវ /crαŋəw, cəŋəw/ sullen, subdued, still

ច្រត់ to lean on (with the hands), bear down on

ច្របាច់ to squeeze (with the hand)

ច្របូកច្របល់ mixed up, mixed together, fused, confused

ច្រម៉ក់ tiny; little one

ច្រមាឃ a kind of tree

ច្រមុះ nose

ច្រវា a loose oar

ច្រវាក់ chain

ច្រវាត់ crisscrossing, helter-skelter, in or from all directions

ច្រវាត់ច្រវែង crisscrossing, helter-skelter, from all directions

ច្រស /crαh/ imitative of the sound of hacking, slashing (with a knife)

ច្រហ to gape, be open, be gaping

ច្រហោង to sit on the haunches

ច្រឡាស to deviate, to go astray; to be recalcitrant, defiant

ច្រឡឹង petite, cute, cozy

ច្រឡឹង a kind of small fish

ច្រឡោត to jump up, leap up, burst out

ច្រឡំ confused, mistaken

ច្រអូស lazy; dragging, drawn out

ច្រាង bristling, sticking up, brush-like

ច្រាន to push (with flat of hand)

ច្រាល to gleam; glowing red, gleaming

ច្រាវ ៗ imitative of crackling or rustling sound

ច្រាស against, in the wrong direction

ច្រាសច្រាល restless, agitated

ច្រាសទឹក upstream, against the current

ច្រុះច្រូង bristling, sticking up

ច្រើន many, much; mostly, usually

ច្រើនតែ usually, mostly

ច្រើនលើកច្រើនសា repeatedly, over and over

ច្រៀក to cut into strips, split

ច្រៀង to sing

ច្រៀវច្រែច chattering and fluttering all around

ច្រេវច្រាវ with a clang, with a clash

ច្រេស mimosa tree

ច្រោក spurting out, surging forth

ច្រាំង river bank

ច្រះផុក name of a poetic style used in the Ream-Kei

ឆ to lie, to deceive

ឆ six (in Pali and Sanskrit compounds)

ឆកាមា /chαα-kaamaa/ six-level heaven

ឆកាមាវចរសួគ៌ /chαα-kaamaawəcαα-suə/ six-level heaven of intangible beings

ឆន្ទៈ /chanteə̆q/ will, desire, wish

ឆវី /chαα-wii/ of (lovely) complexion

ឆស័ក /chααsaq/ 6th year (of the 10 year cycle)

ឆក់ to snatch, to pickpocket

ឆក់ឆួរ (= ឆក់)

ឆត្រ /chat/ umbrella

ឆរ imitative of the sound of gushing, pouring

ឆា to fry in oil; a fried mixture

ឆាសាច់គោ fried beef with vegetables

ឆាន់ to eat (Clergy)

ឆាប swoop down on and carry off (as a hawk); to reach, lick at (of flames)

ឆាបឆួរ (= ឆាប)

ឆាប់ fast, rapid; quick to...

ឆាយ to work up, to cultivate (ground)

ឆាយា shade, shadow

ឆី to eat (Arch)

ឆុត accurate, effective

ឆុតឆាប់ effective, efficacious

ឆុរ /chol/ to slash, hack, chop

ឆូត to slice, split, crease

ឆួល to burn, consume

ឆើតឆាយ attractive, pretty

ឆៀង to go off at an angle, turn aside

ឆៀង sash worn diagonally across the chest

ឆៀងខាងជើង toward the north

ឆៀងឆាប to make repeated passes (as if looking for prey)

ឆៀងមាល័យ sash of flowers, garland of flowers

ឆៀប scratchy, prickling (as a hair in a shirt)

ឆេះ to burn, be on fire

ឆែកឆេរ to search, investigate

ឆៃយ៉ាំ /chayyam ~ sayyam/ a form of dance accompanied by drum beats

ឆោង interval (rare)

ឆោត stupid, naive

ឆោម figure, body

ឆោមឆាយ beautiful

ឆោមឆ្លៅ [My] Beautiful One

ឆោមយង់ handsome, comely

ឆោមស្ងួន [My] Beloved One

ឆោឡោ with a great hubbub and commotion; running around in fright and confusion

ឆៅ raw, uncooked

ឆាំង sound of breaking or crashing

ឆ្ការ to clear off, clear away (with a machete)

ឆ្កួត crazy, idiotic

ឆ្កួតនឹងស្រី crazy about women

ឆ្កួតលីលា deranged

ឆ្កែ dog

ឆ្កែស្រែង a kind of tree

ឆ្កោ a large fish

ឆ្គង clumsy, improper, incorrect

ឆ្គាំឆ្គង crude, improper, inappropriate

ឆ្ងក់ descriptive of rising suddenly, of snapping to a rigid position

ឆ្ងល់ to wonder, be surprised, be in doubt

ឆ្ងាញ់ delicious, tasty

ឆ្ងាយ far, by far

ឆ្នុក stopper, plug

ឆ្នើម above all else, supreme

ឆ្នៀរឆ្នេរ beach, shore

ឆ្នេរ beach

ឆ្នៃ to shape, cut (gems); to estimate, calculate, figure

ឆ្នោត ticket, vote

ឆ្នាំ year

ឆ្នាំកុរ /kao/ year of the Pig

ឆ្នាំក្រោយ the next year, the following year

ឆ្នាំខាល year of the Tiger

ឆ្នាំឆ្លូវ year of the Ox

ឆ្នាំជូត year of the Rat

ឆ្នាំថោះ year of the Hare

ឆ្នាំមមី year of the Horse

ឆ្នាំវកទោស័ក 2nd year of the Monkey (of the 60-year cycle)

ឆ្នាំង pot, pan, pottery

ឆ្មិន deceive the eyes

ឆ្មិន a kind of fish

ឆ្ពោះ toward, directly toward

ឆ្មប midwife

ឆ្មា cat

ឆ្មារ thin, fine, tiny; Fig: insignificant, unfortunate

ឆ្មើង be proud, haughty, stuck-up

ឆ្មៀង look sideways, scan one side

ឆ្មេរ in a dainty or mincing fashion

ឆ្មាំ guard (n)

ឆ្លក spotty, flawed (as an improperly dyed cloth)

ឆ្លកសេចក្តី incomplete, spotty, random

ឆ្លង to cross; across

ឆ្លង shoes (Roy)

ឆ្លងទន្លេ to give birth (Idiom)

ឆ្លា vigorous, energetic

ឆ្លាក់ to carve, sculpt

ឆ្លាត intelligent, clever

ឆ្លាតវៃ extremely intelligent

ឆ្លាម shark

ឆ្លាស់ to alternate, be in alternate order, appear alternately

ឆ្លាស់ឆ្លើយ to answer

ឆ្លាស់ទ្រឹង to alternate topics, be verbally nimble

ឆ្លុះ to shine, appear, give off (light)

ឆ្លុក to intersperse, appear among

ឆ្លុញ a small eel-like fish

ឆ្លើយ to answer; to resound, reverberate

ឆ្លើយកាត់ volunteer an answer, break in

ឆ្លើយរក to find an excuse

ឆ្លើយឆ្លង to spar, banter, exchange words, carry on a dialogue

ឆ្លើយដាក់ to implicate, put the blame on

ឆ្លើយឡើង answer, speak up

ឆ្លៀត to scheme, take advantage of the slightest opportunity, capitalize on any favorable situation, seize an opening (for one's own ends)

ឆ្លៀវឆ្លាត smart, intelligent

ឆ្លេឆ្លា to cast about in a panic

ឆ្លៅ beautiful

ឆ្លាំង catfish

ឆ្វាក់ to tie around, make a double knot

ឆ្វៀលឆ្វាត់ circle around, go around crossing this way and that

ឆ្វៀលឆ្វាយ circling around

ឆ្វេង left (side)

ឆ្អន់ be tired (of), weary (of), disgusted (with)

ឆ្អិន cooked, done; deep, complete (intensifier for red, gold, etc.)

ឆ្អឹង bone

ឆ្អើម to be disgusted by, squeamish about (a smell, taste, etc.)

ឆ្អេះ to have a rancid, ammoniac smell

ឆ្អែត full, satisfied

ឆ្អៅ extremely (intensifier for red, gold, and certain other adjectives)

# ជ

ជក់ to smoke, puff

ជង Chong (a tribal group)

ជជ្ជូរជជ្ជាយ hanging down almost to the ground

ជជ្ជូរជជ្ជាយកេសរ with flowing hair

ជជែក chatter; to argue, discuss, debate

ជញ្ជាក់ to suck, to taste

ជញ្ជាក់មាត់ to click the tongue: tsk tsk

ជញ្ជាប់ជញ្ជឹង pensive

ជញ្ជាប់ to suck

ជញ្ជឹង consider, think

ជញ្ជូន to carry; to transport

ជញ្ជាំ dark

ជញ្ជាំង wall, side

ជណ្ដើរ stairs

ជនក្បត់ /cŭən-kbαt/ traitor

ជន /cŭən/ people, populace

ជនជាតិ /cŭən-ciət/ people, nationality, race, tribe

ជនក /cŭənuə̆q/ father (Lit, Roy)

ជនានុជន /cŭənniənucŭən/ people, population

ជននី /cŭənii/ mother (Lit, Roy)

ជន់ to flood, inundate

ជន្ម /cŭən/ life (Lit)

ជន្មជីព (=ជីពជន្ម) life

ជន្មា /cŭənnəmiə/ life (Lit)

ជន្លួញ walking stick, animal-prod

ជប /cup/ to conjure up, produce by magic

ជប់ to sip

ជប់លៀង to hold a feast, banquet

ជម្ងឺ disease, pain

ជម្ងឺមួយមកចាប់នាង she became ill, caught an illness

ជម្ពូ rose apple

ជម្រៅ depth

ជម្រះ to clear off, scrape clean (with a hoe)

ជម្លោះ a quarrel

ជ័យ /cɨy/ victory; short for 'Thuon Chey'

ជ័យជេដ្ឋាទី ២ /cɨy ceetthaa tii-pii/ Chey Chettha II (King of Cambodia 1618-1624)

ជយភូមិ /cĕəqyĕəqphuum, cɨyyəphuum/ victorious site, auspicious site

ជយវរ្ម័ន /cɨyyəwαrəman/ Jayavarman

ជយវរ្ម័នទី ៥ Jayavarman V, King of Angkor 968-1001

ជយោ /cɨyyoo/ victory; interjection used as a cheer: success! victory!

ជរ /cɔɔ/ embroidery, lace

ជ័រ resin

ជរា senile, decrepit; old age, senility

ជល /cŭəl/ water (Lit)

ជលធី /cŭəlləthii/ ocean, body of water (Lit)

ជលនេត្រ /cŭəlləneet/ tears (Lit)

ជលបុរី Chonburi (Thailand)

ជលស័យ /cŭəlləsay/ ocean, sea, body of water (Lit)

ជល់ to collide; to butt

ជល់ to be effective, to cure

ជល់ភ្នាល់គ្នា to bet (in cockfighting)

ជហ្វា /cĕəqwiə, cəwiə/ curved extension of a temple roof; spire

ជា copulative relator with the meaning 'be, be the same as; being, serving as'

ជា relative conjunction: that

ជា to be well, free; good, proper

ជាការទ្រាំបាន is bearable, supportable

ជាការធម្មតា as usual

ជាការប្រសើរណាស់ is very fortunate; is a stroke of luck

ជាការពិតប្រាកដ obviously, manifestly

ជាខ្នាត as a rule

ជាចុងក្រោយនេះ finally, after all, in the end

ជាជាង... rather, instead

ជាដើម and so forth, as examples

ជាថ្មី again

ជាទម្ងន់ seriously

ជាទីគាប់ព្រះទ័យ satisfying, pleasing (Roy)

ជាទីបង្ការ as a precaution

ជាទីបញ្ចប់ finally

ជាទីបំផុត the very most, extremely; supreme, highest

ជានិច្ច always

ជានិច្ចកាល /ciə-nɨccəkaal/ continually, constantly

ជាបឋម /ciə pathɑm/ first of all, principally, especially; preliminary

ជាផ្លូវការ official, officially

ជាពិសេស especially

ជាមួយ with

ជាមួយនឹង along with, together with

ជាមេត្រី politely, cordially

ជារឿយ ៗ /ciə rɨəy-rɨəy/ often, continually

ជាលាយលក្ខអក្សរ in written form

ជាលំដាប់ gradually, little by little

ជាសង្កាត់ ៗ in various sections

ជាសុខសាន្ត peacefully

ជាស្ថាពរ permanently, absolutely

ជាស្រឡះ be cleared up (of an illness), completely well

ជាស្រេច thorough, accomplished

ជាអនេកប្រការ in many ways

ជាអវសាន /ciə qawəsaan/ finally, in conclusion

ជាអវសានកាល /ciə qawəsaannəkaal/ in conclusion, finally

ជាក់ clear; clearly, truly, really; exactly, precisely

ជាក់ស្ដែង completely, without reservation

ជាង more, more than; better to, rather

ជាង artisan, craftsman

ជាងគេ most, most of all

ជាងទង jeweler

ជាងយន្ត mechanic

ជាងរ៉ាយ (=ឈៀងរ៉ាយ) Chiengrai (Thailand)

ជាងអ្វីទៅទៀត more than anything else

ជាញ to be skilled, expert

ជាតក /ciədɑq/ Jataka

ជាតិ /ciət/ nation, nationality; national

ជាតិ taste, flavor

ជាតិ life, existence, incarnation; nature (the intrinsic character of a person, animal, or thing)

ជាតិដី earth, soil

ជាន់ to step on, tread on

ជាន់ stage, era, floor (in a series)

ជាន់នេះ this time

ជាប់ to adhere, stick to; caught, attached; firmly, tenaciously

ជាប់ incessantly, constantly

ជាប់ចិត្ត attached (to), involved (with)

ជាប់ចោទ be accused

ជាប់ឆ្នោត to win an election

ជាប់ជាយូរខែ for many months

ជាប់ដៃ engaged, engrossed

ជាប់ទៅនឹង connects with

ជាប់នឹងដៃ in the hand

ជាប់ភ្នែកនឹង to be attracted by, notice

ជាប់រវល់ busy

ជាយ border, rim, edge

ជាយា wife (Roy)

ជាលី Jāli (name of Vessantara's son)

ជិត near, close to; closely, tightly; almost, nearly

ជិតខាង close by, nearby

ជិតជុំ all over, completely

ជិត ៗ នោះ close by, nearby

ជិតស្និត close, intimate

ជិនឆ្អន់ to be annoyed (with), tired (of)

ជិនណាយ to get tired of, jaded by, bored with

ជិនបុប្ផា /cɨnnəbopphaa/ name of Preah Chinavong's mother

ជិនស្រី /cɨnnəsrəy/ the victorious one (i.e. the Buddha)

ជិប to sip, to taste

ជិះ to ride, mount

ជិះជាន់ to transgress, break (the law); to oppress

ជី fertilizer, humus

ជី polite term of address

ជីជាតិ natural richness, fertility

ជីដូន grandmother

ជីដូនក្មេក grandmother-in-law

ជីក to dig

ជីកកកាយ to dig furiously, scratch about; to investigate, dig into

ជីពជន្ម /ciip-cŭən/ life (Lit)

ជីពុន /cipun, cəpun/ Japanese

ជីវភាព /ciiwəphiəp/ life, living, existence (Lit)

ជីវា (=ជីវិត) /ciiwaa/ life (Poet)

ជីវិត life

ជីវី (=ជីវិត ) life (Poet)

ជីវំ (=ជីវិត ) /ciiwĕəŋ/ life (Poet)

ជីវ្ហា /ciiwəhaa/ tongue (Roy, Lit)

ជុះ to defecate

ជូជក /cəcŭəq/ Jūjaka (name of the Brahman to whom Vessantara gave his two children)

ជូត to wipe, rub

ជូន to accompany

ជូន to give; to offer (Polite)

ជូនដំណើរ to accompany, go along with; to send off, see off

ជូរ sour

ជួ ill-bred, crude

ជួញ to do trade

ជួញ to draw oneself up, withdraw, shrink

ជួញជិត drawn up close to

ជួត to wear a turban

ជួន some, sometimes; it happened that, by chance; in case, if it should happen that

ជួនកាល sometimes

ជួនកាល...ក៏មាន it sometimes even happens that

ជួនជា it happened that

ជួប to meet, to encounter

ជួបជុំ to meet, come together, reunite

ជួបប្រទះ to meet, happen to meet

ជួបសព្វជាតិ be reunited in every reincarnation

ជួយ to help (to)

ជួយកម្លាំង to help out

ជួយជ្រោមជ្រែង to help, assist

ជួរ /cuə/ row, range, chain

ជួរភ្នំ chain of mountains

ជួល to rent, to hire

ជួស to replace; instead of, to substitute

ជួសជុល to repair

ជើង foot, leg, base

ជើងក្រាន stove; a fireplace composed fo three stones as a tripod for cooking

ជើងគោក by land; army

ជើងទឹក by water; navy

ជើងទៀន any slat or baluster used to support a railing

(lit: candleholder)
ជើងពាន a bowl with a pedestal as base
ជើងភ្នំ foot-hills, low-lying mountains
ជើងម៉ា bench, stool

ជើងសា messenger

ជើងសារជំនួញ dealer, agent (usually of foreign company)
ជើងវាំង immediate surroundings of the palace
ជើងឯក champion

ជើត name of a poetic style used in the Ream-Kei
ជឿ to believe

ជៀងជាក់ clear, precise, exact

ជៀបកប្បាស a kind of small sparrow

ជៀវ chattering, twittering

ជៀវជុំ chattering all around, talking all over the place
ជៀស avoid, stay away from

ជៀសផ្លូវ to go around, to bypass

ជៀសវាង ឬ ចៀសវាង to avoid, to shun
ជៀស្ឋជ័យ supreme, highest; appellation for a king
ជេស្ឋា older sibling (Roy)

ជេរ /cei/ to curse, swear at, scold
ជេស្ឋ /ceeh/ May-June (lunar system)

ជែង to struggle ahead, push ahead, make one's way (through a crowd); to compete
ជោក soaked

ជោគ luck

ជោគជ័យ victory; success

ជោរ susceptible to flattery

ជោរ to brim, well up (of tears); to rise, swell (of tide)
ជោរ too ripe (of a fruit)

ជោរជន់ to overflow, brim with

ជោរជល brim, overflow, swell (with water)
ជោះ to dig out, pry out, probe for (a thorn); to puncture (a blister)
ជុំ circle, revolution, circuit

ជុំជិត close around, round about

ជុំវិញ around

ជំទប់ one of the deputies of a /mee-khum/
ជំនាញ to be expert (in)

ជំនាន់ period, era

ជំនិត close, intimate, favorite

ជំនិះ vehicle, conveyance, thing to ride
ជំនូន gift, offering

ជំនួញ business, commerce; merchant

ជំនួស to substitute for; instead of

ជំនឿ belief

ជំនោរ a puff (of wind), light breeze
ជំនោរ vanity, gullibility, susceptibility to flattery
ជំនុំ to meet, confer, discuss

ជំនុំ used, somewhat worn

ជំនុំគ្នាថា meet and decide that

ជំនុំជំរះកាត់សេចក្តី to adjudicate a case, judge a case
ជំនុំពិចារណា to discuss, consider

ជំនះ victory, success

ជំពាក់ to owe somebody something; entangled (string, thread)
ជំពាក់គុណ to be indebted, obliged (by another's goodness)
ជំពូក ឬ ចំពូក way, type, sort; chapter, section
ជំរាប to inform (Formal)

ជំរាបសួរ greetings, hello; how are you; to greet
ជំរៅ (=ជម្រៅ) depth

ជំរះ to clear with a hoe, cut off at the roots
ជំរះ to resolve, to decide, judge (a case)
ជំរះកាយ to take a bath

ជំហរ /cumhɔɔ/ to brag, boast

ជំហរ /cumhɔɔ/ stance, stand, condition
ជំហាន /cumhiən/ step (n)

ជាំ bruised

ជាំព្រះភក្ត្រ have a darkened countenance
ជះ to throw water; to spend a big sum of money on something
ជ្រក to take shelter under

ជ្រកកោន take shelter, take refuge

ជ្រង sticking up, bristling, standing upright, cropped
ជ្រង to run the fingers through (hair, grass, etc.)
ជ្រងំ dead, complete (intensifier for quiet, calm, peaceful)
ជ្រប់ suddenly

ជ្រមុជ to submerge, duck, put under

ជ្រមូន to cower (?)

ជ្រាប to understand, to learn

ជ្រាល to slope gently

ជ្រាលជ្រៅ (= ជ្រៅ)

ជ្រុង corner

ជ្រុះ to fall; to shed (petals, hair, etc.)
ជ្រូក pig, pork

ជ្រួតជ្រាប to pervade, infiltrate, seep into
ជ្រួស to go beyond; overstep, make a mistake; to miss, pass
ជ្រើស to choose, pick out

ជ្រើសរើសតាំង to elect

ជ្រៀត to intrude, interfere, bother
ជ្រៀតជ្រែក to interfere

ជ្រៃ a kind of palm tree

ជ្រែង to support, prop from an angle
ជ្រែងជាប់ខ្ជាប់ to be firm, stable

ជ្រែងដៃ to put hands on hips (as sign of authority); have the arms full
ជ្រៃ a kind of banian tree

ជ្រោយជ្រែង (= ជ្រែង) to stand with knees bent and arms spread (as if in readiness for attack)
ជ្រោយ cape, point (of land)

ជ្រោះ gorge, mountain stream, spring
ជ្រៅ deep

ជ្រៅជ្រះ deep, profound

ជ្រំ grove, cluster; to cluster, group (?)
ជ្រះ clear, clean

ជ្រះស្រឡះ clearly, completely

ជ្វា Malay, Cham, Indonesian (from Java)

## ឈ

ឈប់ to stop, discontinue

ឈប់ឈរ to stop, cease (usually preceded by negative: unceasingly)
ឈប់សម្រាក to take a vacation, be off (from work, etc.)
ឈមមុខ to face, face up to

ឈរ /chɔɔ/ to stand; to be stationed (at, in)
ឈរឈ្មោះ to be named as; to run (in an election for office)
ឈាន to step

ឈាម blood

ឈាមស្រស់ស្រគាំ healthy complexion, ruddy complexion
ឈឹង still, motionless, dead still

ឈឺ to be ill, to hurt, be in pain

ឈឺក្បាល to have a headache

ឈឺចាប់ sick, ill

ឈឺចិត្ត hurt and disappointed, heart-broken, humiliated
ឈឺឆ្អាល be involved, concerned, take an interest
ឈឺទាស់ any illness contracted by a new mother after childbirth (thought to result from breaking one of the restrictions of the post-partum period)
ឈុត classifier for sets (of dishes, etc.); act (of a performance)
ឈូរ imitative of the sound of rushing, gushing
ឈូរា noisily

ឈូក lotus

ឈូស to plane, to level

ឈួល feel a burning, biting sensation (as from horseradish)

ឈើ wood

ឈើខ្លឹម precious wood, hardwood

ឈើគូស matches

ឈើច្រត់ cane, walking stick

ឈើទាលត្រាញ់ a kind of extremely tall tree

ឈើសំណាត់ driftwood

ឈៀងរ៉ាយ Chiengrai (Thailand)

ឈោង to reach for

ឈ្ងុយ fragrant (esp. aroma of roasted nuts or coffee)

ឈ្ងុយឆ្ងាញ់ fragrant, delectable, appealing

ឈ្ងុយឈ្ងប់ fragrant

ឈ្ងោក to look down

ឈ្ងោកមុខ to look down, be downcast, incline the head down

ឈ្នានីស /cniənih/ to have evil designs toward

ឈ្នួត scarf

ឈ្នួន slate

ឈ្នួល wages

ឈ្នះ to win, succeed, defeat

ឈ្មង handsome

ឈ្មួញ merchant

ឈ្មោល male (of animals)

ឈ្មោះ name; named; (someone) named, the named

ឈ្លក់ to choke, strangle

ឈ្លានពាន to invade, oppress, aggress

ឈ្លូស (small) deer

ឈ្លើយ odd, droll, not appropriate

ឈ្លើយ prisoner of war

ឈ្លេច to squeeze, to crush

ឈ្លោះ to quarrel

ឈ្លោះប្រកែក to quarrel, squabble

ឈ្វេង to think, realize (Roy, Lit)

ញក់ញី to mangle, maul, crumple; to destroy, wreak havoc

ញញឹម to smile

ញញឹមញញែម to beam with joy

ញញឹមប៉ប្រិម to smile broadly, brightly

ញញឹមស្ងួតស្ងប់មុខ to smile wanly, smile dryly

ញញើត to be impressed by, stand in awe of, respect

ញត្តិ /ñatteq/ motion, proposal

ញ៉ម to be meek, submissive, subdued

ញយ often, repeatedly

ញ័រ /ñɔə/ to tremble, shake

ញ័រខ្លួន to tremble

ញាក់ to jerk, to shake

ញាក់សេះ to shake (the reins) of a horse (to make him go)

ញាណត្ថេរ /ñiənəthei/ ecclesiastical title

ញាតិ /ñiət/ relatives, family

ញាតិកា /ñiəteqkaa, ñiətəkaa/ relatives

ញាតិសន្តាន relatives

ញាន (=ញាណ) wisdom, intelligence, knowledge

ញាន (=ញៀន) to be addicted to

ញាប់ fast, quick

ញី female (of animals)

ញី to crumple (tv)

ញឹក often

ញឹកញយ often, repeatedly

ញឹកញាប់ often

ញើស perspiration

ញៀន to be addicted to

ញែក to divide, part with both hands (as hair, tall grass, etc.); to explain in detail

ញ៉ែងញ៉ង coquettishly, with exaggerated movements

ញោច to extend into, jut out

ញោម term of address used by a monk to his parents, or to a person of his parents' age and status

ញាំ /ñam/ to eat (Coll, Familiar)

ញុំាង to cause (to), compel (to), result (in)

# ដ

ដ៏ /dɑɑ/ attributive marker: which, which is, being

ដក pull out, extract

ដកឃ្លា to leave a space (in writing); to pause

ដកដង្ហើមធំ to heave a big sigh

ដកថយ to retract, pull back, retreat

ដកព a kind of tree

ដកកាយ a kind of vine with edible fruit

ដកទឹម a kind of tree with fragrant flowers

ដកស្រង់ to extract, to excerpt, to take out (a passage from a book)

ដក់ contained, held in place (of water)

ដង time, occasion

ដង to dip up, draw up (water, etc.)

ដង range, chain

ដង handle (of a knife); tongue (of a plow)

ដងក្ដារ eave board of a temple, frequently ornate and undulating like a Naga

ដងខ្លួន trunk (of the body)

ដងនោះ once upon a time; then, thereupon, at that time (a standard phrase used in the Ream-Kei to indicate a change in the action)

ដងព្រៃ expanse of forest, jungle

ដងរែក a shoulder pole; the Dang-Raek (Mountains)

ដង្កាប់ pliers

ដង្កោ a kind of tree

ដង្ខោព្រែក Dangkhau Prêk (pl. n.)

ដង្គត់ stump

ដង្គុម bush, brush, underbrush

ដង្គួរ cluster, bunch

ដង្គោល in a big cloud, in a vague mass

ដង្វាយ (=តង្វាយ) offering, gift (Roy, Clergy)

ដង្ហើម breath

ដង្ហែ to parade, accompany in procession

ដង្ហោយ to call from afar

ដដែល same, the same

ដណ្ដប់ cover oneself with

ដណ្ដឹង to ask for one's hand in marriage; to ask, to inquire

ដណ្ដឹងតាមបុរាណ to ask for her hand in the traditional manner

ដណ្ដើម to contest, dispute, fight over

ដណ្ដាំ to cook (rice)

ដទៃ other, foreign

ដន្លង parents of one's son- or daughter-in-law

ដន្លងស្រី female parent of one's son- or daughter-in-law

ដន្លាប់ small round case or compact made of wood or metal, used to carry ointments

ដប bottle, jar

ដប់ ten

ដប់ប្រាំ fifteen

ដប់ប្រាំបួន nineteen

ដប់ពីរ twelve

ដម្បង stick, club

ដម្បូក hill, mound

ដម្រង់ to aim, direct toward

ដម្រឹម to trim, to make even, straighten

ដម្រេក sexual desire, lust

ដំឡើង to assemble, set up

ដរាប always, continuously; inevitably; until

ដរាបដល់ until, all the way to

ដរាបមក up to that point, so far

ដល់ to arrive (at), reach; when, at the time of; until; for, toward

ដល់កម្រិត to the utmost, extremely

ដល់ខ្នាតហើយ to the utmost, maximally, really

ដល់តិច at all, even a little

ដល់ទិវង្គត to die (Roy)

ដល់ទៅម្ល៉េះ even to such an extent

ដល់ខ្ទូវ to the extent of

ដល់ម្ល៉េះ like this, to this extent

ដាក់ to put, place, deposit; to use, put in (ingredients); to set (a trap); to subject someone to

ដាក់ក្ដោង to lower the sails

ដាក់ខ្លួន to stoop

ដាក់គយល្បាត to post a watch, set sentries

ដាក់គ្នា back and forth, reciprocally, against each other

ដាក់ដៃ entrust to, turn over to

ដាក់ទឹកមុខ to adopt a fixed expression

ដាក់បិណ្ឌ ceremony of presentation of food to the monks

ដាក់ភ្នាល់ to put up as collateral for a wager

ដាក់មុខ to look down, to lower one's gaze respectfully

ដាច់ to break apart, break in two, separate (iv); extremely, incomparably, above all others; at the end of

ដាច់ខែ at the end of the month, after the month of...

ដាច់ដាច cut off, isolated; destitute; torn, ragged

ដាច់ពោះ to starve

ដាច់សាច់ sharp, wounding, cruel, (lit: tearing the flesh)

ដាច់ស្រយាល remote

ដាន path, furrow, trace; aisle, walkway

ដាប completely covered, soaked

ដាល to spread, extend

ដាល់ to punch with a fist

ដាវ a sword

ដាស spread all over, covered

ដាសដា all over the place

ដាសដាល all around, all over, thoroughly

ដាសដេរ (=ដេរដាស) full of, covered with; all over

ដាស់ to wake someone up

ដាស់តឿន to remind, admonish, instruct

ដាស់ទុំ deepest part of the night (about 1-3 a.m.)

ដិត to touch, be next to, be touching; stick to, cling to

ដិតដាន close(ly), intimate(ly)

ដី earth, ground

ដីទួល mound, elevated site

ដីល្បប់ alluvial soil

ដីស /dəy-sαα/ chalk

ដីឥដ្ឋ /dəy-qət/ clay

ដឹក to carry, transport, lead

ដឹកដៃ to lead by the hand

ដឹកនាំ to transport, to lead

ដឹង to know; to be aware of

ដឹងខ្លួន to be conscious, aware; regain consciousness

ដឹងខ្លួនមុន to know in advance, realize beforehand

ដឹងចាស់ទុំ to show respect toward one's elders

ដឹងដាន know the facts, know the story

ដឹងដៃដក a woodcutter's ax

ដឹងទុក្ខដឹងសុខា be understanding, cognizant of (another's feelings)

ដឹងទៅដល់ get to, spread to

ដឹងញាត់ដឹងគង់ frugal, shrewd (in household affairs)

ដឹងញូ woodcutter's ax

ដឺ fallow

ដុត to heat, burn, roast; to cremate

ដុតមិនឆេះ won't burn, invulnerable to fire

ដុន elephant command

ដុនដាប serious, severe; penniless, destitute

ដុល unit of weight: approximately 150 kg.(Arch); lump, block, mass

ដុស to rub, grate; scrub (to remove dirt)

ដុសថ្នាំ to prepare a medicinal solution by grating the medicine into water

ដុះ to grow, come up (iv)

ដុះដាល to flourish

ដុះលូតលាស់ to grow, increase, expand

ដូង coconut

ដូច like, as

ដូចកល /douc-kɑl/ just as (Lit)

ដូចគ្នា similar, same; also, likewise

ដូចជា such as; it seems that, it looks as if; (Coll) rather, sort of

ដូចដើម like new, as before

ដូចដែល as formerly

ដូចពោលមក as stated

ដូចម្ដេច how?, why?; however, in whatever way

ដូចម្ដេចបាន how would it be possible?

ដូចសព្វកាល as usual

ដូចស្រមោចរោមស្ករ all over the place (lit: like ants surrounding sugar)

ដូច្នេះ /douccneh/ therefore, thus

ដូច្នោះ /douccnɑh/ thus, therefore

ដូន old lady; female ancestor

ដូនតា ancestors; grandparents

ដូនអាវ Don Av (pl. n.)

ដូរ /dou/ to trade; to change, exchange

ដូរតន្ត្រី instrumental music

ដូររាជ in exchange for the throne, for power

ដួង essence, core, central part; circle, round object

ដួងចិត្ត heart

ដួងជីវិត the love of one's life, loved one

ដួងនេត្រទាំងគូ both eyes (Lit)

ដួងភក្ត្រ /duəŋ-phĕəq/ face (Lit)

ដួច high, remote, lofty

ដួចដល់ touch, reach, get on

ដួល to fall down, fall over

ដួលស្រុប to fall down in a slump

ដួស to ladle out, to spoon out

ដើម plant, stalk; head-word in compounds referring to plants

ដើម origin, beginning; original, first; cause, situation, origin of a problem; originally, in the beginning

ដើមកំណើត origin, beginning

ដើមចេក banana tree

ដើមឈើ tree, trees

ដើមដាន origin, beginning, original [facts]

ដើមដូង coconut palm

ដើមទង background, origin, cause

ដើមទុន capital, investment

ដើមទ្រូង chest

ដើមផ្កា flower, shrub

ដើមហេតុ origin, cause

ដើមឡើយ at first, first of all

ដើម្បី in order to

ដើរ to walk, to go

ដើរលេង to go about to amuse oneself, to go around for fun

ដើរលេងសើច to carouse, be happy-go-lucky

ដៀល to criticize, cast aspersions on, talk (disapprovingly) about

ដេក to recline, to sleep

ដេកពេទ្យ be hospitalized, stay in the hospital
ដេកលក់ to be asleep, go to sleep
ដេកសំរាក to rest in a reclining position; to take a nap
ដេញ to chase, pursue
ដេញដោល to pursue (a question), importune, press (for information), quiz
ដេរ to sew, to make by sewing
ដេរដាស /dei-daah/ all over, everywhere
ដែក iron, metal; piece of metal
ដែកគោល nail
ដែកដុល large lump of iron
ដែន land, country
ដែនដី territory
ដែរ /dae/ also, as well; nevertheless
ដែល relative pronoun: that, which, who; the fact that, the reason that
ដែល ever, to have ever + Verb
ដែលដែរ furthermore, likewise
ដៃ hand, arm, sleeve
ដៃដល់ to mean business, be direct (in one's actions)
ដៃទទេ empty-handed
ដៃបឹង branch or bay of a lake
ដោត to impale, stick through
ដោម peak, summit; tall, high; massive
ដោយ by, with; since, because; relating to, according to; along with
ដោយ to follow, obey, go along with, accept; to acquiesce, submit (of a woman)
ដោយខ្នាត with moderation, in proper proportion
ដោយខ្លួន each one, each on his own
ដោយខ្លួនគេ by himself, on his own accord
ដោយចិត្តនឹងចិត្ត directly, on their own initiative, (without a go-between)
ដោយច្រើន many, in great number
ដោយដំណើរ by the act of; about the situation, relating to the case
ដោយគួរ in accordance with
ដោយបទ sensibly, carefully, with a sense of proportion
ដោយព្រះទូន្មាន as the Buddha instructed
ដោយព្រះសុវត្ថិភាព safely, safe and sound
ដោយយោបល់ល្អិត in great detail
ដោយរដូវ in season, by seasons; as needed, according to the circumstances
ដោយលាក់កំបាំង secretly, surreptitiously
ដោយសង្ខេប briefly, in summary
ដោយសព្វគ្រប់ completely
ដោយសារ to depend on, rely on
ដោយសារ to go along with, accompany; because, because of the fact that
ដោយសារគេ to depend on others
ដោយសារតែ because, only because
ដោយហេតុ because
ដោយហោចទៅ in short, to summarize, at least
ដោយឡែក individual, separate
ដោយអាល័យ affectionately (lit: missing [you])
ដោយឯកឯង by itself, by oneself
ដោះ to loosen, untie, take off; to resolve, solve; to avoid, stay clear of; (Arch) to wake up
ដោះ breast
ដោះខ្លួន to escape, to make a getaway
ដោះដួស to serve, to spoon out
ដោះដៃ back out, abandon a commitment, go back on one's word; to get rid of
ដោះដៃឈប់អាល័យមិត្ត to forsake a friend
ដោះថយ to retreat
ដោះទុក្ខសត្វ /dɑh-tuk-sat/ to eliminate, relieve oneself (Euph)
ដោះប្រស្នា elucidate philosophical

problems

ដោះពាក្យប្ដេជ្ញា free oneself from a promise

ដោះលែង to set free

ដោះសា to make excuses, to justify

ដោះស្រាយ to solve, alleviate

ដុំ piece, lump

ដុំរទេះ cart wheel hub

ដំ to pound, beat

ដំកល់ to set up, put on a pedestal

ដំណក់ (= តំណក់) a drop (of water, rain, etc.)

ដំណាក់ stage, phase, stop; (Roy) residence

ដំណាង (= តំណាង) representative

ដំណាងរាស្ត្រ representative of the people, assemblyman

ដំណាល to relate, recite (events)

ដំណាលគ្នា at the same time

ដំណឹង news, information

ដំណូច (< តូច) smallness, (small) size

ដំណួច bubble, drop, globule

ដំណើប sticky, glutinous (of rice)

ដំណើរ situation, process, custom; travel, trip; gait, walk, manner of walking; account, sequence of events

ដំណៀល (< ដៀល) criticism, gossip, mockery, disapproval

ដំណេក sleep (n)

ដំណែងខ្លួន to change one's form, transform oneself

ដំណែល residue, vestige, left-over

ដំណំ serious

ដំណាំ plants, vegetables

ដំបង stick, club

ដំបន់ area, region, sector, zone

ដំញារ slab, block, surface

ដំបូក mound, hillock

ដំបូង first, original

ដំបូន្មាន /damboun-miən/ instruction, teaching

ដំបូល roof, top

ដំរិះ (= តម្រិះ) education, knowledge; to think, decide (Roy)

ដំរី elephant

ដំរីចងកូប elephant with howdah attached

ដំរីសារ adult elephant, full-grown elephant

ដំរួត (= តម្រួត) stacked up

ដំឡូង potato

ដំឡើង to raise, increase; to assemble, set up

ដំឡៃ (= តម្លៃ) value

ដំអក់ to be sluggish, to procrastinate

ដំអួញ to complain about petty matters, complain for effect only

ដាំ to plant

ដាំ to cook; to boil (water)

ដាំចុះ upside down

ដាំត្បូង inlaid with precious stones

ដ្បិត /tbət/ because; since

ឋាន /thaan/ place, site

ឋានៈ /thaanaq/ position, status

ឋានន្តរសក្តិ /thaanantəraqsaq/ rank, position

ឋិត (= ស្ថិត) to stand, be located

ឌីប្លូម diploma (secondary school)

ឌុន alike

## ឍ

ឍាល /thiəl/ a large drum; a shield
ឍាលិន soldier armed with a shield

## ណ

ណល់ desolate, sad

ណា which?, where?; any, some; whichever, wherever
ណា hortatory final particle

ណាខ្លះ which, where (plural)

ណា ១ /naa-muəy/ which one?; any particular one
ណាមួយ...ណាមួយ... for one thing... for another thing
ណាត់ to make an appointment, agree on a rendezvous
ណាត់សង្គ្រាម to declare war

ណាយ to be bored, tired of; to lag, be lax (in the observance of)
ណារ៉ាន់ Naran (pers. n.)

ណារិន /naarɨn/ Narin (pers. n.)

ណាស់ very, very much

ណាស់ណា (=ណាស់)

ណេះ /neh/ here; this (Coll)

ណែងណង a weight, encumbrance (attached to an animal to restrict his movement)
ណែន silver bar, ingot

ណែន tight, close, packed, full

ណែនណាន់ full, thick, dense

ណែនណាន់តាន់តាប់ crowded, in great crowds, packed together
ណែនាំ to lead, to guide

ណោះ /nαh/ there; that (Coll)

ណ៎ះ, ណ៎ា, ណ៎ាះ /nah!,nəh!/ hortatory final particle: go on!, come on!; you see?
ណ្ហើយ /nəhaəy!/ peremptory particle: there, that's enough, enough said!
ណ្ហើយចុះ oh, well, alright, that's enough

## ត

ត to continue, extend; be continued

តដៃ to fight back

តតាំង to fight

តថ្លៃ to bargain

តនឹង to challenge

តពី continued from

តមក /tαα mɔɔk/ afterward; then, later
តរៀងទៅ forever after

តវ៉ា /tαα-waa/ to contest, protest

តស៊ូ /tαα-suu/ to struggle, resist, bear up
តក់ៗ sound of dripping, drop by drop
តក់ស្លុត stunned, stupified, overwhelmed
តក្កមា /tαqkəmaa/ frightened, alarmed
តក្កសិលា Takkasila (pl. n.)

តង់ (Fr. tente) tent

តង្វាយ gift

តណ្ហា /tαnnəhaa/ love, passion

តត្រុក [to wander] aimlessly

តថាគត /təthaakŭət/ general pronoun for the Buddha
តន់ precious, tender, beloved

តន់ name of the Cambodian author of Sabvasiddhi
តន្តី /tαntəy/ classical (usually refers to texts in Sanskrit)
តន្ត្រី /dαntrəy/ music; musical instrument
តប to respond, retaliate, answer

តបៈ /tapaq/ discipline, self-control
តបៈ /tapaq/ ascetic practice, discipline
តបតទក to sass, talk back to

តប្តលាក្សាមយ /taptəlaqkəsaamayaq/ Taptalâksâmaya (hell for arsonists and poisoners)
តម្កល់ to raise up, set on a pedestal; house, keep
តម្កល់ទុក to keep, to preserve

តម្កើង /dɑmkaəŋ/ haughty, proud; to elevate
តម្បាញ weaving
តម្បារ slab, block; leaf, sheet, surface
តម្រង់ to aim, direct (at); directly, straightaway
តម្រា textbook, manual, text, formulae
តម្រាប់ example, model, sample
តម្រាយ swath, cleared area or path
តម្រិះ education; knowledge; to think, decide (Roy)
តម្រិះប្រាជ្ញា intelligence
តម្រិះវិជ្ជា /dɑmreh-wɨcciə/ education, knowledge
តម្រូវ /dɑmrəw/ to correct; to assign, require
តម្រូវចិត្ត to please, satisfy
តម្រួត stacked up, combined
តម្រួត police
តម្រៀប to arrange, put in order; to set, compose (movable type)
តម្រៀបអក្សរដាក់ពុម្ព compose type to put in the press
តម្លើង (=ដំឡើង) to assemble; set up; to raise, increase
តម្លៃ value
តរុណវេត young (Lit)
តា grandfather, old man
តាជី old man (Polite)
តាក់តែង to decorate, adorn; to settle, to establish
តាក់តែងដោយ is determined by, dependent on
តាង to replace, represent; in place of, instead of
តានតឹង constricted, choked up
តាម to follow; along, by, according to
តាមចិត្ត freely, as one wishes
តាមតែ according to, as
តាមតែកូនគិតចុះ whatever you (Child) think
តាមតែចិត្តនឹកចង់ according to one's whims
តាមត្រង់ honestly
តាមរបៀប in proper order, in sequence
តាមរយៈផ្លូវ by way of
តាមរាជការ officially
តាមវគ្គតាមឃ្លា point by point, by chapter and verse (lit: by stanza and phrase)
តាមហេតុគ្រប់ប្រការ concerning all the events, about the whole situation
តារា /daaraa/ star (Lit)
តារាង list, chart
តាវ៉ៅ starling
តិក្សាយស្កន្ធ /teqsaayeə̆hskɑnteə̆q/ Tiksâyaskanda (hell for thieves of rice)
តិច little, few
តិចតួច few, small in quantity, insignificant
តិណជាតិ /tənnəciət/ herbs, grass
តិរច្ឆាន /deirəchaan/ animal (as opposed to human)
តិះដៀល to ridicule, make fun of, belittle, criticize
តឹង tight; of eyes: fixed, taut, bulging
តុ /tok/ table, desk
តុទូកៅអី furniture
តុក្កតត /tokkətɑɑt/ sound of clucking
តុលា October
តុលាការ court, justice
តុលាការមុខក្រសួង the court concerned
តូ To (given name of King Sri Dhammaraja)
តូច /touc, tuuc/ small
តូចៗ small and numerous
តូចចិត្ត disappointed, angry
តូចតន់ [My] Precious Little [One]
តូចតាច little, small, insignificant (Coll)
តូចព្រះរាជហឫទ័យ disappointed, angry (Roy)
តូរតន្ត្រី /dou-dɑntrəy/ musical instruments; music
តួ body, form; specifier for let-

ters of the alphabet and certain animals; performer, actor

តួយ៉ាង example

តួអង្គ body, person (Roy); character (in a story, play, etc.)

តើ initial question particle; finally, then, after all, so that's it

តើជាគាប់ឯណា is that the proper thing to do? (Rhetorical)

តើអូនយល់ដូចម្ដេច ? what is your opinion, Dear?

តើន awaken, get up (Roy, Clergy)

តឿ dwarfed

តឿន to remind, nag, importune

តៀប a kind of bowl

តេជ /daec, daecə-, daecĕəq/ power (usually in compounds)

តេជដៃ /daecĕəh-day/ prowess, auspicious power

តេជានុភាព /daeciənuphiəp/ power

តេជោ (= តេជះ) /daecoo/

តេជះ /daecĕəh/ power

តែ but, only; just, precisely; whenever, upon

តែ tea

តែខ្លួនទទេ only oneself (without any possessions)

តែថា but if

តែមាត់ in word only (but not in deed)

តែមួយប្រាណ alone, by himself

តែម្ដង all at once, in one operation

តែម្នាក់ឯង by oneself

តែយប់ only at night

តែរាល់គ្នា at all of them

តែសព្វខ្លួន everybody, respectively

តែសព្វថ្ងៃ everyday, incessantly

តែឯង alone

តែង usually, still, typically, continuing to, in the process of

តែង to write up, to draft, to compose; to adorn, prepare

តែងខ្លួន to get dressed, adorn oneself

តែងតួ to adorn oneself

តែង-តែ (= តែងតែ) usually, customarily

តែលតោល adrift, from pillar to post

តោ lion

តោក low altar

តោកយ៉ាក /taok-yaaq/ miserable, wretched, unfortunate

តោង must, necessary to

តោង to grasp, clutch

តោងតែ must, necessary to

តោន ton

តោមរ /taomαα/ scimitar, long-handled machete

តោះតើយ unconcerned, indifferent, cold

តៅ bushel

តំណ joint, juncture, knot; extension

តំណជីវិត generation

តំណាង representative

តំណាងរាស្ត្រ representative of the people, member of the parliament

តំណែង job, position, function; decoration; to decorate

តំនៀល criticism, disapproval, gossip; to criticize, gossip about

តំបន់ place, region; local department

តាំង to establish, to set up, to appropriate; to appoint; to begin to; since, beginning with

តាំងចិត្ត to resolve, intend, be determined to

តាំងតែង to institute, to erect

តាំងតែពី from, since

តាំងពី from, starting from, beginning with

តាំងពីកាលនោះមក ever since that time

តាំងពីផ្ទះ from home

តាំងសតិត្រង់ to think straight, deliberate, stop and think

តះ to wiggle

ត្នោត sugar palm

ត្បុក to rap with the knuckles

ត្បាញ to weave; woven

ត្បិត (=ដ្បិត) /tbət/ since, because

ត្បិតថា since, because

ត្បិតយល់ឯកឯង seeing that [I'm] all alone

ត្បូង diamond, precious stone

ត្បូង head (Arch)

ត្បូងក្សាច់ sandbar, sand dune

ត្បូងពេជ្រ diamond

ត្មាត vulture

ទ័ត្មូវ staringly, wide-eyed

ត្មះ to be ashamed, shamed by

ត្មះតិះដៀល to ridicule, to scorn

ត្រកង to gather up in the arms; embrace with one arm

ត្រកាល precious, extraordinary

ត្រកូល race, lineage, tribe

ត្រកួន edible aquatic vine with leaves

ត្រកៀត an edible aquatic plant with straight stalks

ត្រង to catch, collect; to strain, filter

ត្រងត្រាប់ to follow, accept, imitate

ត្រង់ straight, exact; coincident with, at the point of

ត្រង់ខ្លួន straight (posture)

ត្រងោល bald

ត្រចង់ត្រចះ (=ត្រចះត្រចង់) brightly shining, brilliant

ត្រចើល protrude straight ahead, stand out

ត្រចៀក ear

ត្រចះ exquisite

ត្រចះត្រចង់ brilliant

ត្រជាក់ cool, refreshing

ត្រឈឹងត្រឈៃ cool and shady

ត្រឈៃ cool and shady

ត្រដរ persist (in), insist (on); to carry on, persevere

ត្រដាង to spread out, extend

ត្រដាច wide, expanded, spread out

ត្រដាបត្រដួស miserable, penniless

ត្រដឹង stick up high into the air, pierce the sky

ត្រដួច to loom, tower, rise above all else

ត្រដែត to tower, loom, stand out, rise above all else

ត្រណម regime, prescribed conduct

ត្រប់ eggplant

ត្របក petal

ត្រញាក់ to snap

ត្រញាញ់ to twist, spin

ត្របែក guava tree

ត្រពាំង a pond

ត្រពាំងខ្នារ place name (lit: cross-bow pond)

ត្រពាំងឈូក Lotus Pond (pl. n.)

ត្រពាំងទុង place name (lit: pelican pond)

ត្រពាំងព្រលិត place name (lit: water-lily pond)

ត្រពាំងឫស្សី place name (lit: bamboo pond)

ត្រមោច /trɑmaoc, təmaoc/ lonely, desolate

ត្រយង stilt-walker (bird)

ត្រស់ a kind of plant

ត្រសក់ cucumber

ត្រសក់ផ្អែម name of a street (lit: sweet cucumber)

ត្រសង moving along leisurely in a group

ត្រសាក់ to spread, suffuse (?)

ត្រសាយ extended, spread out, branchy

ត្រសាយត្រសុំ (=ត្រសុំត្រសាយ) spread out, overhanging, providing deep shade

ត្រសិត a kind of bird (?)

ត្រសុក disappearing among, burrowing through

ត្រសៀក blowing gently, wafting

ត្រសេក a kind of tree

ត្រឡប់ to turn around, reverse direction

ត្រឡាច winter melon

ត្រអាល fun-loving, carefree

ត្រា to cease, die down, diminish

ត្រា seal, stamp

ត្រា to be kind, merciful, show mercy, have compassion for

ត្រា scattered around, spread over

ត្រាតែ until

ត្រាប្រណី to have compassion for

ត្រាក់ទ័រ /traqtɔə/ tractor

ត្រាច tree used for resin

ត្រាច់ go, proceed, walk (Lit)

ត្រាជូ balance, scales (for measuring weight)

ត្រាណត្រើយ support, comfort, refuge, consolation

ត្រាប់ to follow, imitate

ត្រាវ taro

ត្រាស់ /trah/ to say, decree (Roy); to attain enlightenment

ត្រិះរិះ to think, reason

ត្រី fish

ត្រី three (in compounds)

ត្រីកោណ triangle

ត្រីខ kind of fish stew

ត្រីគុណ cube, cubic

ត្រីងៀត dried salted fish

ត្រីទឹកប្រៃ salt-water fish

ត្រីទឹកសាប fresh-water fish

ត្រីទូត 3rd-ranking diplomat

ត្រីបំពង deep-fried fish

ត្រីប្រាក់ silver goldfish

ត្រីពិធ /trəy-pɨt/ triple, three-sided

ត្រីពោ a kind of large fish

ត្រីមាស goldfish

ត្រីមុខ primary importance, supreme authority

ត្រីរ៉ស់ /trəy-rɑh/ a kind of fresh-water fish, trout

ត្រីស័ក 3rd (of the 10 year cycle)

ត្រីសូលិ៍ Siva's trident, three-pointed dagger

ត្រីអាំង barbecued fish

ត្រឹប to suck

ត្រឹម at, coincident with, as far as; correct, exact, proper

ត្រឹមតែ just, only, only so far as

ត្រឹមត្រូវ proper, good

ត្រឹមត្រូវតាមច្បាប់ lawful, legal

ត្រឹមនេះ right here, at this point

ត្រុក ៗ to be meek and unassuming, ostensibly stupid

ត្រុន ៗ in a subdued manner, bent over and inconspicuous

ត្រូវ /trəw/ must, have to; correct, exact; to hit, come in contact with; undergo, be subjected to

ត្រូវការ to need, want

ត្រូវចិត្ត to be satisfied with, to like

ត្រូវតែ absolutely must

ត្រូវនឹង consistent with

ត្រូវបានកំណត់ has been fixed, determined, set

ត្រូវបានអនុញ្ញាតឲ្យ have been granted permission to

ត្រូវអន្ទាក់ get caught in a trap

ត្រូវឲ្យ to require

ត្រួត stacked up, compounded

ត្រួតត្រា to supervise, oversee

ត្រួសត្រាយ to clear (jungle, forest, etc.), to prepare

ត្រើយ side, bank (of a river)

ត្រើយ (means of) support

ត្រើយត្រាណ (=ត្រើយ) support, sustenance

ត្រើយនាយ distant shore

ត្រើយម្ខាង the opposite bank

ត្រៀក a kind of palm tree

ត្រៀប to arrange, station, position (troops for battle)

ត្រៀបត្រា in a great crowd, spread around in great numbers

ត្រៀមខ្លួន to be ready, to be prepared

ត្រៀល a kind of vine

ត្រៀលស្វា monkey-vine

ត្រេក to indulge, gratify oneself; passionate

ត្រេកអរ /treik-qαα/ happy

ត្រែ bugle, trumpet

ត្រែង reed

ត្រៃត្រឹង្ស thirty-three (Skt)

ត្រៃបិដក /traybəydαq/ Tripitaka (the Three Baskets of Pali scripture)

ត្រៃបុរី a kingdom in the Himalayas (lit: three cities)

ត្រៃភព /tray-phup/ three stages of existence (i.e. desire, form, and formlessness)

ត្រំ indigo

ត្រាំ to immerse, soak

ត្រាំទឹក to immerse, soak in water

ត្អូញ to complain about trifles, complain for effect

ត្អូញត្អែរ to complain

ថង់ pouch, purse

ថប់ to be stifled, out of breath; pent up, frustrated; have a negative premonition about

ថប់បារម្ភ to worry, be anxious

ថយ to back up, to withdraw

ថា to say; quotative conjunction which occurs after certain verbs of saying, thinking, etc.: that, as follows; if, given the fact that, since

ថា...ចុះ admittedly...but

ថាបើ if

ថាមពល /thaaməpŭəl/ energy, source of energy

ថាមភាព /thaaməphiəp/ strength, power

ថាវី /thaawii/ Thavi (pers. n.)

ថាស round tray; phonograph record

ថាអ្វីរួចតែពីមាត់ to say without thinking

ឋិត to stand, be situated

ថុប to stop, quit (Lit)

ថុល្លា /thollaa/ personal name

ថូ vase

ថើប to kiss

ថេរ long period of time (Lit)

ថេរ (=ឋិតថេរ) firm, solid, permanent

ថេរនៅពុំបាត់ permanently (lit: stay without disappearing)

ថែ to take care of; to care, be concerned

ថែទាំ to take care of

ថែថ្នម care for

ថែន platform

ថែម to add, increase; in addition, more, also

ថែមទាំង while, in addition

ថែរក្សា /thae-rĕəqsaa/ to take care of

ថែវ corridor

ថៃ Thai

ថៃពាក់កណ្ដាល half-Thai

ថោ pottery urn

ថោក cheap; inexpensive

ថោកខ្លួន to debase oneself

ថោកជាងគេ the cheapest, least expensive

ថ្កាន toward, in the direction of

ថ្កើង great, illustrious

ថ្កើងថ្កាន great, illustrious, glorious

ថ្កើងថ្កុង (=ថ្កើងថ្កាន)

ថ្កៀប to grip with pincers

ថ្កុំថ្កើង big, important, impressive

ថ្ងាន់ a kind of tree with edible leaves

ថ្ងាស forehead

ថ្ងូរ to moan, groan

ថ្ងៃ day, sun

ថ្ងៃការ the wedding day

ថ្ងៃកំណត់ fixed date

ថ្ងៃខែ date

ថ្ងៃចន្ទ /tŋay-can/ Monday

ថ្ងៃត្រង់ noon, at noon

ថ្ងៃនេះ today

ថ្ងៃ ៥ កើត 5th day of the waxing moon

ថ្ងៃពុធ Wednesday

ថ្ងៃពេញបូណ៌មី /tŋay-pɨñ-bourəməy/ full-moon day

ថ្ងៃព្រហស្តិ៍ /tŋay-prɑhŏəh/ Thursday

ថ្ងៃមិញ earlier today, previous part of the day

ថ្ងៃមុខថ្ងៃក្រោយ in the future

ថ្ងៃមុន previously, earlier

ថ្ងៃសុក្រ Friday

ថ្ងៃសៅរ៍ Saturday

ថ្ងៃអង្គារ Tuesday

ថ្ងៃអាទិត្យ Sunday

ថ្នមៗ gently

ថ្នល់ street, route

ថ្នល់ជាតិលេខ ៦ National Route 6

ថ្នាក់ class, grade, stage, level

ថ្នាក់ចុងបំផុត final grade (13th year)

ថ្នាក់ថ្នម cherish, pamper, treat gently

ថ្នាក់ថ្នល់ terrace, bank, elevation

ថ្នាក់បណ្ឌិត /tnaq-bɑndɨt/ Doctorate

ថ្នោល boat-pole (for punting a boat)

ថ្នាំ tobacco; medicine, plant, herb

ថ្នាំបំពុល poison

ថ្នាំសង្កូវ medicine, drugs (Coll)

ថ្នះ in order to, with respect to

ថ្ពក់ to hook, catch at

ថ្ពាល់ cheek

ថ្ម stone

ថ្មកែវ marble

ថ្មបាយក្រៀម laterite, Bienhoa granite

ថ្មស /tmɑɑ-sɑɑ/ place name (lit: White Stone)

ថ្មារ (=ថ្មើរ) time, period (of the day)

ថ្មី new, recent, modern; again, over again

ថ្មីទៀត new, different, other

ថ្មីៗនេះ recently

ថ្មើរ time, period of the day

ថ្មើរនេះទៅហើយ at this late hour

ថ្មោងថ្មី (=ថ្មីថ្មោង) fresh, new

ថ្លស់ release, spring back

ថ្លា clear, transparent; (Lit) precious, excellent, perfect

ថ្លាខ្យង crystal clear

ថ្លាថ្លែង to say, speak (Lit)

ថ្លាព្រហ្វា care-free, free of distractions, single-minded

ថ្លាង a large wide pot

ថ្លុក a water-filled hole; buffalo-wallow

ថ្លើម liver, heart, internal organ

ថ្លែង to say

ថ្លែង to shoot, fire (an arrow)

ថ្លែងកោតសរសើរ to praise, honor, respect

ថ្លែងព្រះសង្កថា to give an impromptu speech (Roy)
ថ្លែងសុន្ទរកថា to make a speech

ថ្លៃ price; expensive; priced; term of endearment: dear, precious one
ថ្លៃជាងគេ the most expensive

ថ្លៃថ្នូរ highly valued, prestigious

ថ្លៃថ្លា excellent, precious

ថ្លោះធ្លោយ to slip up, make a mistake
ថ្វាត់ frequent literary particle; sometimes has a perfective function
ថ្វាត់ថ្វាយ (=ថ្វាយ)

ថ្វាយ to give, present, make an offering to; for, toward (Eleg)
ថ្វាយជាព្រះរាជកិត្តិយសចំពោះ presented in royal honor of
ថ្វាយបង្គំ to greet respectfully, bow (with palms joined)
ថ្វាយសព្ទសាធុការ to bless, bestow a blessing
ថ្វី (=ធ្វើអ្វី) why?, for what reason?; for any reason, at all
ថ្វីក៏ why, why is it that...?

ថ្វីដៃ outstanding achievement, meritorious result
ថ្វីបើ even though

ថ្វីមាត់ to have the power of magical speech

## ទ

ទក odd (of numbers)

ទក់ wrinkled and worn (paper, cloth)
ទក្សិណ /teəqsən/ south (Lit)

ទង runner, tendril (of a vine)

ទង់ flag, banner

ទង់ដែង copper alloy

ទង់ទាញ (=ទាញទង់) pull this way and that
ទង់ហ្វ៊ា /tŭəŋwiə/ an alloy of red copper and gold, poor man's gold
ទង្គិច hit, strike against

ទន្ទឹង anxious, worried, feel anxiety about; emotion, grief
ទណ្ឌឃាត /toəndəkhjeət/ to cancel; the symbol ៍

ទត to see, to look at, observe (Roy)
ទតឃើញ to see (Roy)

ទទា partridge

ទទាក់ទទាម be in the way, to interfere
ទទឹក wet, soaked

ទទឹង width; perpendicular, at right angles; opposed to
ទទឹងទាស់ to oppose, be opposed (to)

ទទុង large and indistinct, looming

ទទូរ to cover (part or all of the body) with a cloth
ទទួល to receive, accept, acknowledge; it happened that
ទទួលចាញ់ to concede defeat

ទទួលច្បាំង to accept the challenge (to fight)
ទទួលទាន to eat (referring to oneself)
ទទួលទានបាយ to have a meal

ទទួលបន្ទុក in charge of, responsible for
ទទួលពាក្យ to accept (criticism, orders, etc.) without question, to obey
ទទួលពេលនោះ it so happens that, it happened that
ទទួលព្រះរាជឱង្ការ undertake [to carry out] the king's words
ទទួលស្គាល់ជាផ្លូវការ to recognize officially
ទទួលអនិច្ចកម្ម to die (Formal)

ទទេ empty, void; free, gratis

ទទាំងទទាល to stagger, lurch from side to side
ទទះ to flap (the wings)

ទទ្រើក tremblingly

ទទាត់ដៃជើង to kick the arms and legs
ទន់ tender, soft

ទន់កាយ to feel weak (with fear), irresolute
ទន់ក្បាលជង្គង់ to be weak in the knees

ទន់ខ្លួន to go limp, become weak

ទន់ទាប low

ទន់ភ្លន់ soft, gentle, smooth

ទន្ទើន (=តន្ទើន) repeatedly (Roy)
ទន្ទាប to be low, flat

ទន្ទឹង to wait expectantly

ទន្ទឹងផ្លូវ to await impatiently

ទន្ទឹម to yoke, put side by side, pair off; side by side, abreast
ទន្ទេ gracefully, lithely

ទន្ទេង /tuŏntɛɛŋ/ gracefully, lithely (as a dancer)
ទន្ទេញ to memorize, repeat over and over
ទន្ទាំ to preen, throw out the chest, draw oneself up; gracefully
ទន្ទ្រំ to stomp the feet repeatedly, trample
ទន្លេ large river, waterway

ទន្លេចតុមុខ /tuŏnlee-cattoq-muk/ the Four-Faced River (the intersection formed at Phnom Penh by four rivers: the Tonle Sap, the Upper Mekong, the Mekong, and the Bassac
ទន្លេធំ section of the Mekong River between Phnom Penh and Kampong Cham
ទន្លេបាសាក់ the Bassac River

ទន្លេមេគុង the Mekong River

ទន្លេសាប the Tonle Sap (the Sap River)
ទន្សាយ /tuŏnsaay/ hare, rabbit

ទប់ to stop up, hold back

ទប់ទល់ to oppose, confront, face up to, resist
ទប់ទល់តនឹង opposing, against

ទប់មិនឈ្នះ unable to hold back, unable to stop
ទ័ព /toŏəp/ army

ទ័ពស្រួច vanguard, front-line forces

ទមិឡ Tamil (i.e. pagan, wicked person)
ទម្ងន់ weight

ទម្រង់ necessity [?]

ទម្រន់ to feign weakness, claim to be delicate
ទម្លាក់ to drop, cause to fall

ទម្លាប់ custom, tradition

ទ័យា (= ហឫទ័យ) /tɨyyiə/ heart, mind (Roy)
ទល់ opposed, opposite, at odds with; to prop, support laterally; to reach, touch, be against
ទល់ទុក្ខ facing grief, in misery

ទល់នឹង against, touching

ទល់ផ្ដុក to get hurt (from falling)

ទល់មុខគ្នា face to face, opposite one another
ទល់មុខនឹងមាត់ face to face

ទស /tŭəh/ ten (Skt)

ទសពិធរាជធម៌ /tŭəhsəpɨttəriəccəthɔə/ the ten moral laws or standards for royalty
ទសមុខ the ten-headed one (i.e. Ravana)
ទសសហ័ស (=ទសសហស្ស) /tŭəhsəsahah/ 10,000 (P)
ទស្សនកិច្ច /tŭəhsənaqkəc/ visit, tour, observation tour
ទស្សនា /tŭəhsəniə/ to visit, tour, observe (Lit)
ទស្សនាវដ្ដី /tŭəhsənaawədəy/ journal, magazine
ទា duck

ទាក់ to trap

ទាក់ជើង to trip (iv)

ទាញ to pull, to draw out

ទាញទង់ to pull back and forth

ទាត់ to brush away, push away

ទាត់ទៀង (=ទៀងទាត់) true, exact

ទាន: /tiənĕəq/ charity

ទាន់ while still, in time for; to catch up to, be in time for
ទាន់ចិត្ត to be quick (to satisfy someone's wishes)
ទាន់នេត្រា tangible, visible, immediate
ទាន gift; to give a gift; do the favor of
ទានព្រស formal response (inferior to superior)
ទាប low, short, flat

ទាបថោក cheap, lowly

ទាបនឹងដី flat on the ground

ទាយ to predict, foretell

ទាយលេខ to predict by numbers

ទាយក /tiəyŭəq/ Buddhist layman; the laity

ទារ to ask for; to reclaim

ទារក /tiəruə̆q/ baby (Lit)

ទាល់ until

ទាល់ក្រ destitute, poor

ទាល់ចំណេះ at wits' end, nonplussed

ទាល់តែ until

ទាល់តែសោះ at all, even a little

ទាស់ to be opposed, in opposition; to obstruct, block, prevent; to detract from, mar; to be stalled, stymied, stumped

ទាស់ទាល់ to oppose, be opposed to

ទាស់ទែង to have a dispute, have a disagreement, be at odds

ទាហាន /tiəhiən/ soldier

ទិញ to buy

ទិដ្ឋភាព /tɨttəphiəp/ aspect

ទិទៀន to criticize

ទិន day (Lit)

ទិនករ /tɨnnəkɑɑ/ sun (Lit)

ទិប-ម៉ម Tip Mâm (pers. n.)

ទិព្វ /tɨp/ magic, magical, capable of being evoked by magic

ទិព្វចក្ខុ /tɨppəcaq, -caqkhoq/ magic eyes

ទិព្វសង្វារ Tip Sangvar, Hero of the poem of the same name (lit: Magic Sash)

ទិវង្គត /tiq-wŭəŋkŭət/ death; to die (Roy)

ទិវា day (Lit)

ទិស /tɨh/ direction (Lit)

ទិសទក្សិណ /tɨh-tĕəqsən/ the south (Lit)

ទិសនិរតី /tɨh-niərədəy/ the southwest (Lit)

ទិសបស្ចិម /tɨh-bahcəm, -baccəm/ the west (Lit)

ទិសបូព៌ា /tɨh-bou/ the east (Lit)

ទិសប្រាំបី all around, everywhere (lit: in the eight directions)

ទិសពាយ័ព្យ /tɨh-piəyŏəp/ the northwest (Lit)

ទិសអាគ្នេយ៍ /tɨh-qaqnee/ the southeast (Lit)

ទិសឦសាន /tɨh-qəysaan/ the northeast (Lit)

ទិសឧត្តរ /tɨh-qotdɑɑ/ the north (Lit)

ទិសា (=ទិស) direction

ទី place; having the status, title, or position of; ordinalizing prefix

ទីកន្លែង place, site

ទីកំសាន្ត amuse oneself, enjoy oneself (Roy)

ទីក្រមការជាន់កណ្ដាល middle level of the civil service

ទីក្រុង city

ទីក្រុងព្រះសីហនុ Sihanoukville

ទីគាប់ចិត្ត pleasing

ទីដប់ប្រាំ fifteenth

ទីដែន territory, land

ទីដៅ goal, objective, destination

ទីទួល mound, elevated site

ទីទែន bed (Roy)

ទីទៃ other, different, opposite, respective; separately, respectively

ទីទៃ ៗ separately; each to his own

ទីធ្លា courtyard, clearing

ទីនាំង royal conveyance

ទីបំផុត the extremities; extremely; the end

ទីប៉ុស្តិ៍ /tii-poh/ post office

ទីផ្នុខាងក្រោម base, platform, terrace

ទីពីរ second

ទីពឹង to stay, take refuge, take shelter; guardian, source of support, refuge

ទីពោព្រុយ a large fish

ទីព្រះលានស្តេច the Royal Terrace

ទីភ្ជួយក្រសួង deputy minister

ទីមួយ first, number one

ទីរស់នៅ abode, residence

ទីរួមខេត្ត provincial capital

ទីលាន yard, court, field

ទីលានសី terrace, pavilion

ទីលំនៅ address, residence

ទីវាល open space, field

ទីវិហារស្ថាន temple site

ទីសំណាក់ការ headquarters

ទីស្តីការ administrative office

ទីស្ថាន /tii-sthaan, tii-thaan/ place, establishment

ទឹក water; head-word in compounds describing liquids

ទឹកកក ice; snow

ទឹកក្រូច orange juice

ទឹកខ្មៅ name of a former province (lit: black water)

ទឹកខ្មៅ ink

ទឹកគ្រឿង a spicy, pungent sauce

ទឹកឃ្មុំ honey

ទឹកចិត្ត morale, spirit

ទឹកឆៅ unboiled water

ទឹកជន់ flood, flood-water

ទឹកដោះ breast milk

ទឹកដោះគោ (cow's) milk

ទឹកព្រះនេត្រ tears (of clergy, royalty, or the Buddha)

ទឹកភ្នែក tears

ទឹកមាត់ saliva

ទឹកមុខ expression (on the face)

ទឹកអប់ perfume

ទឹម to yoke (to)

ទឹម to take an aggressive stance with hands on the hips

ទុក to put, keep, leave (aside)

ទុកកន្ទុយសំឡេង to emphasize a word by drawing it out

ទុកចិត្ត to trust, have confidence (in)

ទុកជា to consider as; although, even though

ទុកជាដូចម្ដេច somehow, one way or another

ទុកជាមុន beforehand

ទុកដាក់ to take care of

ទុកដាក់ផ្ញើ to entrust to, trust someone (with)

ទុក...ដូច to consider...as

ទុកយូរ...មិនបាន can't delay

ទុកឲ្យ for, on behalf of

ទុក្ខ to be unhappy, sad; sadness, grief

ទុក្ខទោស suffering, difficulty, problems, trouble

ទុក្ខវេទនា /tuk-weetənie/ misery, grief

ទុក្ខសោក grief

ទុក្ខា (=ទុក្ខ )

ទុគ៌ត /tuurəkŭət/ destitute, miserable

ទុគ៌ម /tuurəkum/ deep, remote, profound

ទុច្ចរិត /tuccərət/ dishonest, evil

ទុង pelican

ទុព្វល /tuppŭəl/ debilitated

ទុរជន (=ទុជ៌ន ) /tuurəcŭən/ evil-hearted person

ទុរគត /tuurəkŭət/ destitute

ទុរន់ទុរា feeble, racked with illness

ទុរេន durian

ទូ cabinet, chest

ទូក boat

ទូកង long curved boat which carries two rows of rowers

ទូង to sound, to strike (gong, drum, etc.)

ទូច-គីម Touch Kim (pers. n.)

ទូទៅ (=ទួទៅ ) all, in general, generally

ទូន្មាន /tuunmiən ~ tuulmiən/ to advise, instruct, teach, discipline
ទូន្មានអាត្មា discipline oneself, instruct oneself (morally)
ទូរ remote, distant

ទូរលេខ /tuurəleik/ telegram

ទូរេ far, distant

ទូល carry on the head

ទូល to tell, to inform (to clergy, or royalty)
ទូលទុក្ខ to undergo suffering, endure grief; recite one's woes
ទូលព្រះបង្គំ I (first person pronoun used in addressing royalty)
ទូលព្រះបង្គំជាខ្ញុំ I (addressing royalty)

ទូលាយ wide, spacious

ទូលំទូលាយ broad, spacious, vast

ទួ all, all of

ទួញ to lament, weep loudly

ទួល hillock, mound

ទើប then, only then; so, consequently
ទើបតែ to have just (+ Verb)

ទើបតែនឹង to have just (+ Verb)

ទើបតែនឹងរះសោះ has just risen (of the sun or moon)
ទើបនឹង (= ទើបតែនឹង )

ទើបនឹងកោរថ្មីៗ newly-shaven

ទើរ to catch, snag, hang up (as a raft against an overhanging limb)
ទើល to stand in the way, to block

ទើលទាក់ unpolished, inappropriate

ទើលទាល់ reluctantly

ទើលភ្នែក to distract, be conspicuous, offend the eyes; to bother
ទៀង precise, exact, straightforward, honest
ទៀង to continue

ទៀងត្រង់ honest, straightforward

ទៀងទាត់ precise, exact; really, truly
ទៀងទុក reliable, precise, dependable

ទៀត again, further, additional

ទៀន candle

ទៀប near, close to; nearly, almost
ទេ final negative particle; final emphatic particle; final question particle (in yes-or-no questions)
ទេដឹង perhaps

ទេតើ /tee-taə/ is a compound particle which always involves an element of disclaimer: 'contrary to what I thought, contrary to what was implied, contrary to appearances, etc.'; the best general translation might be 'on the contrary', but its specific translation will depend on the context: 'just, only, really only, really?, etc.'

ទេពតា /teepədaa/ god, angel

ទេពធីតា angel

ទេពប្រណម្យ /teep-prɑnɑm/ buttress in the form of a praying angel
ទេពមនោរម /teep-mənoorum/ Têp Monorom (name of a ballet)
ទេពសម្ភារ heavenly virtue

ទេព-ហ៊ុន Tep-Hun (pers. n.)

ទេពី (=ទេវី) queen, royal wife

ទេព្តា (=ទេពតា ) gods, angels

ទេព្រក្ស guardian angels

ទេវកថា /teewĕəqkəthaa/ mythological epic, supernatural tale
ទេវង្ស angels, benevolent spirits

ទេវតា /teewədaa/ angel

ទេវតាឃ្វាលគោ devata who guards cattle
ទេវបុត្រ male divinity, god

ទេវរុក្ខ /teewəruk/ spirit of the forest
ទេវលោក /teewəlook/ realm of the gods, divine beings
ទេវវិទូ /teewĕəqwituu/ theologian

ទេស to drift about, look around prospectively

ទេសចរ /teehsəcɑɑ/ tourist, tourism;

to sightsee

ទេសនា /teehsənaa/ to recite the scriptures, give a sermon

ទេសភាព /teehsəphiəp/ view, landscape, nature, aspect

ទើង clear, bright; extremely (intensifier for colors and certain other adjectives)

ទើង to defend

ទើន to sleep; bed, couch (Roy)

ទៃ a long narrow sack tied at both ends and suspended from the shoulder

ទោ two (usually in compounds)

ទោង a swing

ទោមនស្ស /too-mənŏəh/ frustrated, disgusted with oneself

ទោស fault, wrong, guilt, culpability; punishment

ទោសៈ injurious effect of bad actions

ទោស័ក second (of the 10 year cycle)

ទោសោ (=ទោសៈ) anger

ទោះ although, even though; if

ទោះ...ក្តី...ក្តី whether...or

ទោះបី although

ទោះបី...ក៏ដោយ even though, no matter what

ទោះយ៉ាងណា...ក៏ no matter what, even though

ទោះយោបី if, even if, although, no matter

ទៅ to go; to, toward; orientation away from speaker in space or time (aspectual adverb)

ទៅក៏ទៅ fine, okay, let's go

ទៅកាត់ to pass by, go past or through

ទៅកាន់ toward

ទៅខាងក្រោយ backward, toward the back

ទៅចុះ go ahead, do

ទៅជា to become

ទៅដល់ to arrive at, to come upon

ទៅណាមកណា to go anywhere, to go around

ទៅតាម go looking for, go for

ទៅទល់នឹង up until

ទៅមកៗ back and forth

ទៅមករកគ្នា to visit back and forth intimately; back and forth

ទៅមុខ in the future

ទៅលើ bring about, result in, involve

ទៅវិញទៅមក back and forth, reciprocally

ទុំ ripe; rich, deep, extremely (intensifier for red, yellow, gold)

ទុំទាវ Tum-Teav, Cambodia's best-known epic romance

ទំ /tum/ to perch

ទំនង way, manner, method; likely, credible

ទំនងការ procedure

ទំនងការកសាង method of construction

ទំនងជា looks as if, seems that

ទំនងទំនាយ fate, destiny

ទំនងភាព form, aspect, appearance

ទំនប់ dam, barrier

ទំនាយ prediction

ទំនិញ merchandise

ទំនុក poem, verse, song, composition

ទំនុកបម្រុង provide assistance for, undertake (to), take responsibility for

ទំនូល words, message (Arch)

ទំនួញ a lament, wail, cry

ទំនួល ease, fluency, smoothness

ទំនើប modern, recent

ទំនៀមទំលាប់ (=ទំនៀមទម្លាប់) customs, culture

ទំនេរ /tumnee/ free, vacant

ទំនេរដៃ to have free time

ទំព័រ /tumpɔə/ page

ទំពា to chew

ទំពាអៀង to ruminate, chew the cud

ទំរង់ ring (Roy)

ទំរាំ until

ទំលាក់ to put down, set down, cause to fall

ទំលាយ to pierce, penetrate, traverse, push through

ទំហឹង effort

ទំហំ /tumhum/ size, dimension, area

ទំហំដី surface area

ទំហំផ្ទៃ surface, area

ទាំង all of, including, even to the extent of

ទាំង...ទាំង both...and

ទាំងថ្ងៃទាំងយប់ both day and night

ទាំងទើសទាំងទាល់ reluctantly

ទាំងទ្វេ both

ទាំងនេះ all these

ទាំងប៉ុន្មាន ៗ all that there was, all of it, however much

ទាំងពីរ both

ទាំងពួង all together, the whole group

ទាំងមូល all, altogether, the whole

ទាំងស្រុង completely, wholly, entirely

ទាំងហ្វូង ៗ /tĕəŋ-wouŋ, tĕəŋ-wouŋ/ in groups

ទាំងឡាយ all

ទាំងអស់ all, everything; all together

ទាំងអៀនអន់ shyly, diffidently

ទះ to slap, to beat

ទះដៃ clap the hands, to applaud

ទ្រ to support from underneath

ទ្រ a two-stringed musical instrument

ទ្រគោះ crude, improper, excessive, nasty, rude

ទ្រង់ shape, form

ទ្រង់ an auxiliary which precedes verbs describing royal action; also used as a royal 3rd person pronoun

ទ្រង់ to do; to put on; to hold (Roy, Clergy); to possess, embody (Lit)

ទ្រង់គ្រឿង to don one's regalia

ទ្រង់ទ្រាយ shape, form

ទ្រង់ព្រះចិន្តា to think, consider (Roy)

ទ្រង់ព្រះតំរិះ to think, decide (Roy)

ទ្រង់ព្រះមកុដ to put on a crown

ទ្រង់ព្រះរាជបញ្ជា to order, command (Roy)

ទ្រទូង to hold over the head

ទ្រទ្រង់ to support, enhance

ទ្រទ្រង់នូវ to represent, symbolize

ទ្រនុង fin

ទ្រនំ a perch; Fig: home

ទ្រនំអាក្ងូត cock-perch tree

ទ្រព្យ /trŏəp/ wealth, possessions, belongings

ទ្រព្យសម្បត្តិ /trŏəp-sɑmbat/ wealth, possessions, fortune

ទ្រព្យស្រមាល valuables, small belongings (i.e. which can be carried off)

ទ្រព្យា (=ទ្រព្យ ) /trŏəpyiə/

ទ្រម beaten up

ទ្រមក់ sluggish, lazy, drugged with sleep

ទ្រយឹង a tree with edible fruit

ទ្រលោម forming a mass of flames; forming a great cloud

ទ្រវ៉ត្រ្តបុ /trɔwŏəttrəpoq/ Dravattrapu (hell for those who usurp the rights and property of others)

ទ្រហឹង /trɔhɨŋ/ deafening; clamorous (ly)

ទ្រហឹងអឹងកង /trɔhɨŋ-qəɨŋ-kɑɑŋ/ tumultuously, clamorously

ទ្រហោ to wail, moan loudly

ទ្រាប់ to put under, to cushion

ទ្រាប់អង្គុយ use as a seat

ទ្រាយ a kind of deer

ទ្រឹស្តី /trɨhsdəy/ theory

ទ្រុង cage

ទ្រូ a cylindrical fish-trap

ទ្រូង chest, breast

ទ្រើង frame, lattice, trellis

ទ្រើស to be slightly larger (than)

ទ្រើសឈ្លង arrogant, wayward, mean

ទ្រហៀងទ្រហោះ (=ទ្រហោះទ្រហៀង) to cry, wail, screech (of animals)

ទ្រហោះទ្រហៀង to cry, wail, screech (of animals)

ទ្រាំ to withstand, endure

ទ្រាំមិនបាន unable to stand (it)

ទ្រាំង name of a former province (now a /srok/ in Takaew)

ទ្វារ /twiə/ door, opening

ទ្វារកញ្ចក់ mirrored door

ទ្វារខ្មោច Spirit Gate

ទ្វារជ័យ Victory Gate

ទ្វី both

ទ្វីប continent (n)

ទ្វេ two, double

ទ្វេគុណ /twee-kun/ squared

ទ្វេហា (= ទ្វេហារ) both (lit: two persons)

## ធ

ធន /thŭən/ wealth, possessions

ធនធាន /thŭən-thiən/ wealth, belongings; resources, funds

ធនាគារ /thəniəkiə/ bank (Lit)

ធនាគារជាតិនៃកម្ពុជា National Bank of Cambodia

ធម៌ /thɔə/ dharma: the law, the scriptures

ធម៌ when following a kinship term: adopted, foster

ធម៌មេត្តា compassion

ធម្មការ /thŏəmməkaa/ (Ministry of) Religion

ធម្មជាតិ /thŏəmməciət/ nature, natural environment

ធម្មតា /thŏəmmədaa/ usual, ordinary; usually

ធម្មនុញ្ញ /thŏəmmənuñ/ constitution

ធម្មរាជា Dharmaraja (King of Cambodia, 1473-1504, father of Chan Raja)

ធរណី /thɔɔrənii/ ground, earth (Lit)

ធាក់ to kick, pedal (with the sole of the foot)

ធាតុ /thiət/ nature, natural element

ធាតុ /thiət/ cremated remains, ashes

ធាតុអាកាស weather, climate

ធារ immense, huge

ធានា to assure, promise, undertake, guarantee

ធារធំ (=ធំធារ) huge, immense

ធារា pile, heap; Poetic: many, in great numbers

ធារាសាស្ត្រ hydraulics

ធីតា /thidaa/ girl, daughter (Lit)

ធុង barrel, cask

ធុញ to be bored

ធុញថប់ to be bored, discouraged

ធុន model, type

ធុន-សែម Thun Sèm (pers. n.)

ធុរៈ affairs, duties; trouble

ធុលី (=ធូលី) dust, dirt (Lit)

ធូប incense, joss sticks

ធូរ lenient; not tight (rope, tire); relaxed, at ease

ធូរក្នុងចិត្ត relieved, relaxed

ធូលី dust, dirt

ធួ a Chinese game of chance

ធួក-ប៊ិន Thuok Binn (pers. n.)

ធួន to pamper, take care of, be careful with; appropriate, fitting

ធៀប to compare

ធេង completely

ធេងធោង to feel dizzy, wobbly

ធុំ to smell (give off an odor)

ធំ /thom/ big, important

ធំ ៗ big, mature (plural)

ធំដុំ important; grand; serious

ធំទូលាយ spacious

ធំធេង spacious, vast (Eleg)

ធ្ងន់ heavy, serious

ធ្ងន់ធ្ងរ serious, heavy

ធ្នូ bow, crossbow; December

ធ្នុង pectoral fin

ធ្មេច to close the eyes

ធ្មេញ tooth

ធ្មេញត្រី a kind of small tree (lit: fish teeth)

ធ្យាន to meditate

ឈ្យាន have the power to transport oneself magically

ធ្លា clearing, expanse

ធ្លាក់ to fall

ធ្លាក់ទឹកមុខ to adopt a sombre expression, to fall (of the face)

ធ្លាប់ used to; accustomed to

ធ្លាប់តែ used to, always used to

ធ្លាយ to be punctured, pierced

ធ្លុះ to pierce, penetrate

ធ្លុះធ្លាយ perforated, full of holes

ធ្លោយ to overstep, misstep, make a mistake (with unfortunate results)

ធ្លោយប្រាប់ to tell unintentionally, to let slip

ធ្វើ to do; to make; to build; to repair (cars, etc.); to clean (fish); to pretend; to curse

ធ្វើកសិកម្ម to farm, be a farmer

ធ្វើការ to work

ធ្វើកិច្ចមួយ perform an act

ធ្វើក្បាលងីងើ ៗ to look perplexed, confused

ធ្វើខុសឆ្គង to make mistakes, misbehave, be in the wrong

ធ្វើគត់ to kill (Roy)

ធ្វើឃាតកម្មខ្លួនឯង to commit suicide

ធ្វើចិត្តជា to remain patient

ធ្វើជា to pretend (to), pretend (that)

ធ្វើដំណើរ to travel

ធ្វើតាម to follow, to imitate

ធ្វើត្លុកក្រយាច់ to act the clown

ធ្វើទុក្ខទោស to mistreat, to abuse

ធ្វើទុក្ខបុកម្នេញ to abuse, mistreat

ធ្វើបង្ខូច to ruin, destroy

ធ្វើបាប to do wrong, mistreat

ធ្វើបុណ្យ to hold a ceremony, celebration

ធ្វើ...បែក to be able to beat off, overcome

ធ្វើពី made of

ធ្វើពុតជា to pretend that, act as if

ធ្វើពើ to pretend (to)

ធ្វើព្រះរាជដំណើរ to make a trip, travel (Roy)

ធ្វើមុខ make a face

ធ្វើមុខភ្លឹះ ៗ with a stupified expression

ធ្វើលេង do for fun, do as a pastime

ធ្វើស្មើស្មោះ to sulk, be aloof

ធ្វើស្រែ to rice-farm (lit: make rice-fields)

ធ្វើស្លាប់ to play dead

ធ្វើឱ្យ to cause

ធ្វើអ្វី why, what for?

ធ្វេធ្វេស (=ធ្វេស ) be careless, negligent

ធ្វេស to be careless

ធ្វេសធ្វេ (=ធ្វេសធ្វើ ) to be doubly negligent, doubly neglectful

ធ្វេសប្រហែស to neglect, be careless

about

ធ្វេសប្រាណ be off guard, careless of one's safety

នគរ /nɔkɔɔ/ alternative form of អង្គរ

នគរធំ Nokor Thom (pl. n.)

នគរបាល /nɔkɔɔbaal/ police, municipal police

នគររាជសីមា Nokor Raja Sima (the present Thai province of Nakorn Ratchasima)

នគរវត្ត name of a revolutionary newspaper in 1936; older name for Angkor Wat

នង្គ័ល /neăŋkoăl, nəŋkoăl, ŋkoăl/ plow (n)

នទី /nɔɔtii/ river, ocean (Lit)

ននៀល to twist and turn, roll about

ននោង a kind of rough-skinned squash, Chinese okra

នព្វស័ក /nuppəsaq/ 9th year (of the 10-year cycle)

នព្វគុណ /nuppəkun/ nine-tenths pure (of gold)

នភា sky, air (Lit)

នមស្ការ /neăqmahsəkaa/ to pay homage, worship, bow before

នមោ beginning of a sacred incantation which prefaces the recitation of the Pali syllabary

ន័យ /nɨy/ meaning, content

នយោបាយ /nəyoobaay/ politics, policy; political

នរក /nɔruəq, nəruəq/ hell

នរណា /nɔnaa/ who?

នរនាថ /nɔɔniət/ king, protector

នរនោះ /nɔnuh/ that person

នរបតី /nɔruppədəy/ ruler, master; the king

នរលក្ខណ៍ /nɔɔreəq-leăq/ human quality, characteristic

នរូ (=ជន, មនុស្ស) /nɔɔruu/

នរូអ្នកណា whoever, anyone [who]

នរូអ្នកផង whoever, anyone [who]

នរោត្តមបុប្ផានី /nərootdɑm-bopphaanii/ Norodom Bophani (pers. n.)

នា at, in, with regard to

នាក់ specifier for persons of ordinary estate

នាកាល circumstances, situation

នាគ dragon

នាគនាថ៍ (=នាគនាថ) Naga Chief

នាគព័ន /niəq poŏən/ Neak Pean (lit: the encircling Naga)

នាគរាជ /niəqkəriəc/ King of the Nagas, Naga King

នាគា (=នាគ) Naga (as the traditional food for Garuda)

នាគេន្ទ្រា (=នាគ + ឥន្ទ្រា) (Indra's) elephant

នាង Miss; young lady (title or pronoun for women younger than speaker, or for young boys)

នាដៃ ring finger

នាងឆោមឆាយ beautiful maiden

នាងអ្នក people of rank, nobility

នាថ master, chief

នាទី minute; duty, function

នាទីជា to have the duty of

នានា various, different

នា...នា whether...or

នានាប្រទេស foreign, abroad, various countries

នាបី even if; usually (Lit)

នាភី navel (Roy)

នាម name

នាម a small two-man fishing net

នាមា name (នាម + ា ; a device frequently used for rhyming purposes)

នាយ chief, head (functions like នាក់); Mr. (Arch)

នាយ distant, yonder

នាយក /niəyuŏəq/ chief, head, sovereign

នាយកចាត់ការ /niəyuŏəq-cat-kaa/ chief, supervisor

នាយករដ្ឋមន្ត្រី /niəyuŏəq-roŏət-muŏəntrəy/ prime minister

នាយកសាលារៀន principal, headmaster

នាយទ្វារ chief gatekeeper

នាយបំរើ male servant

នាយរ័ដ្ឋកសាធារណការ chief of Public Works

នាយយក្សា ogre chief

នារទេស /niərəteeh/ to exile

នារាយណ៍ /niəriəy/ Narai (another name for Vishnu)

នារាយណ៍កាឡា the power to change one's form

នារាយណ៍បែងភាគ the power to subdivide, multiply oneself

នារី young unmarried girl

នាលោកិយ /niəlookəy/ this life, this world (as opposed to the next world)

នាវា boat, ship

នាសា nose (Roy, Lit)

នាម៉ឺន /niəməɨn/ official, mandarin

នាម៉ឺនមន្ត្រី government officials

នាម៉ឺនសព្វមុខមន្ត្រី all the officials

នាឡិកា /niəlekaa/ watch, clock

និករ group, host (of stars, angels, etc.)

និគម /nikum/ group of villages, community

និគ្គហិត /niqkəhət/ the symbol ំ

និត្យ /nɨt/ closely

និទាន to tell, relate; a story, tale

និទ្រា /nɨntriə/ to sleep; sleep (Lit)

និទ្រាលក់ to sleep (Lit)

និន្ទា to criticize, gossip about

និពន្ធ /nipuŏn/ to write, compose (Lit)

និព្វាន /nipiən/ Nirvana

និមន្ត /nimuŏn/ to walk, to go; to invite (Clergy)

និម៌ល (=និម្មល ) pure, faultless

និមួយ /nimuəy/ each

និមួយៗ each, the various

និម្មល /nimmŭəl/ perfect, faultless

និយម /niyum/ to like, prefer; popular, preferred; suffix: -ism

និយាយ to speak

និយាយដើមគេ to make comments about people, make insinuations about others, to gossip

និរតណ្ហា /niərətɑnnəhaa/ absence of passion

និរតី /niərədəy/ southwest (Lit)

និរទុក្ខា /niərətukkhaa/ absence of pain, lack of suffering

និរទោស /niərətooh/ blamelessness, innocence, absence of guilt

និរន្តរ៍ /niqrŏən/ all the time, always

និរាស to be separated

និរុច្ឆ្វស /niruccwaasaq/ Nirucchvâsa (hell for violent people)

និរុត្តិសាស្ត្រ /niruttəsaah/ philology

និវត្ត /niwŏət/ to return

និស្សិត /nihsət/ student

នីតិកម្ម /niiteqkam, nəyteqkam/ jurisdiction, jurisprudence

នីតិកាល /niiteqkaal, nəyteqkaal/ legislature

នីតិក្រម /niiteqkrɑm, nəyteqkrɑm/ law, statute

នីល /nɨl/ black diamond

នឹក to think of, miss

នឹកខឹង to become angry, get mad

នឹកខ្លាញ់ to be put off by, feel irritated or disgusted by

នឹកឃើញ to remember, realize

នឹកចង់ to desire, to covet

នឹកដើម to think about, call to mind, have occur to one

នឹកនា to miss, remember nostalgically

នឹកព្រួចថា to have a sudden inspiration that, to occur (to one) that

នឹកមមៃ to think continually about something

នឹករលឹក /nɨk-rɔlɨk/ to miss, long for, remember

នឹកសូត្រ to recite mentally

នឹកស្តាយក្រោយ to regret (afterward)

នឹកអស់សំណើច to feel like laughing

នឹង and, with; about, concerning

នឹង still, stationary, stable, steady

នឹង auxiliary of incipient action: will, about to, intend to

នឹងគេ like other people

នឹងធួន quiet, reserved, sedate; stable, steady

នឹម yoke; pair, team (of oxen, etc.)

នឹមនួនល្អង fair, beautiful (of complexion)

នុះ general demonstrative used to refer back to a previously expressed (or implied) action or idea

នុ៎ះ /nuh!/ there!

នុ៎ះន៎ /nuh-nɔɔ!/ there it is!

នុ៎ះហ្ន៎ /nuh-nɔɔ/ there!, there it is!

នូវ /nɨw/ according to, consisting of; with, at, and, including

នួត to massage (Thai)

នួន fair, beautiful (of complexion)

នួននាង girl, maiden

នួនស្រី a variety of jasmine

នឿយ to be burdened, overworked, tired; tiring

នឿយណាយ to tire, flag

នឿយហត់ to be tired; tiring

នេត្រ eye (Lit)

នេត្រា (=នេត្រ ) eye (Lit)

នេន /neen/ novice, title for a novice monk

នេសាទ /nesaat/ to fish; fishing; fisherman

នេះ this, here

នេះឯង this (previously referred to)

នែ there, see there; hortatory particle used by an elder to a child or student

នែចៅ Now, child!; now listen to me, child

នែប near, close, intimate

នែបនិត្យ close, intimate

នៃ of (Formal)

នោះ that, there; the referred to

នៅ /nɨw/ to live, reside, remain, be situated (at); at, in; still, still in the process of, remain

នៅកម្លោះ to be still a bachelor

នៅក្នុងចំណោម among

នៅក្នុងសំណាក់ be under the care of

នៅចាំ to wait (for), be waiting

នៅតែនឹងផ្ទះ just stay home

នៅថ្ងៃមុខ in the future

នៅទីបង្ហើយ at the end, finally

នៅទីបញ្ចប់ in conclusion, finally

នៅផ្ទះគេ in one's home

នៅសងខាង at the sides

នៅឡើយ still, up to the present

នំ confection, anything made with flour

នំគម a sweet pastry

នំចំណី food, snack

នំនែក confections, cakes, sweets

នំអន្សម rice cake made of glutinous rice and pork or banana

នាំ to take, lead; cause, lead to

នាំគ្នា to go together, accompany each other

នាំពា to care, be concerned

នាំពាក្យនិយាយ to bring up for discussion

នាំហេតុ to make insinuations, tattle-tale, incite trouble

## ប

បក to peel; (Coll) to translate

បក់ to blow (of the wind); to fan (with a fan); to heat, flap, rustle (of leaves)

បក្ខា /paqkhaa/ wings; birds

បក្ស /paq/ political party or camp

បក្សពួក party, group

បក្សសម្ព័ន្ធ allies

បក្សា /baqsaa/ (P. plural) birds; male bird

បក្សី /baqsəy/ birds, the bird kingdom

បង older sibling; older friend or relative of one's own generation; I (husband to wife, or older to younger sibling or friend; you (wife to husband, or younger to older sibling or friend)

បងជីដូនមួយ older cousin

បងថ្លៃ older in-law

បងធម៌ /bɑɑŋ-thɔə/ foster brother

បងប្រុស older brother; older male friend or relative

បងប្អូន older and younger siblings, brothers and sisters

បងប្អូនញាតិសន្តាន relatives

បងស្រី older sister

បង់ to discard, abandon, waste, lose

បង់គំនិត to be fooled by, duped by

បង់ត្រី to cast (a net) for fish, to fish with a net

បង់បាត់ disappear, be abandoned

បង់ទម្រៀត needlessly, to no good purpose

បង់សៀត worthless, good for nothing

បង្កង lobster, crayfish

បង្កាត់ start (a fire)

បង្កាត់ net (for catching animals)

បង្កាត់ភ្លើង to start a fire

បង្កាន់ដៃ receipt, deed, affidavit; railing, bannister

បង្ការ to prevent, to deter

បង្កើត to originate, establish, give birth to

បង្កើតរឿង to sow discord, instigate trouble, incite bad feeling

បង្កើន to increase (tv)

បង្កើយ very near

បង្កើល to run aground, beach (tv)

បង្ក្រាប to put down, quell

បង្ខិតបង្ខំ to force; to press (for)

បង្ខូង to inset, make a depression

បង្ខូច to ruin, destroy

បង្ខំ to force, to insist

បង្ខាំង to confine, to shut up

បង្គង bee-limb

បង្គន់ toilet

បង្គាប់ to order; to command

បង្គី a flat basket used to carry earth

បង្គោល pillar, support

បង្គៅ a kind of litchi

បង្រៀន to teach

បង្វិច bundle

បង្វិល to spin, to turn (something) around

បង្វែរ to offer, give

បង្ហាញ to show, point out

បង្ហាត់ to train, drill (tv)

បង្ហូត to draw out, let out on a string or pole

បង្ហួស to go beyond

បង្ហើរ to fly (something)

បង្ហើយ to finish, to complete

បង្ហោះ to fly (something), cause to fly, bear off into the air

បង្អង់ to delay, slow down

បង្អត់ to withhold (usually food), to starve (tv)

បង្អស់ most, last, most of all

បង្អាក់ to hinder

បង្អួច window

បង្អួត to show off

បង្អែម dessert, sweets

បច្ច័យ /paccay/ money (Clergy)

បច្ចាមិត្ត /paccaamɨt/ enemy

បច្ចុប្បន្ន /paccobɑn/ now, the present, modern times

បច្ចុប្បន្នកាល /paccəbɑnnəkaal/ the present

បច្ចេកទេស /paccaekəteeh/ technique; technical

បញ្ច /pañcaq/ five (in compounds)

បញ្ចសីលា /pañcaq-səylaa/ the Five Principles (refers only to the Five Principles of peaceful coexistence)

បញ្ចង់ fine, detailed, carefully done

បញ្ចប់ to end, bring to a close

បញ្ចិន្ទ្រិយ /pañcəntrii/ the five senses (Fig. consciousness, wisdom, intellect)

បញ្ចុក to feed by hand

បញ្ចុះ to reduce, lower, put down

បញ្ចុះខ្មោច to bury a corpse

បញ្ចុះបញ្ចូល to persuade, solicit, enlist (support)

បញ្ចុះបឋមសិលា to lay the corner stone (i.e. the first stone)

បញ្ចូល cause to enter, put into

បញ្ចូលអារក្ខ instill a spirit (in a medium); cause (a medium) to be possessed by a spirit

បញ្ចើត to flaunt, show off

បញ្ចៀស indirectly (adv); to avoid (tv)

បញ្ចេញ express, issue, expel; to show off

បញ្ចេញបញ្ចូល to change, alter (lit: to invent and add)

បញ្ចេញរាង to show off (one's body)

បញ្ចេញសម្លេង to utter

បញ្ចោរ to curse, vilify

បញ្ចោរបញ្ចៀស to slander, malign, insinuate

បញ្ចាំ to pawn, pledge; prepared, made ready, put in place beforehand

បញ្ចាំចិត្ត to betroth, be betrothed

បញ្ឆិតបញ្ឆៀង to equivocate, allude to (indirectly)

បញ្ឆោត to deceive

បញ្ជា to order

បញ្ជាក់ to clarify, explain

បញ្ជាការ command (n)

បញ្ជី list, register, record, table (n)

បញ្ជីជាតិ birth certificate

បញ្ជូន to send

បញ្ជូនទៅឱ្យ to send to, on behalf of

បញ្ជោះ to provoke, egg on, taunt

បញ្ឈប់ to bring to a stop, to stop (tv)

បញ្ឈរ to stand on end (tv); cause to stand

បញ្ឈរទ័ព arrange troops in formation

បញ្ញាវ័ន្ត /paññəwan/ intellectual, educated person

បញ្ញា /paññaa/ intelligence, reason, wisdom, insight, knowledge

បញ្ញាធិការ superior intelligence, great intelligence

បញ្ញាសជាតក /paññaasaq-ciədɑq/ Fifty Jatakas (50 apocryphal birth stories not included in the Tripitaka, but very popular in Cambodia, Laos, and Thailand)

បញ្ញាសម្បទា the possession of wisdom

បញ្ញាក់ (=ភ្ញាក់) /pəññeəq/ to startle

បញ្ហា /paññəhaa/ problem, issue

បដិមា /patdemaa/ image, statue

បដិវត្តន៍ /paqdewŏət/ revolution, revolutionary

បដិសណ្ឋារៈ /padeqsɑnthaareəq/ greeting, welcome

បដិសណ្ឋារកិច្ច /pədeqsɑnthaarəkec/ greetings

បដិសន្ធិ /padeqsɑnthiq/ conception, rebirth, creation, ongoing cycle

បដិសេធ /patdesaet/ to cancel, kill; the symbol ៍

បណ្ឌវៈ /pandəweəq/ the Pandavas

បណ្ឌិត learned man, scholar

បណ្ណសាលា /pannasaalaa/ hermitage,

hut of leaves

បណ្ណាការ /pannaakaa/ provisions, equipment
បណ្ណាគារ /pannaakiə/ bookstore
បណ្ណាគារគិម-សេង Kim - Seng Bookstore
បណ្ណាល័យ /pannalay/ library
បណ្ដា among, including, various, all
បណ្ដាក់គ្នា to do in relay, pass the buck
បណ្ដាជន /bɑndaacŭən/ people; population
បណ្ដារាស្ដ្រ people
បណ្ដាល (=បណ្ដាលឲ្យ) to lead to, cause
បណ្ដុះ to raise, to cultivate
បណ្ដុះបណ្ដាល to nurture with care
បណ្ដូល core, heart (e.g. of an artichoke); Fig. ideal, essence, epitome
បណ្ដើរ to walk, parade (tv; as a hen her brood); simultaneously
បណ្ដើរគ្នា to walk together, accompany one another
បណ្ដើរ...បណ្ដើរ simultaneously, at the same time
បណ្ដេញ to drive out, expel
បណ្ដែត to float, to put afloat
បណ្ដែតបណ្ដោយ to procrastinate, be nonchalant
បណ្ដែរបណ្ដាំ to admonish, exhort, recommend
បណ្ដោយ length; along, along with
បណ្ដោយខ្លួនឲ្យ to allow oneself to
បណ្ដោយទឹក downstream, along with the current
បណ្ដោយឲ្យ to go along with, permit
បណ្ដោះ to spirit (something) away; to free, remove secretly
បណ្ដោះអាសន្ន temporarily
បណ្ដាំ order, instruction, message
បត់ to fold; to turn
បត់ចន្ទាស crooked, twisted
បត់ចុះបត់ឡើង to zigzag
បត់ជើង to relieve oneself (lit: to fold the legs)
បឋម /pathɑm/ first, primary; early
បឋមសិក្សា /pathɑmməsəksaa/ primary school, primary education
បថមោក្ខ (=បដិមោក្ខ) /patdəmaok/ remedy, solution (i.e. to life's suffering)
បទ /bɑt/ set, verse, song, composition; meter, rhyme pattern; path, way, behavior; because
បទកខ /bɑt kɑɑ khɑɑ/ Alphabetic Progression Style (Meter)
បទកង្កែបលោតកណ្ដាលស្រះ Style of a Frog Jumping into the Middle of the Pond
បទកង្កែបលោតស្លាក់ពេជ្រ Style of a Frog Choking on Jewels
បទកាកគតិ /bɑt kaaqkəteq/ Crow's Gait Meter
បទកែកន្ទណក a poetic meter used in the Ream-kei
បទគួរសម /bɑt-kuə-sɑm/ appropriate behavior
បទគោព័ទ្ធស្នឹង Style of a Cow [wrapping his rope] around the Tether-stake
បទចក្រវាឡ Space-Binding Style (deriving from the fact that each line begins and ends with the same word, like book ends)
បទឆ័ត្របីជាន់ Three-Tiered Umbrella Style
បទផាប់ទង Intertwined Meter
បទត្រឡាចឡើងទ្រើង Style of Melons Climbing a Trellis
បទត្រីពិធព័ន្ធ Triply Interrelated Style
បទថយក្រោយ Reverse [Word Order] Style
បទវិទានននយោបាយ political criticism
បទនមោ Namo Meter
បទនាគកៀវក្រវាត់ Encircling Naga Meter
បទនាគបរិព័ទ្ធ Encircling Naga Style
បទនាគរាជប្លែងឫទ្ធិ Style of Naga King Magically Transforming [Himself]
បទបន្ទោលកាក Frog's Gait Meter
បទផ្កាឈូករីក Blossoming Lotus Style
បទពំនោល Narrative Meter
បទព្រហ្មគីតិ /bɑt prumməkɨt/ Song of Brahma Meter

បទព្រះចន្ទ្របាំងឆ័ត្រ Style of the Moon Hidden by an Umbrella

បទភុជង្គលីលា Snake-Crawl Meter

បទមករខ្ជាក់កែវ Style of a Sea Monster Spewing Jewels

បទយតិភង្គ Hyphenated Style (deriving from the fact that each line ends with the first part of the word which is completed at the beginning of the next line)

បទរមាំងដើរព្រៃ Style of Deer Walking in the Forest

បទរលកខ្ទប់ច្រាំង Style of Waves Beating against the Shore

បទរវ៉ែង false charge, mistaken action

បទសទ្យាបល្ហួន Mellifluous Conversation Style (?)

បទសារថីទាញរថ Style of the Driver Pulling a Cart

បទសិង្ហតោលេងកន្ទុយ Style of a Lion Playing with His Tail

បទស្ដេចផ្ទំ name of a wedding song (lit: Song of the Sleeping King)

បទអក្សរល្ហួន Slithering Letters Styles

បទអក្សរសង្វាស Related Letters Style

បទអញ្ជើញគ្រូ Chant for the Invocation of the Spirits

បទអាក្រក់ /bɑt qaakrɑa/ crime, scurrilous conduct

បទុម /patum, botum/ lotus

បទុមា (=បទុម ) lotus flower

បន់ to pray; to petition

បន់ស្រន់ to pray, to petition

បន្ត /bɑntɑɑ/ to continue, extend

បន្ត ៗ /bɑntɑɑ-bɑntɑɑ/ successively, in turn

បន្តក់ to drip; the symbol ់

បន្តិច a little, rather; in a little while, a little later, soon, shortly; watch out or I'll...

បន្តិចទៀត a little later

បន្តិច...បន្តិច for awhile...then for awhile

បន្តិចបន្តួច just a little, somewhat

បន្តិចម្ដង ៗ /bɑntəc mədɑɑŋ, bɑntəc mədɑɑŋ/ a little at a time, little by little

បន្តិចម្នាក់ ៗ /bɑntəc mənĕəq, bɑntəc mənĕəq/ each for awhile

បន្តុះ /bɑntoh/ to criticize

បន្តែ (=បណ្ដែ ) /bɑndae/ pledge, promise

បន្ថយ to lessen, decrease (tv)

បន្ថើ to soften, to lighten

បន្ថែ to take constant care of

បន្ថែម to add, supplement, increase (tv)

បន្ថែមពាក្យថា added, said further

បន្ថំ to rush, hurry (tv)

បន្ទន់ to soften, to relax (tv)

បន្ទប់ room

បន្ទប់ដេក bedroom

បន្ទប់ទទួលភ្ញៀវ living room (guest-receiving-room)

បន្ទប់ទឹក washroom

បន្ទប់បរិភោគបាយ dining room

បន្ទប់រៀន classroom

បន្ទរ to join in (in a song)

បន្ទាត់ rules, discipline; line, straightedge, rule

បន្ទាន់ urgent

បន្ទាប់ next, following

បន្ទាប់មក afterward, next (in succession)

បន្ទាយ fortress; military installation

បន្ទាយឆ្មាក a fortress with extended wings or parapets

បន្ទាយស្រី Banteay Srei (lit: women's fortress)

បន្ទាល់ witness, proof

បន្ទូល speech, words (Roy)

បន្ទោបង់ be relieved of, to ease (Polite)

បន្ទោស to scold

បន្ទំ to sleep (Roy)

បន្ទំ to cause to stand out in deep relief

បន្ទះ sheet, strip, plate

បន្ធូរ to relax, release, loosen

បន្ទួន to repeat, to do repeatedly

បន្លប់ to distract, confuse, trick

បន្លា thorn, sticker

បន្លាច to scare, frighten

បន្លាស់ a change, substitute, replacement; specifier for changes (of clothing, etc.)

បន្លឺ to make a sound, cause to be heard, utter; to sound

បន្លែ vegetable

បន្លែបង្កា vegetables (Coll)

បន្លែបន្លប់ to distract someone's attention, confuse, mislead

បន្លំ to trick, mislead; falsify; obtain under false pretenses

បន្សល់ទុក to leave (something) behind (a legacy, amount, etc.)

បន្សាប to weaken, dilute

បបរ rice soup, porridge

បបួល to agree; to persuade

បបែល ray fish

បព៌ត /baarəpoə̆t/ mountain (Lit)

បពិត្រ /bapɨt/ Lord, Majesty, Excellency

បពិត្រធិបតី Your Highness

បព្វកថា /boppəkəthaa/ introduction, foreword

បព្វជិត /boppəcɨt, bappəcɨt/ monk (Lit)

បព្វតា (=បុព្វតា ) mountain, hill (Lit)

បម្រាស to struggle (to get away)

បម្រុង for, intended for; to intend, resolve, determine (to); to make preparations, be prepared

បម្រើ to serve

បម្រះ (=បម្រាស់ ) to struggle, to wiggle

បម្រះរួច to escape, to free oneself

បរ /baa/ to drive, conduct (a car, etc.)

បរបាញ់ /baa-bañ/ to hunt (animals)

បរប៉ៃលិន /baa-paylɨn/ Bar Pailin (a town)

បរទារកម្ម /baarətiəkam/ adultery

បរទេស /baarəteeh/ foreign, foreign countries

បរម /barommə-/ bound attribute: highest, best, most excellent

បរមបពិត្រ /barommabapɨt/ title

បរមរាជវង្សានុវង្ស /barommariəccəwŭəŋ-saanuwŭəŋ/ family (Roy)

បរមរាជវាំង /barommariəccəweə̆ŋ/ palace, royal residence

បរមវិស្ណុលោក /barommawihsnulook/ Paramavishnuloka (posthumous name for Suryavarman II)

បរមសុខ /barommasok/ great joy, perfect peace of mind; to be well (Roy)

បរលោក /baarəlaok, balaok/ the next world, the life beyond

បរាជ័យ /paraacɨy/ to be defeated

បរាសិត /paraasət/ parasitic

បរិក្ខារ /baarikhaa/ equipment, commodities

បរិច្ចាគ to contribute, sacrifice

បរិច្ចាគៈ /baaricaakeə̆q/ generosity

បរិបូណ៌ /baaribou/ plentiful, full, complete (with)

បរិពារ /baaripiə/ entourage

បរិភោគ /baariphook/ to eat (Eleg)

បរិយាយ to elaborate, to develop in detail

បរិវារ /baariwaa/ entourage

បរិវិតក្ក /pareqwitok/ thought, consideration; to ponder, consider (Roy)

បរិវេណ /pariween/ perimeter, confines

បរិសុទ្ធ /baarisot/ pure, unalloyed, perfect

បរិហារ to fulminate, to talk, rant, to comment

បរិឡាហ៍ burning, fiery hot

បល្លង្ក /ballaŋ/ pedestal, throne

បវរ /baa-wɔɔ/ excellent, superior

បស្ចិម /bahcəm~pachəm/ west (Lit)

បស្ចិមប្រទេស /pachəm-prateeh/ western countries, the West

បសាទ /pasaat/ sense, feeling

បសាទរូប /pasaattəruup/ the organs of perception

បា father (Arch); familiar 2nd person masculine pronoun: you; male (of animals)
បាក់ to break (iv); broken, irregular
បាក់ជើងម្ខាង have a broken leg
បាក់បែក broken up
បាក់ស្បាត terror-stricken
បាច to broadcast, to spread, to scatter; to splash, scoop (water)
បាត bottom
បាតដៃ palm of the hand
បាត់ to lose, disappear
បាត់ដាន to lose track, lose the trace
បាត់ដំបង Battambang (province)
បាត់ទ្រង់ to be ruined, destroyed (financially, socially, etc.)
បាត់បង់ disappear, be lost
បាត់ស្មារតី to lose consciousness
បាតុកម្ម demonstration
បាត្រ large spherical bowl (used by Buddhist monks)
បាទ polite response particle used by men; (in response to a yes-no question, it means 'yes')
បាទ an old monetary unit
បាទ line, phrase (of verse or scripture)
បាទ sole (of the foot), palm (of the hand)
បាធ្យាយ /baatyiəy/ teacher, master, preceptor, mentor
បាន to get, have, achieve, result (in); preceding a verb: to get to, have the opportunity to; following a verb: can, able, possible
បានការ to achieve, get results, be successful, amount to something
បានការពេល to be an opportune moment, to have an advantage
បានគ្នា to take each other (as husband and wife)
បានជា results in, is the reason that
បានជាគ្នាលេង as a playmate
បាននឹង have an aptitute for, predilection for, natural ability in
បានផល to make a profit, obtain results, get a yield
បានឫក្ស propitious
បានសេចក្ដីថា this means that
បាប sin, immoral action
បាពួន Bapuon (an 11th-century temple inside Angkor Thom)
បាយ cooked rice, food; to eat, have a meal
បាយកក left over rice
បាយខុនគូ name of a traditional wedding composition
បាយព្រឹក breakfast
បាយម៉ាត a kind of small tree with aromatic foliage
បាយសី an ornamental offering made of the stalk and leaves of the banana tree
បាយ័ន /baayŏən/ The Bayon (central temple of Angkor Thom)
បារ to scrape up, dig out (with the hands)
បារមី /baarəməy/ excellence, perfection; power, virtue, chastity authority, status
បារមីតា /baarəməytaa/ greatness, excellence, authority
បារម្ភ /baarɑm/ to worry, be concerned
បារី cigarette
បារីស្លឹកសង្កែ local cigarettes (made with /slək sɑŋkae/)
បារាំង French, France; western, a westerner
បារាំងសែស French
បាល់ /bal/ ball
បាល់ទះ basketball
បាល័ដ្ឋ (=បាទ្បាត់) /baalat/ a clerical title
បាល័ដ្ឋស្រុក deputy district chief
បាលី Pali (language)
បាវ servant
បាវ bag
បាវព្រាវ servant
បាសក /baasɑq/ layman, laity
បាសាក់ Bassac (river); name of a former province

បាសាន name of a former province

បាឌុប bachot (French baccalaureate degree)

បាឡាត់ស្រុក assistant to the district chief

បាលី (=បាលិ) Pali (language)

បិណ្ឌ /bən/ food offering presented to the monks

បិណ្ឌបាត្រ /bən-baat/to go about accepting gifts of food (of monks)

បិត (=បិទ) to close

បិត to whittle

បិតា /bəydaa/ father (Eleg)

បិទ to close; to stick, attach (to)

បិសាច /bəysaac/ ghost, spirit

បី three

បី to cradle in the arms

បី adverbializing particle: of a... kind, in a...manner, as if (Lit)

បី ៗ by threes

បីដូច seem as if, just as if

បីបម to provide tender loving care

បីបាច់ to take care of

ប៊ីយែរ /biyɛə, byɛə/ (Fr. bière) beer

បឹង lake, pond

បឹងបួ lakes and ponds

បឹងរាំង Beng Rang (a section of Phnom Penh)

បុក to pound (with a pestle or stick)

បុកស្រូវ to husk rice (with a mortar and pestle)

បុគ្គល /bokkuəl/ person, individual

បុគ្គលិក /bokkəlɨk/ personnel, employee(s) (Lit)

បុច្ឆា /pocchaa/ to question (Lit)

បុញ្ញាភិសង្ខារ /paññaaphiqsɑŋkhaa/ accumulation of merit

បុណ្យ /bon/ ceremony, celebration, feast; magical power, supernatural power, power of virtue

បុណ្យការងារ Labor Day

បុណ្យចូលឆ្នាំ New Year's Celebration

បុណ្យចូលវស្សា /bon-coul-wŭəhsaa/ celebration of the beginning of the Buddhist Lenten period

បុណ្យចេញវស្សា /bon-cəñ-wŭəhsaa/ celebration of the end of Buddhist Lent, or of rainy season

បុណ្យឆ្លង dedication ceremony (for a public or religious building)

បុណ្យតាំងតុ celebration of the reigning monarch's birthday (one facet of which is the erection of tableaux from each province in the palace grounds)

បុណ្យបារមី power

បុណ្យប្រកាសរដ្ឋធម្មនុញ្ញ Constitution Day (ceremony [commemorating] the promulgation of the constitution)

បុណ្យផ្កា a fund raising ceremony in which contributions, usually in the form of paper money, are attached to an artificial tree)

បុណ្យភ្ជុំបិណ្ឌ /bon-pcum-bən/ ceremony of commemoration of one's ancestors

បុណ្យព្រេង fate

បុណ្យរំលាយសព cremation ceremony

បុណ្យសក្តិ status, rank, position

បុណ្យអង្គការសហប្រជាជាតិ United Nations Day

បុណ្យឯករាជ្យជាតិ National Independence Celebration

បុណ្យអុំទូក Water Festival (featuring longboat races)

ប៊ុត /but/ Bouth (pers. n.)

ប៊ុតនាង name of a bookstore in Phnom Penh

បុត្រ son (Eleg)

បុត្រី daughter (Eleg)

បុប្ផ flower (Eleg)

បុប្ផទេវី /bopphaa teewii/ Boppha Devi (Sihanouk's daughter)

បុប្ផវតី /bopphaawədəy/ Bopphavadi (pers. n.)

បុព្វកថា /boppəkəthaa/ introduction, foreword

បុព្វជាតិ /boppəciət/ past lives, former incarnations

បុព្វតា (=ភ្នំ) /boppətaa/ mountain, hill (Lit)

បុព្វសិទ្ធិ /boppəsətthiq/ prerogative

បុព្វេ /boppee/ past, former times

បុរស /borɑh/ man (Lit)

បុរសស្ត្រី /borɑh-satrəy/ ladies and gentlemen (Eleg, lit: man and woman)

បុរាណកាល /boraanəkaal/ ancient time, antiquity

បុរាណរាជ្យ earlier reigns

បុរាណសម័យ the old days, ancient times

បុរីរម្យ /boqriqrum/ delightful city

បុរិសទោស /borihsatooh/ human fault, mortal defect

បុរីរដ្ឋរាជធានី /borəy-roŏt-riəccəthaan/ royal capital

បុរោហិត /boraohət/ Brahman priest

បុស្ប /bos, boh/ flower (Lit)

បុស្បនាគ /boh-niəq/ large hardwood tree

បុស្បបង្គ /bohsəboŋ/ lotus (i.e. flower [which rises from the] mud)

បុស្បី (= បុស្ប ) /bohsəbəy/ flower (Lit)

បូ bow (of ribbon or cloth)

បូក to add (of numbers, things)

បូកគោ Bokor (a resort area)

បូជា to offer, present

បូជាសព to cremate, hold a cremation

បូណ៌ /bou/ full (of the moon)

បូណ៌មី /bourəməy/ full-moon

បូបុស្ប bow-shaped blossom

បូព៌ /bou/ east (Lit)

បូព៌ទិស /bourətɨh/ east, eastern (Lit)

បូព៌ា /boupiə/ east (Lit)

បូយបូណ៌ហ្រទ /bouyeə̆qbourənahrəteə̆q/ Pûyapûrnahrada (hell for those who steal liquor, and for adulterers)

បូរាណ old, ancient, former; former times

ហ៊ូហ៊ង Hou Hong (pers. n.)

បួង to put the hair up in a French roll; to gather hair in a bundle

បួងសួង to pray

បួន four

បួនជ្រុង quadrangle; square

បួនជ្រុងទ្រវែង rectangle

បួនជ្រុងស្មើ square

បួស to enter the monk-hood

បើ if

បើកាលណា whenever, if

បើកុំតែ if it weren't for, only (because)

បើកុំប៉ុណ្ណោះ if it weren't for that, otherwise

បើក្រៅតែពី apart from, excluding

បើដូច្នេះ in this case

បើដូច្នោះ in that case

បើទុកជា...ក្តី even though; no matter what

បើនឹង whether, if

បើប្រសិនជា if, if perchance

បើមិនយូរក៏ឆាប់ sooner or later

បើម្ល៉េះហើយ therefore, that being the case

បើម្ល៉ោះសម undoubtedly, inevitably

បើយ៉ាងយូរណាស់ at the longest

បើសិនជា if

បើសិនណាជា if perchance

បើអញ្ចឹង then, in that case, therefore

បើក to open

បើក to drive (used with vehicles)

បើកក្តោង to sail

បើកពពារ to swell the neck or hood (of a snake)

បើកឱ្យ allow, permit

បៀ playing cards

បៀក to dip up and spread; to

prepare (a quid of betel)

បៀត close to, next to, to afflict, attain
បៀតបៀន to harm, afflict, oppress

បៀម to hold in the mouth

បៀវត្ស /biəwoət/ salary

បេក្ខជន /paekkəcuən/ candidate

បេង a mahogany-like hardwood tree

បេតី /paetəy/ to love; love (Poetic)
បេឡា /peilaa/ fund (n)

បេឡាជាតិសម្រាប់បរិក្ខារ National Development Fund
បេះ to pick (flowers, fruits)

បេះដូង heart

បេះបិទ exactly, identically

បែក to break, divide (iv)

បែកខ្ញែក to be separated

បែកខ្ញែកខ្ចាត់ខ្ចាយ separated, dispersed

បែកចែក to divide

បែកញើស to break into sweat

បែកបាក់ to separate, break apart

បែកញាក់ to disperse, break up (iv)

បែកផ្កាត្រែង (Idiom) to break violently (of waves)
បែកផ្សែង to break into spray, throw up a mist
បែង to divide, share

បែប sort, type, kind

បែបបទ /baep-bɑt/ good manners, savoir-vivre, proper etiquette
បែបផែន overall plan; way, method

បែបយ៉ាង example, model, sample

បែរ to turn, turn aside

បែរជា change to, become; instead

បែលហ្សិក /baelzik/ Belgium (Fr. Belgique)
បោក to hit, to beat; to wash (clothes); to deceive

បោក្ខរណី /paokkhaarənəy/ lotus-pond

បោច to pluck, pull off (feathers, grass, etc.)
បោយដៃ to summon with the hand, to beckon
បោល to gallop, to run (of animals)

បោលពុំចេះទាន់ទើរួយ run without ever catching up
បោស to sweep, to brush, to graze

បោសជ្រះ to sweep, clean up

បោសអង្អែល to caress

បោះ to throw, pitch; to drive in (stakes, nails, etc.); to stamp, to print, to publish; to pitch (a tent); to encamp

បោះ(ទ័ព) to encamp, to pitch camp
បោះឆ្នោត to vote

បោះជំហាន to take steps, to make progress
បោះបង់ to abandon; to leave unfinished
បោះបង់ចោល to abandon

បោះបង្គោល drive a stake, put in a stake
បោះបរ to drive (Arch)

បោះបោក throw around, beat up, bang against (the ground, each other, etc.)
បោះពុម្ព /bɑh-pum/ to print, to publish
បោះពុម្ពលើកទី ៧ seventh edition

បោះពួយ to dive (from the sky), make a pass at
បោះយុថ្កា to drop anchor

បៅ to suck (teat or rubber nipple)

បំណង desire, intention; to intend

បំណាច់ since, because

បំណាច់ service (rendered)

បំណុល debt

បំបាក់ to cause to break

បំបាត់ cause to disappear; to trick, to swindle
បំបាត់ជីវិត to destroy life

បំបាត់មាត់ to shut someone up

បំបិទ to hide (tv)

បំបិទបំបាំង to hide, keep (something) secret

បំបួស to ordain, send [one's child] into the monk-hood

បំបែក to break (tv)

បំបែរ turn away, shunt aside, ward off

បំបោល to cause (animals) to run

បំបោល to cause (horse, ox, etc.) to run, to stampede

បំបៅ to nurse (offspring)

បំបាំង to hide (tv)

បំផាយ to cause to gallop

បំផឹក to give to drink, cause to drink

បំផុត most, last

បំផ្លាញ to destroy

បំផ្លិចបំផ្លាញ to destroy

បំពក់ to stoke, add fuel to (a fire)

បំពង to deep-fry in oil

បំពង់ pipe, tube; quiver, arrow-holder

បំពង់ក the throat

បំពាក់ clothing worn above the waist; to affix, attach (a decoration, medal, etc.)

បំពាន transgress, violate, infringe (intentionally or persistently)

បំពារ to push against

បំពុល to poison

បំពេ to lull by singing, to lullaby

បំពេញ to fill, fulfill

បំពេញព្រះផ្នួស to fulfill the rites of ordination

បំពេរ to sing a lullaby, to sing to sleep, to serenade

បំព្រង fresh and pretty

បំភាន់ to deceive, trick, fool

បំភ្លឺ to illuminate

បំភ្លុក to overturn, upset

បំភ្លេច to forget intentionally, to ignore

បំរុង in order to, with the intention of

បំរុងការណ៍ to be prepared for any eventuality

បំរើ to serve

បំរើសេះ messenger, circuit rider

បាំង to block, bar, shield, protect

បាំងទើជ to shade the eyes with the hand

បាំងស្កូល commemoration

បះ to raise up (iv)

បះ to strike (of workers)

បះបោរ to revolt

ប៉ក់ Pak (pers. n.)

ប៉ង to expect, intend, assume, hope

ប៉ិប្រប fresh and pretty

ប៉ផុរ soft, smooth

ប៉ផ្លេក shiny, glistening

ប៉ម watch-tower, guard tower

ប៉ា Father (term of address or reference)

ប៉ាឈឺន name of a Cambodian politician

ប៉ាន to cover, to plate

ប៉ាន Paan (pers. n.)

ប៉ារី /paarii/ Paris

ប៉ាហ៊ី charlatan, purveyor of folk remedies

ប៉ិច Pech (pers. n.)

ប៉ិន skillful, clever, adept

ប៉ិនប្រសប់ clever

ប៉ី /pəy/ flute, clarinet

ប៉ុណ្ណឹង only, that's all, only to that extent

ប៉ុណ្ណេះ only, that's all, this is all

ប៉ុណ្ណោះ only, that's all

ប៉ុន to equal, be the same as (in size, amount, degree, etc.)

ប៉ុណ្ណា to what extent, how much

ប៉ុន្តែ but

ប៉ុន្មាន how much, how many; however much, to whatever extent

ប៉ុស្តិ៍ /poh/ post-office

ប៉ែក part, section

ប៉ែតសិប eighty

ប៉ែន-នុត Penn Nouth (pers. n.)

ប៉ោ a Chinese game of chance

ប៉ោង swelled, inflated

ប៉ះ touch, come in contact with; to patch

ប្តី husband

ប្តឹង to bring a complaint, to sue

ប្តូរ to exchange

ប្តួល to knock over, cause to fall over

ផ្តើម to begin; to create

ប្តេជ្ញា /pdacñaa/ to swear (that), resolve (that)

ប្រក់ to roof, thatch; roofed with

ប្រកក់ឆ្មប ceremony for thanking the midwife and for naming and piercing the ears of the new baby

ប្រកប to combine, endow; to do, engage in, be involved in

ប្រកបដោយ combined with, provided with; consisting of

ប្រកបនឹងកិច្ច to fit the facts

ប្រកបរបរកសិកម្ម engaged in agriculture

ប្រកាច់ to twitch, to have muscular spasms

ប្រកាន់ to hold to, insist on; to object to; to reserve, preempt; to be conservative, stuffy

ប្រកាន់ដៃ (=បង្កាន់ដៃ) railing, handrail, bannister; receipt

ប្រកាប់ do battle, spar (with knives, swords, etc.)

ប្រការ way, kind, point

ប្រកាស to proclaim, announce

ប្រគូក to hail from afar; to play a wind instrument

ប្រកួត to compete

ប្រកែក to object, argue, refuse, quarrel

ប្រខាំ to bite each other

ប្រគង crisscrossing, lying across each other

ប្រគល់ to hand over

ប្រគេន to offer, to give (to clergy)

ប្រគំ to play (orchestra)

ប្រចណ្ឌ, ប្រច័ណ្ឌ /pracan/ jealous (of one's spouse or lover)

ប្រចាប់ to blame, accuse, hold responsible; to wrestle back and forth, wrangle over

ប្រចាប់គ្នា to struggle, wrestle, grab each other

ប្រចឹក to peck at reciprocally

ប្រចាំ attached to, concerning; every

ប្រចាំ pass the buck (to), leave it up to

ប្រចាំការ full time (lit: to be on hand to watch over business)

ប្រឆាំង to oppose, resist, contest

ប្រជាជាតិ people, populace

ប្រជាធិបតេយ្យ /praciəthɨppətay/ democracy

ប្រជាប្រិយ /praciəprəy/ traditional, folk, of the people

ប្រជាពលរដ្ឋ /praciə-pŭəlləroə̆t/ citizens, populace

ប្រជាភិថុតិ /praciəphithoqteq/ demagoguery

ប្រជារាស្ត្រ /praciəriəh/ people, populace

ប្រជែង to dispute querulously

ប្រជុំ to gather, convene

ប្រជុំជន densely populated (area)

ប្រជ្រុយ mole, wart

ប្រញាយ scatter in all directions, pell-mell

ប្រញាប់ to hurry (to)

ប្រញាប់ប្រញាល់ to hurry

ប្រញិបប្រញាប់ to hurry

ប្រដាប់ tool, utensil, instrument;

to fashion, work, adorn

ប្រដាប់ដោយ provided with, decorated with, dressed in

ប្រដាប់ប្រដា tools, instruments, provisions

ប្រដាល់ to hit each other, to box

ប្រដូច to compare

ប្រដៅ to advise, instruct, counsel

ប្រដៅជេរ (=ជេរប្រដៅ) to exhort, harangue, admonish

ប្រឌិត to create, to invent

ប្រឌិតញាណ /pradɨttəñiən/ creativity, imagination

ប្រណម្យ /pranam/ to greet with hands together (to royalty)

ប្រណិធាន /pranethiən/ promise, intention, oath; to promise, swear

ប្រណិប័តន៍ /pranebat/ to respect, obey

ប្រណី to pity, be compassionate

ប្រណាំង to compete, to race

ប្រតិបត្តិ /pratebat/ to follow, carry out, execute (orders); behavior, conduct

ប្រតិព័ទ្ធ /pratəpoət/ to love, be involved with; relationship, involvement

ប្រត្យក្ស /pratyaq/ clear, obvious, evident

ប្រថពី /prathəpii/ earth (Lit)

ប្រថាប់ to stay, put up; to stamp (Roy)

ប្រថុយ have a go at it, try and see

ប្រទក្សិណ /prateəqsən/ to encircle clockwise

ប្រទាក់ connected, enmeshed, intersecting

ប្រទាក់គ្នាខ្វាត់ខ្វែង intersecting, crossing

ប្រទាន to give (Roy)

ប្រទីប /pratiip, pratɨp/ lantern; a miniature temple decorated with candles and set afloat

ប្រទូស្ត /pratuuh/ to argue, quarrel, be obstinate

ប្រទូស្តវិញឈ្លង to argue back, oppose, be obstinate

ប្រទេច to curse, slander, vilify

ប្រទេស country (head-word in names of countries)

ប្រទេសកម្ពុជា Cambodia

ប្រទេសក្រៅ abroad, foreign countries

ប្រទេសជាតិ nation, country

ប្រទះ to come upon, to meet

ប្រទះឃើញ to come upon

ប្រធាន president, chairman

ប្រធានអគ្គនាយក /prathiən qaqkeəq-niəyŭəq/ Presidential director

ប្រប stay close to, sidle along, keep next to; near

ប្របៀត to squeeze in, huddle together

ប្របែល (=បបែល) ray fish

ប្របាំង to hide oneself, conceal oneself, cover oneself

ប្រផ្សុរ fine, smooth, silky, powdery

ប្រផេញ a kind of fern

ប្រផេះ gray

ប្រពន្ធ /prapŭən/ wife, female companion

ប្រព័ន្ធ to intertwine

ប្រពាក់ to overlap, be superimposed

ប្រពាក់ប្រពួន piled up higgledy-piggledy

ប្រពាត to enjoy oneself, relax, go for an outing (Roy)

ប្រពៃ proper, correct

ប្រពៃណី customs, tradition; traditional

ប្រព្រឹត្ត /praprɨt/ to behave, act, follow

ប្រភេទ kind, variety, genre

ប្រមាណ to guess, estimate; about, approximately

ប្រមាត់ /pramat, pəpat/ gall-bladder

ប្រមាថ /pramaat, pəmaat/ to blaspheme, scorn, show disrespect for

ប្រមាថមើលងាយ to look down on, scorn, be disrespectful to

ប្រមុខ head, chief

ប្រមុខរដ្ឋ chief of state

ប្រមូល to gather, to find

ប្រមែប្រមូល /pramae-pramoul, pəmae-pəmoul/ to gather

ប្រយង្គ /prɑyɑŋ/ the plant Panicum Italicum
ប្រយ័ត្ន to be careful (to)
ប្រយ័ត្នការណ៍ be careful
ប្រយ័ត្នក្រែង in the event that, in case
ប្រយ័ត្នក្រោយ be careful (lit: keep a lookout behind)
ប្រយ័ត្នខ្លួន you be careful!
ប្រយ័ត្នប្រយែង be careful
ប្រយុទ្ធ to fight
ប្រយូរវង្ស royal lineage
ប្រយោគ complete sentence, statement
ប្រយោជន៍ /prɑyaoc/ useful; usefulness, purpose, importance; for the purpose of
ប្រយោជន៍ជាតិ national interest
ប្រយោជន៍នឹង for the purpose of
ប្រល័យ to ruin, destroy; to die; death, destruction, ruin
ប្រល័យ to kill
ប្រល័យជន្ម to kill; to commit suicide
ប្រលោម to soothe, comfort, cajole
ប្រលោមលោក novel
ប្រវត្តិ /prɑwoət/ history (of a specific event, place, etc.)
ប្រវត្តិសាស្ត្រ /prɑwoəttəsaah/ (the study of) history
ប្រវា to grab at, grasp, flail
ប្រវាល expanse, wide surface
ប្រវេណី (=ប្រពៃណី) custom, tradition
ប្រវែង to have the length of...
ប្រសប់ skilled, skillful, clever (at)
ប្រសា son- or daughter-in-law
ប្រសាសន៍ to say (Eleg)
ប្រសាសនោបាយ /prɑsahsnoubaay/ politics
ប្រសិទ្ធិ /prɑsət/ to offer, wish, extend, endow
ប្រសិទ្ធិពរជ័យ to extend wishes of success
ប្រសិទ្ធិភាព /prɑsətthəphiəp/ effectiveness
ប្រសិន if perchance
ប្រសិនណាជា if
ប្រសិនបើ if
ប្រសូត name of a village
ប្រសូត្រ to give birth (Roy)
ប្រសើរ praiseworthy, extraordinary; good, proper
ប្រស្នា enigma, philosophical problem, abstract question
ប្រស្មា (=ស្មា) shoulder
ប្រស្រ័យ reminisce; to like, desire (Lit)
ប្រហារ to kill; (Skt. to beat, hit, kick)
ប្រហារជីវិត to kill (Lit)
ប្រហុក fermented fish, preserved salted fish
ប្រហើរ musky, having the odor of civet
ប្រហែល about, approximately; perhaps
ប្រហែស to be careless, neglectful
ប្រហោង vacant, empty; a void, a hole
ប្រហោងពោះ to have an empty or sinking feeling in the stomach
ប្រហោងពោះពុង to have an empty or sinking feeling in the stomach
ប្រឡង to take an examination; to compete
ប្រឡងជាប់ to pass an examination
ប្រឡងធ្លាក់ to fail an examination
ប្រឡាក់ to be soiled, stained, dirty
ប្រឡាយ ditch, canal, stream
ប្រឡូក to be entangled (in a fight, etc.)
ប្រឡេះ to shell (corn); shell out, rub off, gather
ប្រឡែង to tease, pick at playfully
ប្រអប់ box
ប្រឱបគ្នា to embrace each other
ប្រា a kind of fish
ប្រាក់ silver, money

ប្រាក់កាស /praq-kah/ money

ប្រាក់ខែ salary

ប្រាក់ចំណូលបុណ្យ contribution (to the ceremony)

ប្រាក់ជំនួយ supplementary allowance, subsidy

ប្រាកដ /praakɑt, pəkɑt/ exact, clear, definite

ប្រាកដបង្កើតកេរ្តិ៍ច្បាស់ it will surely redound to my honor

ប្រាកដប្រជា surely, truly, definitely

ប្រាក់បំណាច់ bonus, commission, allowance

ប្រាង្គណ៍, ប្រាង្គ /praaŋ/ prang, stupa, tapering monument; temple or palace with a tower

ប្រាជ្ញ /praac/ intelligent

ប្រាជ្ញប្រាយ intelligent, witty

ប្រាជ្ញា /praacñaa/ intelligence

ប្រាជ្ញាសារពេជ្ញតាញាណ /praacñaa-saarəpɨc-tañiən/ enlightenment

ប្រាណ body, self

ប្រាណប្រែ (=ប្រែប្រាណ) to change

ប្រាថ្នា /praatnaa/ to wish, intend; wishes, desire (n)

ប្រាប to subdue

ប្រាបប្រាម to subdue, to bring under subjection

ប្រាប់ to tell; to inform

ប្រាប់ប្រាយ (=ប្រាយប្រាប់)

ប្រាប់ផ្លូវ to give directions

ប្រាប់ឱ្យ to tell someone to do something

ប្រាម to warn

ប្រាយ to start, spurt, lunge (of a horse)

ប្រាយប្រាប់ to tell

ប្រារព្ធ /praarup/ to originate; to relate, to commemorate, to perform

ប្រាស away from, different from, separated; to run off, scurry away

ប្រាសចាក devoid of, separated from

ប្រាសយកតែអាយុ to run for one's life

ប្រាស់លះលែងទោសទុក្ខ to exonerate, excuse, exculpate

ប្រាសាទ /praasaat, prasaat/ palace; ancient monument, temple

ប្រាស្រ័យ (=ប្រស្រ័យ) to like, to respect; to talk, to reminisce

ប្រឹក្សា /prəksaa/ to advise, consult

ប្រិត economical, thrifty

ប្រិតប្រៀន to instruct rigorously; rigorous, careful

ប្រិមប្រិយ /prəm-prəy/ lovable, pleasing, smiling, happy

ប្រិយ pleasing, pleasant

ប្រី to persuade

ប្រឹង try to, make an effort (to); to feel like

ប្រឹងតែ persist in, keep trying

ប្រឹងប្រែង to try hard to, make a strong effort

ប្រឹថពី (=ប្រថពី) the earth (Lit)

ប្រុង to be on guard, ready to, intend to

ប្រុងនឹង to intend to, about to

ប្រុងប្រយ័ត្ន /proŋ-prɑyat, proŋ-pəyat/ to be careful

ប្រុងវិញ្ញាណ be alert, fully conscious; pay full attention

ប្រុស man; masculine

ប្រុសកំដរ groomsmen

ប្រូង with a splash (sound of falling into the water)

ប្រួញ to shrink up, draw up

ប្រួញប្រាណ draw oneself up, make oneself inconspicuous

ប្រើ to use; to send, commission

ប្រើការ to actually do, put into practice; to use, utilize

ប្រើប្រាស់ to use, make use of

ប្រើពុតជា to pretend that, act as if

ប្រើឱ្យ to charge, to entrust with a duty

ប្រើស /prəh/ a kind of deer

ប្រើស /prəh/ conical bamboo entry to a fishtrap

ប្រៀនប្រដៅ to educate, instruct, advise

ប្រៀប to compare

ប្រៀបធៀប to compare, consider

ប្រៀបបាននឹង like, can be compared with

ប្រេង oil

ប្រេងកាត kerosene; petroleum

ប្រេត /praet/ demon, ogre, monster, inhabitant of hell

ប្រែ to change, translate; to become

ប្រែក្រឡាប់ to turn around (and)

ប្រែខ្វ (=ប្រែ )

ប្រែជា change to, become; to do instead

ប្រែប្រាជ្ញា to scheme, look for excuses

ប្រែប្រាណ to change position, move one's body

ប្រែប្រឹង (=ប្រឹង ) try hard to

ប្រែះៗ crackling sound

ប្រៃ salty

ប្រៃសណីយ៍ post office

ប្រោស to revive (tv)

ប្រោស to like, love, be pleased with

ប្រោសប្រណី to be compassionate, considerate

ប្រោះ to restore to life, resurrect (by magic); to keep alive in water

ប្រាំ five

ប្រាំង dry, hot and dry

ប្រាំបី eight

ប្រាំបីម៉ឺន eight 10,000's (80,000)

ប្រាំបួន nine

ប្រាំពីរ /prampii/(spoken /prampɨl/) seven

ប្រាំពីរដប់ seven times (completions)

ប្រាំពីររយ seven hundred

ប្រាំមួយ six

ប្រាំម៉ោងកន្លងមក five hours later

ប្រះ to bolt away, dash off; throw oneself down (as from fatigue, exhaustion)

ប្លន់ to rob, hold up

ប្លាម៉ា a kind of fish

ប្លាម៉ូ a kind of fish

ប្លាយ approximately

ប្លូច to slip into

ប្លេងប្លោង to bob, pitch and roll

ប្លែង to change, change form (by magic)

ប្លោត descriptive of a sudden jump or leap

ប្អូនថ្លៃ younger in-law

ប្អូន /pqoun/ younger sibling; younger friend or relative of one's own generation; I, me (wife to husband, or younger to older sibling or friend); you (husband to wife, or older to younger sibling or friend)

ផ្អែក to lean against, put against

ផង too, in addition; mild imperative: please, will you?

ផង (=របស់ ) of, belonging to (Coll, rare)

ផងគ្នា together, respectively, each other

ផត់ fine, powdered

ផនស៊ី Phân-Si (pers. n.)

ផល /phɑl/ product, fruit, result

ផលកម្ម /phɑlləkam, phɑl-kam/ fate, destiny (karma)

ផលដំណាំ agricultural products

ផលប្រយោជន៍ importance, usefulness

ផលា /phɑllaa/ fruit

ផលានុផល /phɑllaanuphɑl/ crops, harvest, produce

ផលិត /phɑllɨt/ to produce

ផលិតកម្ម /phɑllɨttəkam/ production

ផលិតផល /phɑllɨttəphɑl/ products

ផល្គុន /phɑlkun, phəkun/ February-March (lunar system)

ផល្លា (= ផស)

ផស /phɑɑh/ imitative of the sound of a dull thump or knock

ផាឌីប broad-cloth

ផាមួង plain silk cloth

ផាមួងជរជើង sarong with an embroidered border

ផាហ៊ុម coverlet, spread, small blanket (Thai)

ផាត់ repay, redeem

ផាត់ to blow (of wind; Lit)

ផាត់ to powder, dab on powder

ផាត់ to brush back (the hair, etc.), brush aside, push aside

ផាត់ផាយ (= ផាយផាត់ ) to blow (Lit)

ផាត់ផើយ to blow (Poetic)

ផាយ at full speed

ផាយផាត់ to blow (of wind; Lit)

ផឹក to drink

ផុង to sink, go under, plunge, submerge

ផុត to escape, avoid, be free of; to come to the end of, pass out of; to barely miss, almost reach, be just out of reach

ផុតអំនួត be dead (lit: have nothing more to boast about)

ផុយ crumbly, ready to disintegrate

ផុល to boil up, roil

ផុស to emerge, spring up

ផូង ៗ sound of beating

ផូរផង់ soft, smooth, fine, beautiful (of complexion)

ផួយ blanket

ផើងផ្កា flower pot

ផើម to be pregnant (vulgar, condescending)

ផេះ ashes

ផែ pier, wharf, dock

ផែន sheet, disc, flat surface

ផែនការ plan, project

ផែនដី ground, territory; world; kingdom

ផែនថ្ម stone surface

ផែល to jump on (horse, bicycle, etc.), to jump astride

ផែល to float, drift from side to side

ផែល ៗ with a slow undulating movement, weakly

ផែះ (=ផេះ) /pheh/ ashes

ផ្កា flower

ផ្កាក្រពុំ name of a modern novel (lit: unopened flower)

ផ្កាមាស artificial flower made of gold and traditionally presented to an overlord as a symbol of vassalage

ផ្កាស្លា betel flower

ផ្កាប់ face down, on the stomach

ផ្កាប់ផ្ងារ turning over and over

ផ្កាយ star

ផ្កាយព្រឹក morning star

ផ្គង to devise a plan, figure a way to, effectuate (a plan, etc.)

ផ្គង to direct (something) toward, to aim; toward

ផ្គង (=ប្រុងប្រៀប ) to crouch, steel oneself against attack

ផ្គង់ផ្គត់ (=ផ្គត់ផ្គង់ ) to support, contribute to, add to

ផ្គងផ្គុំ criss-crossed, crossed

ផ្គត់ to support, provide support

ផ្គត់ផ្គង់ to assist, support

ផ្គរ thunder

ផ្គាប់ to please

ផ្គាប់ផ្គុន to please, indulge the wishes of, cater to, curry favor with

ផ្គូផ្គង to provision thoughtfully, to solicitously provide with necessities

ផ្គាំ string of beads

ផ្ងារ face up, on the back

ផ្ងាររពោះ stomach up

ផ្ងើយ to lift upward, incline upward

ផ្ងូត to bathe, give a bath to

ផ្ចង់ to satisfy, fulfill, gratify; concentrate on

ផ្ចង់ប្រុងអាត្មា be stoical, put up a brave front, steel oneself

ផ្ចាល to rebuke, reprove

ផ្ចិត to take great pains, do carefully

ផ្ចិតផ្ចង់ careful, diligent; to pursue diligently

ផ្ជាប់ attached to, against

ផ្ញើ to send; to consign (to), entrust (to), leave (with); for, on behalf of, for the purpose of

ផ្ញើជន្មផ្ញើខ្លួនប្រាណ to entrust [one's] life and limb (to)

ផ្ញើទុកនឹង to leave with, entrust to, consign to

ផ្ញើសំរាំ to nest, build a nest (of bees)

ផ្តន្ទា /pdɑntiə/ to curse, wish bad luck

ផ្តន្ទាទោស to sentence, to fix punishment

ផ្តល់ to provide

ផ្តល់ទៀ to happen to

ផ្តាច់ to break (tv); cut off from, deprive of, separate from

ផ្តាច់ better; to surpass

ផ្តាច់ផ្តិលជន្ម to kill (Lit)

ផ្តាស lax, careless, foolish; indecorous, unseeming

ផ្តាសា /pdahsaa/ to curse, put a curse on

ផ្តិល /ptəl/ metal drinking bowl

ផ្តួចផ្តើមគំនិត to initiate, instigate

ផ្តួល to overthrow, knock down, cause to fall over

ផ្តើម to begin, originate

ផ្តេក to lay, lay down, put to bed

ផ្តេសផ្តាស careless, irresponsible, nonchalant

ផ្តែផ្តាំ to admonish, counsel, leave final instructions

ផ្តោះផ្តង to hint, imply, express one's intentions indirectly

ផ្តៅ rattan

ផ្តាំ to warn, admonish; to delegate, leave instructions (with someone) to

ផ្តាំប្រដៅ to advise, to instruct

ផ្តាំផ្ញើ to have final words with, leave final instructions with

ផ្តាំហើយផ្តាំទៀត to instruct over and over

ផ្ទក់ a kind of small fish

ផ្ទញ់ផ្ទាល់ to embarrass, take advantage of, push to the wall

ផ្ទប់ from both sides

ផ្ទាត់ to thump

ផ្ទាត់ក្រចក to snap the fingernails

ផ្ទាន់ផ្ទុញផ្ទាល់ to gloat, take pleasure in another's misfortune

ផ្ទាប់ next to; to put next to

ផ្ទាល់ next to, against; personally

ផ្ទាល់នឹង against

ផ្ទាល់ខ្លួន private, personal, one's own

ផ្ទាល់ដៃ with one's own hands

ផ្ទឹម to compare, put side by side

ផ្ទុក to load

ផ្ទុញផ្ទាល់ to treat with contemptuous mirth

ផ្ទុយ contrary, opposite

ផ្ទុយគ្នាស្រឡះ completely different; contrarily

ផ្ទួន to repeat; again, over again

ផ្ទួន ៗ repeatedly

ផ្ទួនពាក្យ to repeat (in agreement)

ផ្ទៀង to give ear, pay strict attention

ផ្ទៃ surface

ផ្ទៃក្រឡា surface

ផ្ទៃដី area (of land)

ផ្ទៃរឿង theme

ផ្ទោង a small tubular fish

ផ្ទំ to sleep (Roy)

ផ្ទំផ្ទឹមខ្នើយ share the same pillow, be intimate

ផ្ទាំង slab, side, wall

ផ្ទះ house, home

ផ្ទះថ្ម masonry building

ផ្ទះទាប ground-level house with mortar walls

ផ្ទះបាយ kitchen

ផ្ទះពេទ្យ doctor's office

ផ្ទះធំទ្រនំខ្ពស់ a large and impressive house; Fig. wealth

ផ្ទះសំបែង home; house and property

ផ្នត់ fold, crease, line

ផ្នូក mound, hillock

ផ្នូកខ្សាច់ sand dune

ផ្នូរ grave, tomb

ផ្នួង knot (of hair), chignon

ផ្នួងសក់ chignon

ផ្នួស state of being a monk, entry into the monkhood

ផ្នែក part, section

ផ្លាញ (= បំផ្លាញ )

ផ្លាស់ to change, to transfer (tv)

ផ្លាស់គ្នាម្តងម្នាក់ to take turns

ផ្លាស់ប្តូរ to change, to exchange

ផ្លិត a hand fan

ផ្លិងៗ to glow dimly

ផ្លូវ street, road, way

ផ្លូវការ official, officially sanctioned

ផ្លូវគោក land route

ផ្លូវថ្នល់ streets and roads

ផ្លូវទឹក water route

ផ្លូវធ្លា main street

ផ្លូវបែក crossroads

ផ្លូវទៀបថ្ម stone walkway

ផ្លូវលំ trail, path

ផ្លេក to flash

ផ្លេកផ្លោះ to jump up, leap over; dash, swoop

ផ្លេច quickly, with a dart, like a flash

ផ្លេចផ្លាញ to destroy

ផ្លែ fruit

ផ្លែឈើ fruit

ផ្លែក (= ប្លែក ) different, strange

ផ្លែង to shoot an arrow (Roy)

ផ្លោះ to make a flying leap, to jump up, leap over

ផ្លោះផ្លើរ to jump, leap, dash, swoop

ផ្លោះផ្លេក (= ផ្លេកផ្លោះ )

ផ្លោះផ្លោង flying over, soaring over

ផ្លោង to throw over

ផ្លុំ to blow on

ផ្សង to venture, prospect, adventure; as a venture, prospectively; to invoke the aid of, rely on (supernatural forces)

ផ្សប់ផ្សាយ to disperse, spread around, diffuse

ផ្សព្វ to permeate, soak through

ផ្សព្វផ្សាយ to disperse, spread around, diffuse

ផ្សា to burn, sting, smart

ផ្សាខ្លោច (= ខ្លោចផ្សា ) anguished; to suffer, feel mental pain

ផ្សាយ to spread, broadcast, scatter (tv)

ផ្សាយផ្សព្វ to diffuse, suffuse, spread

ផ្សារ market, shopping area

ផ្សារកណ្តាល name of a market near Wat Onalaom (lit: 'central market', but no longer central)

ផ្សារក្រោម the Lower Market

ផ្សារថ្មី Central Market (lit: new market)

ផ្សារធំ Central Market (lit: big market)

ផ្សារស៊ីឈ្លីប name of a section of P.P. (lit: hoaxing market)

ផ្សឹក to excommunicate (Clergy)

ផ្សុនផ្សង to hang back, hesitate, delay, wait around

ផ្សេង to be different

ផ្សេងៗ various, various other, different (plural)

ផ្សែផ្សំ to combine, scrape together

ផ្សែង smoke (n)

ផ្សែងផ្សា acrid smoke

ផ្សោត a kind of dolphin

ផ្សំ combine, put together, add to, accumulate

ផ្សំផ្គុំ match up, put together; marry off

ផ្សំដំណេក to sleep together, to consummate a marriage

ផ្អួស stale

ផ្អុក to have something occur to one

ផ្អើល to be startled, surprised

ផ្អើលភ្ញាក់ be excited, alarmed

ផ្អៀង to incline to one side

ផ្អៀងផ្អង to incline, tilt (the head or body)

ផ្អេះ sad, listless, pathetic

ផ្អែក to depend on, lean against

ផ្អែម sweet (of taste)

ផ្អែមល្ហែម dulcet, sweet, gentle, melodious

ព carry on one hip

ពក bump

ពង egg; to lay an egg; to blister

ពងទាប្រៃ salty duck-egg

ពងមាន់ (chicken) egg

ពង្រ a kind of tree with edible fruit

ពង្រត់ to abduct

ពង្រីក to expand, increase (tv)

ពង្ស /pŭəŋ/ family (Lit)

ពង្សនរា /pŭəŋnəriə/ name of Bhiruna's faithful horse

ពង្សាវតារ chronicle, genealogy; Coll. history

ពញា /pŭəñiə, pəñiə/ title; replaced later by /qokñaa/

ពញាជ័យ title

ពញាពិស្ណុលោក /pəñiə-pihsnulook/ a title

ពញារោង legendary Cambodian prince, builder of Sukhothai

ពញាល្វែក Chan Raja

ពញាសួគ៌ាលោក /pəñiə-suəkiə-look/ title

ពញាអុង cousin of Chan Raja, son of Sri Raja

ពញ្ញាក់ /pŭəññeəq/ to startle, surprise

ពណ្ណរាយ /pŭənnəriəy/ to shine, excel; brilliance, excellence (Lit)

ព័ណ៌ /poə/ color, complexion

ពណ៌នា /poənəniə, poərəniə/ to tell, explain, describe; description

ពត៌មាន /poədamiən/ news

ព័ទ្ធ /pŏət/ to surround, encircle

ព័ទ្ធព័ន្ធ /pŏət-pŏən/ entangled, enmeshed

ព័ទ្ធសីមា to establish a boundary (usually ceremonial, to ward off spirits)

ពន់ past, beyond (Arch)

ពន់ប្រមាណ extremely

ពន់ពេក extremely, very much, too much

ពន់ព្រលប់ late evening, twilight

ពនាល័យ forest, forest abode

ពនិតា /pŭənnitaa/ woman, wife (Poetic)

ពន្ធ /pŭən/ tax

ពន្ធប្រថាប់ត្រា stamp tax, seal tax

ព័ន្ធ /pŏən/ related, intertwined, tied together

ពន្យល់ to explain

ពន្លក shoot, sprout; tender one, infant

ពន្លត់ extinguish, shut off (a motor, etc.)

ពន្លឹក strong, loud, great; amazing, extreme

ពន្លឺ light, brightness

ពពក cloud

ពពា puffed up neck or hood of a snake such as the cobra, when it is about to strike
ពពាក់ in a huddle, piled up, overlapping one another
ពពាក់ពពូន in a huddle, piled up, overlapping one another
ពពាយ a kind of vine with edible fruit
ពពាយនាយ to advertize by shouting, to shout one's wares
ពពិល a leaf-shaped candle-holder used in ceremonies
ពពីមពពើម gropingly, hesitantly (in the darkness)
ពពីរ rim of the lips, lips

ពពូល grey-green bird similar to a pigeon
ពពួក group; herd

ពពេច a small bird

ពពែ goat

ពល្ងើ (=ល្ងើ) stupid, slow-witted

ពម put into the mouth, take a bite

ពរ /pɔɔ/ blessing, good wishes, benediction
ពរសព្វសាធុការ every good wish

ព័រ /pɔə/ Pear (a tribal group)

ពល /pŭəl/ corps, group of people; strength
ពលក្ការ /pŭəlləkaa/ Puollakaa (pers. n.)
ពលថ្មើរជើង army, ground forces

ពលភាព /pŭəlləphiəp/ power, strength
ពលរដ្ឋ /pŭəllərŏət, pŭəl-rŏət/ citizenry, population
ពលរាជនិមន្ត /pŭəl-riəc-nimŭən/ royal messenger corps
ពលា /pŭəlliə/ force, strength

ពលាការ (=ពលិការ) offering, tribute; tax
ពស់ snake

ព.ស. (=ពុទ្ធសករាជ)/puttəsaqkəraac/ Buddhist Era (A.D.+543)
ពសុធា /pŏəhsəthiə/ earth (Lit)

ពស្តុ (=វត្ថុ) /pŏəh/ thing (Skt)

ពស្ត្រ /pŏəh/ clothing

ពស្ត្រអម្ពរ (=អម្ពរពស្ត្រា) clothing

ពាក់ to put on, wear above the waist
ពាក់កណ្ដាល center; half-way point, part, half
ពាក់កណ្ដាលអធ្រាត្រ /pĕəq-kandaal qatriət/ middle of the night, midnight
ពាក់មុខខ្លា to glower, scowl (lit: wear a tiger's face)
ពាក្យ /piəq/ word, speech

ពាក្យក្រងកែវ rhythmical prose (lit: style of interwoven jewels)
ពាក្យកាព្យ /piəq-kaap/ poetry, verse

ពាក្យដំនៀល criticism, censure

ពាក្យទំនៀម proverb, proverbial saying
ពាក្យបណ្ដាំ instruction, warning

ពាក្យបុរាណ old saying, proverb

ពាក្យប្ដេជ្ញា promise, oath

ពាក្យពោលទាំងផ្ដាស damning talk

ពាក្យពេចន៍ words, wording

ពាក្យពេជ្ញញាណ words of enlightenment (i.e. of the Buddha)
ពាក្យរាយ prose

ពាក្យសន្យា promise, covenant

ពាក្យសុំ application

ពាង /piəŋ/ a drum, kettle, large stone jar
ពាជី horse (Lit)

ពាណិជ្ជ /piənɨc/ commerce (Lit)

ពាណិជ្ជករ /piənɨccəkɑɑ/ merchant (Lit)
ពាធា to hurt, harm, do damage to (Lit)
ពាន to storm, go over (a wall, etc.)

ពានពារ to hit, strike, go against

ពាន់ thousand

ពានរ /piənɔɔ/ monkey (Lit)

ពានរិន្ទ /piənərɨn/ name of Bhiruna's faithful monkey
ពានរេន្ទ្រ (=ពានរ + ឥន្ទ្រ) /piənəreen/ King of the Monkeys (i.e. Hanuman)

ពាម (= ពាមកំពត ) Kampot

ពាមកំពត name of a former province (now Kampot city)

ពាមឆ្កោត Peam Chhkaot (pl. n.)

ពាយឃាយ negligent, nonchalant, unconcerned

ពាយព្យ /piəyoə̆p/ northwest (Lit)

ពារ to go against, hit against

ពារាណសី Benares

ពាល young wicked person, ruffian; wicked, profligate, sinful; brash, immature, raw (of youth)

ពាល់ to touch

ពាលា (=ពាល ) profligate, sinful

ពាលី Bâli, a monkey king

ពាស to spread over, cover

ពាសពេញ all over, completely covering

ពិការ wounded, incapacitated, have a physical defect

ពិឃាត to kill, execute, murder

ពិចារណា /picaarənaa/ to think, consider

ពិចិត្រ (=វិចិត្រ )

ពិចិត្ររេខា ogre queen, Preah Chinavong's mother-in-law

ពិជ័យ victory

ពិដោរ odor, aroma, fragrance; fragrant (Lit)

ពិត true, real

ពិត to tell, inform (to a monk)

ពិតៗ really, truly, genuinely

ពិតមែនតែ even though

ពិទូរ្យ title (lit: Lapis lazuli)

ពិធិ luck, destiny

ពិធី ceremony, celebration

ពិធីកាត់សក់ hair-cutting ceremony

ពិធីចូលត្រណម ritual productive of magical power

ពិធីចម្រើនព្រះជន្ម Royal Birthday Ceremony

ពិធីច្រត់ព្រះនង្គ័ល Royal Plowing Ceremony

ពិធីបុណ្យ ceremony, festival, affair

ពិធីអាពាហ៍ពិពាហ៍ /pithii qapiə-pipiə/ wedding ceremony

ពិន highest point, pinnacle; Supreme One

ពិនរាជ /pɨnnəriəc/ father of /wɨy-roə̆t/ and king of the ogres

ពិនិត្យ to oversee, examine

ពិនិត្យពិច័យ /pinɨt-picay/ to audit, to check; carefully

ពិនិច្ឆ័យ to examine, observe carefully, consider carefully

ពិន្ទុង a kind of whale

ពិបាក difficult

ពិព័ណ៌ (=ពិព័រណ៌ ) /pipɔə/ to show, exhibit; exhibition, display

ពិពិធ various, different

ពិពិធពិពណ៌ multicolored

ពិភព /piphup/ world

ពិភាក្សា /piphiəqsaa/ to discuss

ពិភាល់ have misgivings, be puzzled, surprised, to wonder

ពិមាន dwelling of the gods, sumptuous building; conveyance for a god

ពិរុទ្ធ /pirut/ blame, wrong; to examine, verify

ពិរុណ God of Rain

ពិរោធ anger; to be angry (Roy)

ពិលាស charming, graceful

ពិស poison, venom

ពិសា , ពីសា to eat (polite, with reference to others); delicious

ពិសាខ April-May (lunar system)

ពិសិដ្ឋ sacred

ពិសី , ពីសី precious, special

ពិសេស /piseh/ special

ពិសាល (=ពិសេសពិសាល ) excellent, special

ពិសី precious

ពិសុទ្ធ perfect, flawless

ពិសោធន៍ /pisaot/ to test, experiment; experienced

ពិស្តារ /pɨhsdaa/ excellent; effective

ពិស្រុត famous, renowned

ពិស្ណុការ /pɨhsnaokaa/ Vishnu

ពី from, since

ពីកាលណា when, since when...

ពីដើម originally, from the beginning

ពីដៃ from the hands of, from the grasp of

ពីណា somebody, anybody, who, whom (Coll)

ពីព្រលឹម very early, at dawn

ពីព្រោះ because

ពីព្រោះក្ដី because of the fact of

ពីមុន before, formerly

ពី...មួយទៅ...មួយ from one...to another

ពីយប់ while dark, very early

ពីស្ថានព្រះឥន្ទ from the realm of Indra (i.e. magic, supernatural)

ពីអង្កាល when (in the past)

ពិគ្រោះ to discuss

ពីជនិយម /pɨccəniyum/ natural laws of vegetable life; vegetation

ពីរ two

ពីរបី two or three

ពីរោះ beautiful, sweet (to the ear)

ពីលាប (=ពិលាប) to lament, mourn and weep (Lit)

ពីសា (=ពិសា) to eat (Eleg); delicious (Lit)

ពីសី (=ពិសី) precious, special

ពឹង to solicit help from, to depend on

ពឹងពាក់ to depend on, solicit help from

ពឹតទឹត keep on, persist (in)

ពុកចង្កា beard

ពុករលួយ corrupt, dishonest

ពុងពោះ (=ពោះពុង) stomach (Coll)

ពុត to bend, be devious; deviousness, weakness, fault

ពុតត្បុត pretense, hypocrisy (Coll)

ពុតរល្ល a kind of flower

ពុតធ្វើជា to pretend (to be)

ពុទ្ធ /put/ Buddha

ពុទ្ធង្គុល /putthuŏəŋkoul/ Buddha's lineage (i.e. Preah Chinavong)

ពុទ្ធដីកា /putdəykaa/ speech; to say (of Buddha or Clergy)

ពុទ្ធរដ្ឋ /puttərŏət/ Buddhism

ពុទ្ធសាសនា /puttəsahsnaa/ Buddhism

ពុទ្ធសាសនបណ្ឌិត /puttəsaahsnaq-bandɨt/ Buddhist Institute

ពុទ្ធោ /putthoo!/ a mild oath: heaven!, oh my goodness!

ពុន to carry suspended from a pole across the shoulder

ពុម្ព the press; model, sample, figure, symbol

ពុរ /pul, poo/ bruised, pulpy

ពុល to be poisoned

ពុះ to boil, be boiling

ពុះពារ to overcome, surmount

ពូក mattress, cushion

ពូកែ clever, smart, skillful (at)

ពូជ seedlings; background, family, lineage

ពូជសារ stock, lineage (Coll)

ពូជពង្ស family, lineage

ពូជពង្សនិងត្រកូល family background, pedigree

ពូជពង្សវង្សា /puuc-puŏəŋ-wuŏəŋsaa/ lineage, background, pedigree

ពូជសត្វ breeding animals (of pure strain or high quality)

ពូជស្រូវ seed rice

ពូត to wring, to twist; to mold into a ball

ពូន to hill up, mound

ពូនចុះពូនឡើង to crowd this way and that, push back and forth

ពួក group, category, people

ពួករាជនិយម royalists

ពួច small pitcher

ពួន to hide (iv)

ពួននឹង to hide from

ពួរ rope, cord

ពើ to feign, pretend, be affected

ពើប to meet

ពើបពះ to meet by accident

ពើបពះប្រទះ happen to meet, run into

ពៀង carry in the arms

ពៀប to be low in the water from a heavy load (of a boat)

ពៀរ retribution, painful consequences

ពេក extremely, very much, too much

ពេកពន់ (= ពន់ពេក )

ពេជ /pɨc/ precious stone, diamond

ពេជ-ហេង Pech Heng (pers. n.)

ពេជ្ឈឃាត (=ពេជ្ឈឃាដ ) /pɨccəkhiət/ executioner

ពេជ្ជញាណ /pɨccəñiən/ precious, supreme, enlightened

ពេជ្រ /pɨc/ diamond

ពេញ full, complete

ពេញច្បាប់ legal, lawful

ពេញជំទង់ of marriageable age

ពេញទំហឹង to the fullest extent, to to the utmost, with all one's effort

ពេញបរិបូណ៌លក្ខណៈ: legally, with full rights and attributes

ពេញបូរមី full moon

ពេញចិត្ត with all one's heart

ពេញពីពោះ whole-heartedly, from the bottom of my heart

ពេញព្រះរាជហឫទ័យ satisfied, happy (Roy)

ពេញមុខ overt, official, regular; be open, face up to

ពេញលេញ /pɨñ-lɨñ/ fully, completely

ពេញអង្គ in full session

ពេញអំណាច in full force

ពេទ្យ /pɛɛt/ doctor; medical science

ពេទ្យចេះវិជ្ជាបារាំង western-educated doctor

ពេន to encircle, coil around

ពេប to pucker in anticipation of crying

ពេល time, period

ពេលឈប់សំរាក vacation

ពេលថ្ងៃត្រង់ noon, at noon

ពេលបុណ្យ festival-time

ពេលព្រលឹម at dawn, dawn

ពេលល្ងាច evening, at evening-time

ពេលា time

ពេលាពួនហើយ the time is ripe, the auspicious moment has arrived

ពែង cup, glass

ពោត corn (maize)

ពោធិ៍ /poo/ banyan (tree)

ពោធិកំបោរ /poo-kɑmbao/ name of a rebel leader

ពោធិ៍ចិនតុង /poocəntoŋ/ Pochentong (name of a town)

ពោធិញ្ញាណ /poothiññiən/ enlightenment

ពោធិ៍ព្រឹយ a kind of banyan tree

ពោធិសត្វ /poothisat/ Bodhisatva

ពោធិសាត់ /poosat/ Pursat (province)

ពោធិ Bodhisatva

ពោរ full, overflowing, abundant

ពោល to say (Lit)

ពោះ stomach

ពោះពុង stomach (Coll)

ពោះម៉ាយ widower

ពោះវៀន intestines

ពោះវៀនបត់ចន្លាស intestines (Fig: crooked or dishonest person)

ពៅ youngest sibling

ពៅពន្លក [My] Tender Young [One] (lit: tender youngest sibling)

ពុំ negative auxiliary (Lit)

ពុំចេះ never

ពុំចាំគិត not concerned, doesn't matter, don't have to worry

ពុំ...ដល់ម្នាក់ទទឹ្យណា not even one

ពុំឃ្លៀងឃ្លាត vigilantly

ពុំដឹងខ្លួនប្រាណ to be unconscious, unaware

ពុំដឹងសេចក្តី inexperienced, immature

ពុំដែល never

ពុំដែលធ្លុះណ៉ា there's never been anything like this before

ពុំស្រាស្បើយ unabated

ពុំនោះ or rather (Lit)

ពុំនោះសោត if not that, then...; or else

ពុំមែន not really, not truly

ពុំរួច to be unable to

ពុំលង់ straightaway, without delay

ពុំលែង certainly, surely, inevitably

ពុំសូវ not very

ពុំឱ្យ in order not to (be)

ពុំងា term of endearment for a woman: darling, precious one

ពុំនៀវ (=ពៀវ)

ពុំនះ defiant(ly), in defiance of

ពំនាក់ care, protection, guardianship

ពាំ to carry in the mouth

ពាំង to shield, block

ពះ hey (Arch)

ព្នង the Pnong tribe; hill tribes in general

ព្ន័យ (=ពិន័យ) to fine, penalize

ព្នៅ a kind of tree whose edible fruit is used for glue

ព្យ័គ្ឃ៍ /pyeə̆q/ tiger (Lit)

ព្យ័គ្ឃ៍ផ្ត្រី King of the Tigers

ព្យាង្គ /pyieŋ/ syllable

ព្យាធិ /pyiəthiq/ disease

ព្យាបាទ malice; to intend harm, feel ill-will toward; to persecute, harass

ព្យាបាល to care for, tend, treat

ព្យាម fathom, distance across the outstretched arms, 4 cubits

ព្យាយាម to try, endure; effort, endurance

ព្យុះ a strong wind, storm

ព្យូហយាត្រា /pyuuhaqyiətraa/ to defile

ព្យួរ /pyuə/ to suspend, hang, be suspended

ព្រងើយ to be indifferent; blithely, imperturbably

ព្រ័ត rope made of plaited leather

ព្រ័ត (=ព្រាត់) to break, violate, transgress

ព្រនង់ a stick, club

ព្រន័យនិ eyes (Roy)

ព្រនាក់ to shoulder

ព្រម to agree (to); to accept; as well as, including, even

ព្រមគ្នា in unison, all together

ព្រម ៗ គ្នា all together

ព្រមទាំង along with, together with

ព្រមព្រៀង to agree

ព្រមមូលអរខ្លី finally decided

ព្រលប់ evening, twilight

ព្រលិត water-lily

ព្រលឹម dawn

ព្រលឹង soul

ព្រលូង a kind of fish

ព្រហាម dawn

ព្រហើន /prɔhəən/ arrogant, disrespectful

ព្រហ្មណ៍ /prum/ Brahma

ព្រហ្មញ្ញសាសនា /prummaññəsahsnaa/ Brahmanism

ព្រហ្មទណ្ឌ /prummətŏən/ penal, criminal (law, code)

ព្រហ្មស្ថាន /prumməthaan/ the realm of Brahma
ព្រហ្មិន្ទ /prummɨn/ Brahma + Indra

ព្រា a long-handled knife used for cutting bushes and small trees
ព្រាង to draft, compose; to probe, test (with words)
ព្រាត់ to be bereaved, deprived of; separated from
ព្រាត់ព្រាយ scattered

ព្រាត់ប្រាស់ to be bereaved, deprived of
ព្រាន hunter

ព្រានព្រៃ hunter

ព្រាយ demon, malevolent spirit

ព្រាល a kind of tree whose bark is used for rope
ព្រាវៗ impressionistically, by guesswork, vaguely
ព្រាហ្មណ៍ /priəm/ a Brahman

ព្រិប imitative of the sound of steps
ព្រីង a kind of tree with edible fruit
ព្រឹក morning

ព្រឹកមិញ this morning

ព្រឹកព្រាង (=ព្រឹក)

ព្រឹក្ស (=ព្រឹក្សា) tree, forest (Lit)

ព្រឹក្សា tree, forest (Lit)

ព្រឹក្សា (=ប្រឹក្សា) to advise, consult
ព្រឹត្តការណ៍ /prɨttəkaa/ situation, event
ព្រឹទ្ធ old (Lit)

ព្រឹទ្ធាចារ្យ /prɨtthiəcaa/ old age; elders
ព្រិលៗ hazy, obscure, vaguely, indistinctly
ព្រឺ to have goose-bumps, have one's hair stand on end (from fear)
ព្រឺព្រួច feel a chill of emotion

ព្រុស sound of falling or thrashing about
ព្រុសប្រាស sound of falling or thrashing about
ព្រូស a variety of mangosteen

ព្រួច to want, have a (sudden) desire for

ព្រួចព្រឺ to feel a thrill, have a sensation of excitement
ព្រួញ arrow

ព្រួត to join forces against, to gang up on
ព្រួតគ្នា to join together (to), to combine one's efforts (to)
ព្រួយ to worry, be anxious, sad

ព្រួយចិត្ត sad, worried, anxious

ព្រួយប្រាណ to be sad, worried

ព្រួយព្រះទ័យ to worry (Roy, Clergy)

ព្រួយរិះគិត hard to get along, difficult to manage
ព្រួល white fish

ព្រើត with a start, suddenly

ព្រើស to rejoice, be extremely happy
ព្រេង the past, ancient times, antiquity; ancient, former
ព្រេងនាយ former times, the old days

ព្រេងព្រឹទ្ធ the past, ancient times, antiquity; ancient, former
ព្រេងសំណាង fortune, luck, destiny

ព្រែ undyed silk

ព្រែក /prɛɛk/ canal, creek

ព្រែកក្តាម Prek Kdam (site of the ferry-crossing between Phnom Penh and Kampong Cham)
ព្រែកជីក man-made canal

ព្រែកទឡ្ញា name of a village

ព្រែកអ្នកលឿង a town along the Mekong

ព្រៃ forest, jungle

ព្រៃតាហ៊ូ place name (lit: Grandfather Hu Forest)
ព្រៃនគរ /prɨy-nɔkɔɔ/ Saigon

ព្រៃព្រឹក្ស forest

ព្រៃព្រាល place name (lit: fibre-tree forest)
ព្រៃស្លា name of a village (lit: areca-palm forest)
ព្រៃស្វាយ name of a village

ព្រោង sparkling, gleaming (usually from many points)
ព្រោងព្រាច glimmering here and there

ព្រោងព្រាត shining from many points
ព្រោងព្រាយ gleaming here and there, sparkling from many points
ព្រោះ /prŭəh/ because

ព្រោះតែ just because of

ព្រោះ to sow, scatter, broadcast

ព្រុំ-ធុស Prum Thos (pers. n.)

ព្រំដែន border

ព្រំបុរី border, territorial limit

ព្រំប្រទល់ border, territorial limit

ព្រះ the Buddha

ព្រះ /prĕəh/ prefix used before nouns of a sacred or esteemed nature, and before verbs whose subjects are persons of sacred or royal estate
ព្រះករុណា /prĕəh-kaqrunaa, prĕəh-konaa/ term of reference for a king; polite response part. (to clergy); you (to clergy)

ព្រះករុណាជាអម្ចាស់ជីវិតលើត្បូង King (lit: sacred one [who] is the lord of life over [our] heads)
ព្រះករុណាពិសេស the king

ព្រះកាណ៌ /prĕəh-kaa/ ear (Roy)

ព្រះកេស head (of royalty, clergy, or the Buddha)
ព្រះក្រយាស្ងោយ royal food

ព្រះខាន់ (=ខ័ន ) Preah Khan (royal sword)
ព្រះខែ the moon

ព្រះគណ្ឌ cheek (Roy)

ព្រះចន្ទ /prĕəh-can/ moon (Lit)

ព្រះចន្ទចរត្រង់ the moon is directly overhead
ព្រះចន្ទរាជា /prĕəh-can-riəciə/ (King) Chan Raja (1516-1568)
ព្រះចមពល /prĕəh-cααm-pŭəl/ the king (Lit)
ព្រះចិន្តា /prĕəh-cəndaa/ royal heart, mind; to think (Roy)
ព្រះចេស្តា /prĕəh-ceihsdaa/ the king

ព្រះចៅ the king

ព្រះចៅកំបង់ពិសី (King) Kambong Pisei

ព្រះចៅចក្រពត្រាធិរាជ /prĕəh-caw-caqkrəpoətraathiriəc/ title of Ramathibodi II
ព្រះចៅឡាន (King) Chao Lan

ព្រះចៅអធិរាជ /prĕəh-caw-qathiriəc/ emperor
ព្រះជន្ម /prĕəh-cŭən/ age (Roy)

ព្រះជន្មាយុ /prĕəh-cŭənnəmiəyuq/ age (Roy)
ព្រះជ័យអស្មារ្យ name of a king (obscure; perhaps legendary)
ព្រះជាម្ចាស់ the Buddha

ព្រះជាយា royal wife

ព្រះជេដ្ឋា older brother (Roy)

ព្រះដំណាក់ royal residence

ព្រះតម្រាស់ royal speech

ព្រះតម្រិះ to think, decide (Roy)

ព្រះត្រពាំង name of a former province

ព្រះថនា breast (Roy)

ព្រះតេជគុណ /prĕəh-daecəkun/ you (to priest or high official)
ព្រះតេជព្រះគុណ /prĕəh-daec-prĕəh-kun/ you (addressing a priest or high-ranking official)
ព្រះតំរិះ to think, decide (Roy)

ព្រះទន្ត /prĕəh-tŏən/ royal tooth

ព្រះទ័យ mind; heart (Roy)

ព្រះទិនករ /prĕəh-tɨnnəkαα/ the sun (Lit)
ព្រះទីនាំង royal conveyance

ព្រះទីនាំងនាវា royal ship or barge

ព្រះទេពី wife (Roy)

ព្រះទំរង់ (finger) ring (Roy)

ព្រះទ្រង់រិទ្ធិ /prĕəh-trŭəŋ-rɨt/ he who has authority, i.e. the king
ព្រះធម៌ the holy law; the scripture; (Buddhist)law; Vrah Dharma (god of justice)
ព្រះធរណី /prĕəh-thɔɔrənii/ earth (Lit)
ព្រះនគរ royal city

ព្រះនាង princess, queen; she, her

(Roy)

ព្រះនាងចន្ទរត្ថា Queen Chan Rattha

ព្រះនាងចមព្រះញាតិ title of concubine

ព្រះនាងផែសុមាលី Queen Phae Somali

ព្រះនាងមុនីមេខលា Princess Muni Mekhala

ព្រះនាម name; be named (Roy)

ព្រះនារាយណ៍ Lord Narai (Vishnu)

ព្រះនាសិក nose (Roy)

ព្រះនេត្រ /prĕəh-neet/ eyes (Roy, Clergy)

ព្រះនេត្រា eye (Roy)

ព្រះនេហ្វ /prĕəh-nee/ name of a god

ព្រះបញ្ជា to order, command (Roy)

ព្រះបន្ទូល royal speech; to say (Roy)

ព្រះបរមខត្តិយាមហាចន្ទរាជា Chan Raja

ព្រះបរមនាថ appellation for Rama

ព្រះបរមបពិត្រ /prĕəh-bɑrommәbɑɑpɨt/ title for the king

ព្រះបរមរាជវាំង /prĕəh-bɑrommәriәc-cәwĕәŋ/ royal palace

ព្រះបរមរាជា (King) Boromaraja

ព្រះបរមវង្សា Royal Family

ព្រះបាទ title for a king; foot (Roy); response particle (inferior to superior)

ព្រះបាទត្រៃបុត្តី King Traipotti

ព្រះបាទទសរថ /-tŭəhsәrŏәt/ King Dasaratha (Rama's father)

ព្រះបាទនរបតី King Mithila

ព្រះបាទនរោត្តម King Norodom (king of Cambodia 1860-1904, son of Ang Duong)

ព្រះបាទផៃសុរិយា King Phai Soriya

ព្រះបាទព្រហ្មទត្ត /-prummәtŏәt/ King Brahmadatta

ព្រះបាទម្ចាស់ response particle (to superior or a high-ranking official)

ព្រះបាទសម្តេចនរោត្តមសីហនុ King Norodom Sihanouk

ព្រះបាទសម្តេចព្រហ្មទត្ត King Brahmadatta

ព្រះបាទសម្តេចព្រះលំពង់រាជធិបតី King Lampong Rajadhipati

ព្រះបាទអង្គឌួង King Ang Duong

ព្រះបាទអម្ចាស់ /prĕəh-baat qɑmmәcah/ you (to royalty)

ព្រះបិតុលា /prĕəh-peqtolaa/ paternal uncle

ព្រះបីតិ to be delighted, ecstatic; delight, ecstasy

ព្រះបំរើ royal servant

ព្រះផ្នួស ordination (as a monk)

ព្រះពន្លា royal camp

ព្រះពន្លាភាក់ royal camp

ព្រះពលទេពសេនាបតី /prĕəh-pŭəl-teep-seenaapәdәy/ military commander

ព្រះពាយ the wind (Lit)

ព្រះពិស្វាមិត្រ Visvamitra (the rishi companion and counsellor of Rama)

ព្រះពុទ្ធ the Buddha

ព្រះពុទ្ធដីកា [what] Buddha said; words of Buddha

ព្រះពុទ្ធបាទ /prĕəh-puttәbaat/ Buddha's foot

ព្រះពុទ្ធរូប /prĕəh-puttәruup/ image of the Buddha

ព្រះពុទ្ធរូបចូលនិព្វាន reclining Buddha

ព្រះពុទ្ធសាសនា /prĕəh-puttәsahsnaa/ Buddhism

ព្រះពុទ្ធអង្គ /prĕəh-puttәqɑŋ/ Buddha

ព្រះពោធិសត្វ /prĕəh-poothisat/ bodhisatva (reincarnation of the Buddha)

ព្រះភគវន្តមុនី /prĕəh-phĕəqkәwŏәntaq-munii/ the Buddha

ព្រះភគិនេយ្យ /prĕəh-phĕəqkinɨy/ niece (Roy)

ព្រះភិរុណសុរិយវង្ស Bhiruna

ព្រះភូបាល the king (Lit)

ព្រះភូសា clothing, costume (Roy)

ព្រះមកុដ /prĕəh-mәkot/ royal crown

ព្រះមហាក្សត្រ /prĕəh-mɔhaa-ksat/ king

ព្រះមហាក្សត្រិយានី /prĕəh-mɔhaa-ksat-trәyaanii/ queen

ព្រះមហារាជ the king

ព្រះមហានគរ Angkor

ព្រះមហេសី /prĕəh-məhaesəy/ queen

ព្រះមុនីរាជ appellation for King Mithila

ព្រះរ័ម៉ហូ official female representative of the royal household

ព្រះម្ចាស់ថ្លៃ the Buddha

ព្រះយម /prĕəh-yĕəqmĕəq, prĕəh-yum/ Vrah Yama (god of death)

ព្រះយមរាជ /prĕəh-yumməriəc/ Yama, God of Death

ព្រះរាជកិត្តិយស /prĕəh-riəccəkəttəyuŏh/ honor, glory, greatness (of the king)

ព្រះរាជក្រម /prĕəh-riəccəkrαm/ (royal) decree, law

ព្រះរាជដំណើរ royal journey

ព្រះរាជតំណាង royal representative

ព្រះរាជទាន /prĕəh-riəccətiən/ to give (Roy); royal gift

ព្រះរាជទីនាំង /prĕəh-riəc-tii-nĕəŋ/ royal conveyance

ព្រះរាជទីនាំងនាវា royal barge

ព្រះរាជទ្រព្យ /prĕəh-riəccətrŏəp/ royal wealth, possessions

ព្រះរាជធានី /prĕəh-riəccəthiənii/ royal capital

ព្រះរាជនិពន្ធ royal author

ព្រះរាជបញ្ជា /prĕəh-riəccəbαñciə/ royal command

ព្រះរាជបញ្ញត្ត /prĕəh-riəccəbαññat/ to decree, order (Roy)

ព្រះរាជបរិពារ preĕəh-riəc-bααripiə/ royal entourage

ព្រះរាជបុត្រ /prĕəh-riəccəbot/ prince

ព្រះរាជបំណង the king's wishes

ព្រះរាជពង្សាវតារ royal chronicle, royal genealogy

ព្រះរាជពិធី royal ceremony

ព្រះរាជមន្ទីរ royal offices

ព្រះរាជរោង royal reception hall

ព្រះរាជវង្សានុវង្ស /prĕəh-riəccəwuŏəŋ-'saanuwuŏəŋ/ royal family

ព្រះរាជវរានុកូល royal family

ព្រះរាជវិនិច្ឆ័យ /prĕəh-riəc-winɨcchay/ to decide, pass judgement, adjudicate (Roy); royal judgement

ព្រះរាជវាំង /prĕəh-riəccəwĕəŋ/ royal palace

ព្រះរាជសារ royal letter, royal communication

ព្រះរាជហឫទ័យ /prĕəh-riəccəhaqrɨtɨy/ royal heart, mind

ព្រះរាជអាជ្ញា royal order; royal authority

ព្រះរាជអាណាចក្រ /prĕəh-riəc-qaanaa-caq/ kingdom

ព្រះរាជឱង្ការ /prĕəh-riəccəqaoŋkaa/ to say (Roy); royal speech

ព្រះរាជា the king

ព្រះរាជាណាចក្រ /prĕəh-riəciənaacaq/ kingdom

ព្រះរាជានុញ្ញាត /prĕəh-riəciənuññaat/ royal permission

ព្រះរាជិនី /prĕəh-riəccinii/ queen

ព្រះរាជូបត្ថម /prĕəh-riəccuupəthαm/ royal assistance

ព្រះរាជោវាទ /prĕəh-riəccoowiət/ royal influence

ព្រះរាម Râma (husband of Sîtâ, and central figure of the Râmâyana epic)

ព្រះរាមា (=ព្រះរាម) Râma, hero of the Râmâyana

ព្រះរាមាធិបតី Rama Thibodi, king of Ayuthia 1350-1369

ព្រះរាមាសួរ (King) Ramesuen, son of Rama Thibodi

ព្រះរៀម elder brother (Roy)

ព្រះលោហិត blood (Roy)

ព្រះវរកាយ beautiful body (Roy)

ព្រះវររាជទេពី queen

ព្រះវស្សា year; rain (Roy, Clergy)

ព្រះវិតក្ក /prĕəh-witαq/ to worry (Roy)

ព្រះវិស្ណុ Lord Vishnu

ព្រះវិហារ sacred temple

ព្រះសង្ឃ /prĕəh-sαŋ/ Buddhist monk

ព្រះសណ្ដាប់ to listen (Roy)

ព្រះសម្មាសម្ពុទ្ធ /prĕəh-sammaasamput/ the Enlightened One (Buddha)

ព្រះសម្រួល to be at ease, composed, relaxed, to laugh (Roy)

ព្រះសវនីយ /-saqwənəy/ to talk (Roy)

ព្រះស៊ីសុវត្ថិ /prĕəh-siisowat/ King Sisowath

ព្រះសីហនុ /prĕəh-siihanuq/ King Sihanouk

ព្រះសុដន់ breast (Roy)

ព្រះសុរាម្រឹត /preə̆h-soraamərɨt/ King Suramarith

ព្រះសុរិយ /-sourəy/ the sun (Lit)

ព្រះសុរិយា /preə̆h-souriyaa/ the sun (Lit)

ព្រះសុរិយោទ័យ (King) Soriyotey

ព្រះសុរិយោទ័យ name of a Prince

ព្រះសុរិយោវង្ស /preə̆h-souriyaowŭəŋ/ King Soriyovong(1416-25)

ព្រះសុវណ្ណកោច្ឆៈ /preə̆h-sowannəkaocchaq/ golden chair, royal chair

ព្រះសំរួល (=ព្រះសម្រួល ) to laugh (Roy)

ព្រះស្ដែង term of address used by superior to inferior (Lit)

ព្រះស្នំក្រមការ /-krɑmməkaa/ the king's concubines

ព្រះស្មារតី consciousness (Roy)

ព្រះស្រីរាជា Sri Raja (king of Cambodia 1459-1473)

ព្រះស្រែនជ័យ title

ព្រះហរិ /preə̆h-haqrii/ appellation for Vishnu

ព្រះហស្ត /preə̆h-hŏəh/ hand (Roy)

ព្រះអគ្គមហេសី /preə̆h-qakeə̆q-məhaesəy/ first or official queen

ព្រះអគ្គី God of Fire

ព្រះអង្គ 2nd and 3rd personal pronoun referring to royal or sacred persons; specifier for royal or sacred persons, and for Buddha images

ព្រះអង្គឌួង (King) Ang Duong (1847-1860)

ព្រះអង្គម្ចាស់ title of children of the king

ព្រះអង្គម្ចាស់ក្សត្រី /preə̆h-qɑŋ-mcah-ksatrəy/ Princess

ព្រះអធិបតី /preə̆h-qathɨppədəy/ leader, ranking official, person in authority

ព្រះអនុជ /preə̆h-qanoc/ younger brother (Roy)

ព្រះអរិយគាមណី /preə̆h-qariyeə̆q-kɨəmənii/ ecclesiastical title

ព្រះអាទិត្យ the sun (Lit)

ព្រះឥន្ទ្រ /preə̆h-qən/ Indra

ព្រះឥសូរ /preə̆h-qəysou/ Siva

ព្រះឱស /preə̆h-qaoh/ mouth (Roy)

ព្រះឱស្ឋ /preə̆h-qaoh/ mouth (Roy)

ព្រះអើយ My God!, alas!

ព្រះអំណរ to be pleased, happy (Roy)

ភក់ mud

ភក្ដីភាព /pheə̆qkdəyphiəp/ devotion, faithfulness

ភក្ត្រ /pheə̆q/ face (Lit)

ភក្ត្រា (=មុខ) /pheə̆qtraa/ face (Lit)

ភ័ណ្ឌ /phŏən/ goods, treasures, wealth

ភ័ន្ដ /phŏən/ to be mistaken, make a mistake

ភ័ន្ដភាំង /phŏən-pheə̆ŋ/ bewildered, stunned, dazed

ភព /phup/ world

ភព្វវាសនា /phŏəp-wiəhsnaa/ fortune, fate

ភ័ព្វ /phŏəp/ luck, fate

ភមរី /phumməriі/ a shiny black beetle

ភ័យ /phɨy/ to fear, be afraid

ភ័យភ្លែស to be frightened, terrified

ភរ /phɔɔ/ to lie, prevaricate

ភរភូត (= ភូតភរ) to lie, prevaricate

ភរិយា /pheə̆qriyiə/ wife (Eleg)

ភស្តុតាង /phŏəh-taaŋ/ proof, evidence, witness

ភស្ដា /phŏəhsdaa/ lord, master; husband

ភាគ section, part

ភាគច្រើន majority

ភាគរយ percent

ភាណ term of address, husband to wife (Arch)

ភាតរភាព /phiətəraqphiəp/ fraternity

ភាព form, aspect, quality

ភាពទំនង way, manner, likeness, aspect

ភាយ to spread, diffuse, suffuse

ភារា (= ក្រុង) captain of a ship

ភាសា language

ភិក្ខុ /phiqkhoq, phikhoq/ ordained priest

ភិក្ខុសង្ឃ /phikhoq-sɑŋ/ ordained priest

ភិតភ័យ to be frightened, in terror

ភិនភាគ region, area; appearance

ភិសម័យ /phihsəmay/ love, affection

ភីលៀង servant, companion, nanny (Roy)

ភឹស expulsion of breath (verbal specifier)

ភុជង្គ /phuucuŏəŋ/ snake (Lit)

ភុជង្គនាគ /phuucuŏəŋ-niəq/ Naga

ភូជង្គ (= ភុជង្គ) snake, serpent (Lit)

ភូឈួយកុងស៊ី /phuu-chuəy-koŋsəy, phəchuəy-koŋsəy/ deputy minister

ភូត to lie, prevaricate

ភូតភរ to lie, prevaricate

ភូធរ king (Poetic)

ភូមា /phuumiə/ Burma, Burmese

ភូមិ /phuum/ village

ភូមិច្បារអំពៅ village of Chbar Ampouv

ភូមិថ្ម Phum Thmâ (pl. n.)

ភូមិភពអាយតនិយ in this world

ភូមិភាគ /phuum-phiəq/ area, zone, region

ភូមិន្ទ្រ (= ភូមិន្ទ) king

ភូមិន្ទ /phuumɨn/ king; royal

ភូមិសាស្ត្រ /phuumisaah/ (the science of) geography

ភូមី king

ភូវនេយ្យ /phuuwənɨy/ master, lord

ភើប to lift or pull with a jerking motion

ភេត្រា seagoing sailing vessel

ភេទ aspect, genre, gender

ភេរី a kind of big drum

ភេសជ្ជៈ /pheesəceə̆q/ beverage, refreshment

ភោគទ្រព្យធម្មជាតិ natural resources

ភោគផល produce, products

ភោគសម្បទ possessions, treasures, wealth

ភោក្តា to eat; food (Lit)

ភោជនីយដ្ឋាន /phoocəniiyəthaan/ restaurant (Lit)

ភោជន /phoocuŏn/ food (Lit)

ភោជនាហារ /phoocəniəhaa/ food (Lit)

ភាំង have a mental lapse, go blank

ភាំងវិញ្ញាណ to have a lapse, blank out

ភ្ងា beloved

ភ្ជាប់ to attach, put together, stick together; stuck

ភ្ជួរ /pcuə ~ pyuə/ to plow

ភ្ជុំ to unite, bring together

ភ្ជុំបិណ្ឌ to commemorate one's ancestors

ភ្ញាក់ to wake up; to start, be startled, surprised

ភ្ញាក់ខ្លួន to become aware, realize, wake up (to a fact)

ភ្ញាក់ផ្អើល to be startled, taken aback, shocked

ភ្ញាក់រលឹក to wake up, become aware

ភ្ញាក់ស្មារតី to awaken, become aware

ភ្ញី entwined flowers, flowering vine

ភ្ញីផ្កា garland of flowers

ភ្ញៀវ guest

ភ្នក to have a sudden inspiration, have it occur to one to

ភ្នក់ bonfire, an outdoor fire

ភ្នាក់ងារ agent, person designated

ភ្នាក់ដៃ handrail

ភ្នាល់ to bet, wager

ភ្នៀង plow-base

ភ្នែក eye

ភ្នែកស to show fear, have a startled reaction

ភ្នែន crosslegged sitting position

ភ្នំ mountain, hill

ភ្នំក្រវាញ the Cardamom Mountains

ភ្នំគោវទ្ធន៍ /pnum-koowəthŏən/ Mount Govadhana

ភ្នំដងរែក the Dang Raek Mountains

ភ្នំបាក់ខែង Mt. Bakheng (site of a 9th century Angkor temple)

ភ្នំពេញ Phnom Penh

ភ្នំព្រះសុមេរុ /-someeruq, -somae/ Mt. Meru (of Hindu mythology)

ភ្នំភ្នែង a small tree used for firewood

ភ្នំមន្ទរ /pnum-mŭəntəreə̆q/ Mount Mandara

ភ្នំសិវបទ /pnum səywəbɑt/ Mount Sivapada

ភ្នំសុមេរុ /pnum-somae, -someeruq/ Mount Meru

ភ្លង a kind of red hardwood tree

ភ្លាត់ to have a lapse, commit an unintentional act

ភ្លាត់ភ្លាំង shocked, speechless, dumbfounded, in a state of suspended consciousness

ភ្លាត់មាត់ to say in spite of oneself

ភ្លាម immediately

ភ្លាម...ភ្លាម as soon as...immediately

ភ្លឹង (straight) as a ramrod

ភ្លឺ light, bright

ភ្លឺស្រែ ricefield dike

ភ្លុក tusks

ភ្លូ a kind of tree

ភ្លូក to turn over, upset

ភ្លូត a tree with edible fruit

ភ្លើង fire; electricity

ភ្លើងអគ្គិសនី electricity; electric light

ភ្លៀង rain; to rain

ភ្លេង music, composition, song

ភ្លេច to forget

ភ្លេចត្រចៀក to forget oneself momentarily

ភ្លេចវិញ្ញាណ to lose one's senses, be in a fog

ភ្លេចស្មារតី be unaware, be oblivious (to), unmindful (of), become lax (in)

ភ្លែត quickly, immediately

ភ្លៅ thigh

ភ្លាំង a kind of tree

## ម

ម. abbreviation for /maet/(meter)

មក /mɔɔk/; Coll. /mɔɔ/ to come; orientation toward speaker in space or time

មកលេង to visit, pay a visit

មកឃើញ to realize, come to see

មកអាយ come here (Arch)

ម័កប៉ែន a sweet-smelling fruit

មករ /məkɑɑ/ fish (Lit)

មករា /meə̆qkəraa ~ maqkəraa/ January

មកុដ /məkot/ crown

មគធភាសា /meə̆qkətheə̆q-phiəsaa/ Pali language (language of Magadha)

មង fishing net

មង្គល /mŭəŋkŭəl/ success, good luck, happiness

មង្គលការ /mŭəŋkŭəl-kaa/ wedding

មច្ឆា /macchaa/ fish (Lit)

មជ្ឈដ្ឋាន /macchəthaan/ milieu, circle

មជ្ឈមណ្ឌល /maccheə̆q-mŭəndŭəl/ center, base (Lit)

មឈូស coffin

ម៉ដ្ឋហ្មង /mɑt-mɑɑŋ/ fine, smooth (of texture)

មណី /mənii/ jewel, precious stone (Lit)

មណីរតន៍ /məniiroə̆t/ precious stone (Lit)

មណ្ឌប /mŭəndup/ small ornate pavilion, usually crown-shaped

មណ្ឌល /mŭəndŭəl/ circle, solar disk, center, district;

around, encircling

មណ្ឌលគិរី /mŭənduŭəl-kirii/ Mondulkiri (Province)

មណ្ឌលគរុកោសល្យ Teacher Training Center

មណ្ឌលនីតិកម្មពាមជ្រៃទៀ Peam Chralay legal district [?]

មណ្ឌលសុខភាព health center

មត់ agree beforehand, prearrange

ម៉ត់ចត់ seriously, carefully

ម៉ត់ម៉ង (=ហ្មត់ហ្មង) clean (Lit)

មតិ /matteq/ opinion

មទ្ទវៈ /mattəweə̆q/ propriety, modesty

មធ្យ័ត /mattyat/ rigorous, careful, painstaking

មធ្យម /mattyum/ average; medium

មធ្យមសិក្សា secondary school

មធ្យោបាយ /mattyoobaay/ way, means

មន Mon (an ethnic group in Southeast Asia)

មនុស្ស /mənuh/ man, mankind, person

មនុស្សក្រៅ outsider, non-family

មនុស្សណា anyone; whoever

មនុស្សទាបថោក person of low character

មនុស្សទោស prisoner

មនុស្សធម៌ /mənuhsəthɔə/ humanity; humanism

មនុស្សផ្តេសផ្តាស vagabond, bum

មនុស្សមានពូជ person from a good family, person of good breeding

មនុស្សម្នា people

មនុស្សយើង we humans

មនុស្សលោក human world, human beings

មនុស្សល្បែង gambler

មនោរម្យ /mənoorum/ enchanting, delightful, idyllic, blissful

មន្ត /mŭən/ magical formula; scripture

មន្តវិជ្ជាការ magic formula

មន្ត្រី /mŭəntrəy/ government official

មន្ត្រីសង្កាត់ official of a municipal division

មន្ត្រីអ្នករាជការ (royal) government officials

មន្ទរ /mŭəntəreə̆q/ Mandara (name of the mountain with which Vishnu churned the milk ocean)

មន្ទិល /mŭəntɨl/ to doubt, suspect

មន្ទីរ /mŭəntii/ office, building

មន្ទីរក្រសួង ministry

មន្ទីរពេទ្យ /mŭəntii-pɛɛt/ hospital

មន្ទីរព្យាបាលរោគ hospital (Eleg)

មន្ទីររាជសហករណ៍ Royal Office of Cooperatives

ម.ម. (=មីលីម៉ែត្រ) millimeter

មមូរមមា in great numbers, in a crowd

មមៀច gnat

មមឹម distracted, preoccupied

មយូរ peacock (Lit)

មរកត /mɔɔrəkɑt/ emerald

មរណៈ /mɔɔrənaq/ to die (Lit)

មរណកាល /mɔɔrənaqkaal/ death (Lit)

មរណភាព /mɔɔrənaqphiəp/ death; to die (Lit, Eleg)

មរណា /mɔɔrənaa/ death; to die (Lit)

មរតក /mɑɑrədɑq/ heritage

ម.ស. (=មហាសករាជ)/məhaasaqkəraac/ an era which began in 78 A.D.

មហា /mɔhaa, məhaa/ in compounds: big, great; Coll: really, immensely, extremely

មហា title of a learned monk, usually retained after having left the priesthood

មហាក្សត្រ /məhaa-ksat/ king

មហាក្សត្រិយ៍ /məhaa-ksatrəy/ king

មហាជន /məhaacŭən/ the general public

មហាតទ្លឹក /məhaa-tlək/ royal servant

មហាទូលាយ very large, vast

មហាធ្ងន់ extremely heavy, extremely

important

មហានគរ great city; Angkor

មហានិកាយ /məhaanikaay/ liberal sect of Buddhist priests in Cambodia (lit: large branch)

មហាភារត /məhaaphiərətaq/ Mahābhārata

មហាមន្ត្រី title for an official

មហាមាត្យ title for a palace official

មហាយាន /məhaayiən/ Mahāyāna

មហាវិថី /məhaa-withəy/ boulevard

មហាវិថីព្រះបាទនរោត្តម Boulevard Preah Bath Norodom

មហាវិថីព្រះសុរាម្រិត Boulevard Preah Suramarith

មហាវិទ្យាល័យ university, college

មហាវេស្សន្តរជាតក /məhaa-weesəndɑɑ-ciədɑq/ Mahā Vessantara Jātaka

មហាសេដ្ឋី /məhaa-saetthəy/ wealthy man, mandarin

មហាហង្ស a kind of tree

មហាហិង្គុ /məhaahɨŋ/ the plant asafetida

មហាឧត្តម /məhaa-qotdɑm/ excellent, impressive

មហាឧបរាជ /məhaa-qupperaac/ Vice-King

មហិង្សា (= មហឹសា) /məhəŋsaa/ male water buffalo (Lit)

មហិមា /məheqmiə/ extremely; gigantic, enormous, huge

មហិមានុភាព great power

មហឹសា /məhəŋsaa/ water buffalo bull (Lit)

មហេសី /mɔhaesəy/ queen

មហោរី /məhaorii/ orchestra; stringed instrument (Lit)

មហោស្រព /məhaosrɑɑp/ music (Lit)

មា uncle (younger brother of either parent)

មា in large numbers, many (Lit)

មាក់ងាយ to belittle, look down on, scorn

មាក់ប្រាត a kind of tree with edible fruit

មាក់ប្រាង (= ម៉ាក់ប្រាង) a golden plum

មាគ៌ា /miəkiə/ route, road; Fig: way, line, policy

មាឃ /miəq/ January-February (lunar system)

មាឃបូជា /miəq-bouciə, miəqkəbouciə/ Māgha Pūjā (a festival commemorating the last assembly of the Buddha with his disciples)

មាឃវ៉ាន់ /maqkəwan/ name of a street in Phnom Penh

មាណព /miənup/ a young unmarried man (Lit)

មាត់ edge, opening; mouth; voice; Coll: to talk, say, utter

មាត់ក to speak, utter, make oneself heard

មាត់ក្រសាស់ name of a village

មាត់តែថា just saying, saying insincerely

មាត់តែស្រដី just talking, just saying [that]; say one thing while doing another

មាត់ទន្លេ bank of the river, waterfront

មាត់របង gateway

ម៉ាត់ /mat/ mouthful, chew, plug; word, utterance

មាតា /miədaa/ mother (Lit)

មាតិកា important point; heading, title

មាត្រា part, section, division, article, point

មាឌ size, stature (of the body)

មាន to have, to exist; there is, there are; to be rich, have property

មានការ to have business

មានកាល sometimes, it happens that

មានកំណត់ cautiously, sparingly, keeping account

មានគំនិត thoughtful, conscientious

មានគំនិតគំនូរ to be thoughtful, circumspect, sensible

មាន...ចិត្តពីរ to be unfaithful, have divided loyalties

មានចិត្តល្អ to be kind-hearted

មានចិត្តប្រតិព័ទ្ធនឹងគ្នា to fall in love, be strongly attracted to each other

មានចិត្តលោភ greedy

មាន...ជាដើម such as...for example

មានសំណឹង let others know, inform those around you (hence: thoughtful)

មានតែ the only possibility is that, there's only that...
មានតែថមទាំង even (to the extent of)

មានធម៌សប្បុរស good, kind, generous

មានបាន to happen to, to have occasion to
មានបើ perhaps

មានបើហេតុអី what happened?; how is it that...?
មានប្រសាសន៍ to say (Eleg)

មានប្រសិទ្ធិភាព effective

មានពាក្យ to criticize, have something [critical] to say
មានផ្ទៃ to be pregnant

មានផ្ទៃពោះ to be pregnant

មានពូជ to be of good breeding, be of respectable background
មានព្រះតម្រាស់ to say (Roy)

មានព្រះបន្ទូលថា to say (Roy)

មានភព្វសំណាង to be fortunate, lucky

មានមារយាទ to be of good character, to be worthy
មានមួយឆ្នាំនោះ there was a year

មានមេត្តា to have pity, compassion

មានលាភ to be lucky, fortunate

មានវិញ្ញាណ to be alive, have one's wits
មានទៅតវគ្គ well organized (of speech, writing, etc.)
មានសំដី to be voluble, talkative

មានអី why not?, of course! (Coll)

មាន់ chicken

មាន់គក a large rooster

មាន់ឈ្មោល rooster, cock

មាន់ញី hen

មាន់ទា chickens and ducks, poultry

មាន់ព្រៃ wild bantam

មានះ stubbornness, heedlessness, recalcitrance; stubborn, heedless, recalcitrant; to persist in
មាយា wiles, antics, affectation, pretension; to pretend, be affected, be coquettish
មាយើង name of the hero of the epic poem of the same name
មារ Māra, enemy of Buddha

មារយាទ /miəyiət/ conduct

មាល pure

មាលតី /miələdəy/ gardenia

មាលមាស pure gold

មាល័យ /miəlay/ garland of flowers

មាលី flower (Lit)

មាលប្បាយ /miələbaay/ extremely (Poetic)
មាស gold, golden; precious, valuable
មាសម័យ pure gold

មាសស្នេហ៍ My Beloved

មាសា (= មាស) month (Lit)

ម៉ាស៊ីន /maasiin ~ masɨn/ engine, motor, machine
មិច to wink

មិញ /mən̄, mɨn̄/ past, just past, just referred to
មិត to try hard to, redouble one's efforts to
មិត្ត /mɨt/ friend (Lit)

មិត្តជិតខាង neighbor

មិត្តភក្តិ /mɨt-phĕəq/ have intimate relations with
មិត្តភាព /mɨttəphiəp/ friendship

មិថិលា /miqthelaa/ Mithilā (a former kingdom in northeastern India)
មិថុនា June

មិន negative auxiliary: not

មិនកើតទេ inappropriate, not right, isn't done
មិនខាន without fail, surely

មិនគិតគន់ thoughtlessly, heedlessly, recklessly
មិនគិតប្រាណ heedless of one's own safety
មិនចង់រួច barely able to

មិនចេះ never, customarily don't

មិនចេះដាច់ពីមាត់ unceasingly (of speech, etc.)

មិនចេះអស់មិនចេះហើយ constantly, incessantly

មិនចំឈ្មោះ without specifying names

មិនជាយ៉ាប់ប៉ុន្មានទេ not so bad, fairly comfortable

មិនជាប់នៅ elusive, impermanent

មិនដាក់ភ្នែក fixedly (of staring)

មិនដាច់ endlessly

មិនដាច់ពីមាត់ unceasingly, incessantly, continually (of singing, speaking, eating, etc.)

មិនដឹងស័ព្ទសោច doesn't know what [he's] talking about

មិនដូចចិត្ត not satisfactory

មិនដែល never; customarily don't

មិនដែលខាន never failing

មិនដែលដាច់ incessantly

មិនដែលនឹងធ្ងន់ never tiring, never flagging; tirelessly, indefatigably

មិនដែលមាន it never happens that...

មិនតែប៉ុណ្ណោះ not only that, but...

មិនតែប៉ុណ្ណោះសោត not only that, but...

មិនតែម្ល៉េះ not only that, furthermore

មិនត្រឹមតែ...ទេ not only...

មិនថាអញ្ចឹងឬ? isn't that right?

មិនទាន់ not yet

មិនទាន់ចាញ់ឈ្នះផង inconclusive, outcome (of a battle) not yet decided

មិន...ទេ discontinuous negative: not

មិនទំនង unlikely, doesn't make sense

មិនធ្វើដឹងមិនធ្វើឮ to ignore, not pay attention (to)

មិនបាច់ not necessary (to), no need (to)

មិន...ប៉ុន្មានទេ not...to any extent, not so very...

មិនមែន not really

មិនយូរប៉ុន្មាន not too long

មិនឈប់ពេលណា all the time, incessantly

មិនលែងទៀយ unceasingly, inevitably

មិនសូវ hardly, not very

មិនសូវផ្លាស់ប្តូរប៉ុន្មានទេ doesn't change very much

មិនស្កាមាត់ hardly tasted it; hunger still not abated

មិនអីទេ don't mention it; it's nothing; don't worry

មិនា March

មិល្លីម៉ែត្រ /millimaet/ millimeter

មីង aunt, younger sister of either parent, or general term for women of parents' generation

មីមុត Mimot (name of a district)

មីរ in a great crowd, spread densely all over, stippled, teeming; cloudy, overcast, somber, dark

មីសួរ rice noodles

ម៉ឹងម៉ាត់ vigorously

ម៉ឹង tightly (Coll)

ម៉ឺន ten-thousand; title of nobility

មុខ face; front, in front of; kind, variety, dish

មុខកំពូល name of a district in Kandal Province

មុខក្រសួង status, function, duty; those in charge, those concerned

មុខងារ duty, position

មុខជា probably, undoubtedly

មុខដាច់ upper gabled roof (of a temple or palace)

មុខមាត់ facial features

មុខរបរ trade, profession

មុខយ៉ាងមាំ serious face, stern face

មុង mosquito net

មុជ to dive, submerge oneself

មុត to cut, pierce, penetrate; sharp (of a knife)

មុតមាំ strongly, intensely, staunchly

មុន before

មុនក្រោយ one after the other

មុននឹង before (doing something)

មុនី scholar, learned person, sage

មុនីវង្ស /məniiwŭəŋ/ Monivong (King of Cambodia 1927-1941)

មុសា to lie, prevaricate; untrue, false

មុសាវាទ to lie, prevaricate

មូរ្ខ sullen, rude

មូរ to roll up (tv)

មូល to be round; circle, group

មូលដ្ឋានសឹក military base

មូលមក to come together, convene

មូលមិត្តមេត្រី share [each other's] love

មូលមួយផងគ្នា unite, be united

មូលមេត្រី to love fully, to feel unreserved friendship

មូសិកទន្ត /museqkətoən/ the symbol ៉

មួន tight, steady, stable

មួម៉ង furious, irritated

មួយ one

មួយ ៗ slowly, deliberately; each one, the various

មួយខែពីរ one or two months

មួយចំណែក...មួយចំណែក on the one hand..., and on the other hand...

មួយឆ្នាំ ៗ /muəy cnam, muəy cnam/ each year

មួយផងមួយកាល once in a while

មួយថ្ងៃ ៗ /muəy tŋay, muəy tŋay/ each day, every day

មួយថ្ងៃមួយយប់ a full day, 24 hours

មួយថ្ងៃទាល់ល្ងាច all day long

មួយទៀត furthermore

មួយពាន់ one thousand

មួយភ្លែត /muəy-plɛɛt, məplɛɛt/ a moment, just a bit, awhile

មួយមុខ only, exclusively

មួយ...មួយ first...then

មួយយប់ទាល់ភ្លឺ all night long

មួយយប់មួយថ្ងៃ all day, 24 hours

មួយយ៉ូ shout used to mark a rowing cadence

មួយរយ one hundred

មួយរូប one person

មួយរំពេច immediately; for a moment, awhile

មួយស្ទុះ for a moment, awhile

មួយសែន one hundred-thousand

មួយស្របក់ for a moment, awhile

មួយអង្គឯង alone (Roy)

មួល to turn, twist (a knob, etc.)

មើល /məəl/; Coll:/məə/ to look at; treat (an illness); after a verb: tentatively, and see how it works, give it a try

មើលងាយ to belittle, look down on, scorn

មើលទៅឃើញ to seem, appear

មើលចំណាំ to watch critically

មើលប្រមាណគ្រប់គ្នា take everybody into consideration

មើលផ្លូវ to await (lit: watch the road)

មើលពុំយល់ not recognize, not realize, not see (Fig)

មើលមុខ know the person, consider the merits of the individual

មើលមុខមើលក្រោយ look at [it] from every perspective

មើលយល់តែមុខឯង think only of oneself

មើលយាម to tell fortunes, predict destiny

មើលល្អ ៗ ទៅ to consider various aspects

មើល...ឱ្យជា to cure

មើលឱ្យស្ដែង to look carefully, determine clearly

មើលអ្វីមិនឃើញ unable to see anything

មឿង (= ឃ្លាំងមឿង) a 16th century Cambodian hero

មៀងភ្នែក to glance sidelong, look out of the corner of one's eyes

មៀន a kind of small litchi

មេ female (of animals); bitch;

Arch: mother

មេ chief, head; headword in compounds

មេការ supervisor; head of provincial public works

មេកំណែន corvée chief

មេគណខេត្ត /mee-kuən-khaet/ head priest of the province (ecclesiastic counterpart of the provincial governor)

មេឃុំ commune chief

មេចោរ leader of the bandits

មេជើង big toe

មេដឹកនាំ leader, chief

មេដែក magnet

មេដៃ thumb

មេទន្ទេញ lesson to be memorized and recited

មេទ័ពក្រោយ commander of the rear guard

មេទ័ពឆ្វេង commander of the left flank

មេទ័ពធំ commander of the main army

មេទ័ពមុខ commander of the vanguard

មេទ័ពស្តាំ commander of the right flank

មេបញ្ជាការ commander

មេបញ្ជាផ្នែកសឹករង adjutant commander

មេបា spirits of one's ancestors; Arch: parents, guardians

មេម៉ាយ widow

មេស្រុក chief of a khum (not of a srok)

មេរៀន lesson

មេអាចម៉ង a kind of dice used for gambling

មេគុង Mekong (River)

មេឃ sky

មេឃា (= មេឃ) sky (Poetic)

មេច to pinch

ម៉េច /məc/ how?, why?

មេដាយ medal (Fr. médaille)

មេត្តា to pity; be good enough to

មេត្តាធម៌ compassion

មេត្តាប្រោស... please...

មេត្រី to like, to love; friendship, affection

មេត្រីភាព /meetrəy-phiəp/ friendship

មេទោរទ្រហទ /meetoorəteəq/ Medohrada (hell for wanton women)

មេសា April

មែ polite response particle used by women to royalty

ម៉ែ mother; term of address for woman of same age

ម៉ែ interjection of surprise

ម៉ែឪ father and mother, parents

មែក branch, limb

ម៉ែត្រ /maet/ meter

មែន to be right, true, correct

មែនទេ? right?

មែនទែន really, truly

មែនហើយ right, that's right, that's true

មែ ៗ constantly

ម៉ោក imitative of sound of rapping, knocking, thumping

ម៉ោង hour, time

ម៉ោងដប់ពីរព្រឹក twelve o'clock noon

ម៉ោងដប់ពីរភ្លឺ midnight

ម៉ោងដប់ពីរយប់ (= ម៉ោងដប់ពីរភ្លឺ ) midnight

ម៉ោងប្រាំកន្លះ five-thirty o'clock

ម៉ោងមួយភ្លឺ one a.m.

មោនី Moni (pers. n.)

មោហៈ /moohaq/ state of irrationality, insensitivity, moral blindness, numbness

មោហ៍បាំង /moo-baŋ/ in a blind rage

មោហ៍មឹត in a rage, blind with anger

មោហោ (= មោហៈ ) ignorance, blindness

មោះ it is, that is, being (Arch)

មោះ mistake, misfortune, problem

មោះមុត courageous

មំសី (= មំសៈ) /mĕəŋsəy/ flesh, meat (Roy, Clergy)

មាំ firm, strong, solid, sturdy

មាំទាំ firm, stable

មាំមួន firm, solid, permanent

មករ /məkαα/ mythical sea monster

ម្ខាង on one side

ម្ខើ៉ if it happens that (Lit)

ម្ចាស់ lord, master, owner

ម្ចាស់ក្សត្រី queen

ម្ចាស់ថ្លៃ my lord, my good fellow

ម្ចាស់ផ្ទះ master or mistress of the house, owner

ម្ជុល needle

ម្ជូរ sour or pungent food

ម្ដង once; once and for all, definitively, for a change

ម្ដង ៗ once in a while

ម្ដងទៀត once more, once again

ម្ដាយ mother

ម្ដាយធំ aunt (older sister of either parent)

ម្ដេច /mdəc/ why?, how?

ម្ដេចក៏ then why?, how is it that?

ម្ដេចក៏ទៅជា why is it that...?, why did you...?

ម្ដេចម្ដា whatever, whatever it may be

ម្ទេស chili pepper

ម្នាក់ one person

ម្នាក់ ៗ each one, one after the other

ម្នាល term of address used by superior to inferior (Arch)

ម្នាស់ pineapple

ម្នីម្នា hurriedly

ម្នេញ to worry, be bothered, suffer (mental anguish)

ម្ភៃ /məphɨy, mphɨy/ twenty

ម៉្យាង /məyaaŋ/ one kind, one way

ម្រាក់ female friend (Arch)

ម្រាម finger, toe

ម្រឹគ four-legged wild animal (tiger, deer, etc.)

ម្រឹគា (=ម្រឹគ) four-legged wild animal

ម្រឹគីម្រឹគា female and male four-footed wild animals

ម្រេច (black) pepper

ម្លប់ shade

ម្លិះរួត a variety of jasmine

ម្លឹង so, such, to that extent

ម្លឹង so, such, to that extent

ម្លឹង ៗ so, such, to such an extent

ម្លូ betel leaf

ម្ល៉េះ like this, in this way; so, to such an extent

ម្ល៉េះសម /mleh sαm/ must, probably, undoubtedly

ម្ល៉ោះហើយ thus, therefore, in this way

ម្ល៉ោះ thus, therefore, like that

ម្សៅ flour

ម្ហូប food, a meal

ម្ហូបចំណី food, various kinds of food

## យ

យ៉ porch, balcony

យក /yɔɔk/; Coll: /yɔɔ/ to take, to bring

យកចិត្តគេ to strive to please, to ingratiate oneself with another

យកចិត្តទុកដាក់ to pay attention, devote oneself to

យកជាការ to rely on, depend on, have confidence in, take seriously

យកជាគ្នា to associate with each other, be friends

យកជាបែបយ៉ាង take as an example

យកជីវិត to save one's (own) life

យកតែបុណ្យទៅចុះ for one's own good

យកលំនាំតាម to imitate, draw inspiration from
យកអាសា to help, assist, wait on; to protect, defend
យក្ខិណី /yeə̆qkhenəy/ female ogre
យក្ស /yeə̆q/ giant, ogre
យក្សា (= យក្ស) giant, ogre
យក្សាសូរ (= យក្ស + អសុរ) /yeə̆qsaasou/ giants, demons, ogres
យង់ intensifier for adjectives of clarity, brightness, etc.
យង់យល់ to see
យតិភង្គ /yattephŭəŋ/ hyphen
យន្ត /yŭən/ machine, engine (Lit)
យន្ត (= យ័ន្ត) /yoən/ magical design
យន្តហោះ /yŭən-hɑh/ airplane
យប់ evening, night
យប់ថ្ងៃមួយរោច first night of the waning moon
យមបាល /yumməbaal/ Yamapāla, guardians of Hell
យមុនា Yamunā (the Jumnā river in northeastern India)
យប់មិញ last night
យប់យន់ evening (Poetic)
យមរាជ /yumməriəc/ Minister of Justice
យល់ to learn, to understand; to recognize, know; to see
យល់គុណ grateful; to feel gratitude
យល់ជា be considered to be
យល់ដោយមុខ selectively, on an individual basis, with discrimination
យល់ថា be considered that
យល់មុខ to show favoritism
យល់ទាស់ to oppose, disagree
យល់ព្រម to agree, consent
យល់យង់ bright, luminescent
យល់សប្តិ /yŭəl-sɑp/ to dream
យល់ស្រប to agree

យស /yŭəh/ honor, glory, fame, rank
យសសក្តា /yŭəh-saqkədaa/ high position or rank
យសោធរគិរី /yasaothəreə̆qkirii/ name for the Bayon
យសោធរបុរៈ /yasaothəreə̆qboraq/ Yasodharapura (original city of Angkor)
យសោធរេស្វរៈ /yasaothəreeswaraq/ Yasodharesvara (honorary name of King Yasovarman)
យសោវរ្ម័ន /yasaowɑɑrəman/ Yasovarman (King of Angkor 889-900)
យាង to go (Roy)
យាងយាល to go (Lit, Roy)
យ៉ាង kind, way; like, as
យ៉ាងខ្លី briefly
យ៉ាងណាក្តី whatever, whatever kind
យ៉ាងតិច at least
យ៉ាងតិចណាស់ at the very least
យ៉ាងថ្កុំថ្កើង importantly, impressively
យ៉ាងមធ្យម on the average
យ៉ាងម៉េច how?
យ៉ាងមាំទាំ seriously, resolutely
យ៉ាងយូរបំផុត at the longest
យ៉ាងលាយឡំគ្នា mixed, intertwined; complex, subtle
យ៉ាងសម្បើម impressive, remarkable
យ៉ាងសម័យ modern, up-to-date
យ៉ាងស្មោះ sincerely
យ៉ាងហោចណាស់ at least, at the minimum
យ៉ាងហ្នឹងហើយ that's right, it's true
យាត (= យាត្រា) to go (Roy, Lit)
យាត្រា to go; trip (Roy, Lit)
យាត្រាមក to come (Roy)
យាន vehicle
យ៉ាប់ difficult, hard; slow, inept
យាប្លង Johnson grass (an aquatic grass)

យាម plow-handle

យាម prediction; auspices, signs of the future

យាម to guard

យាមល្បាត to patrol

យាយ grandmother; title of respect for old ladies

យាយជី nun

យាយី to harm, hurt

យារ to be drawn out, extended, delayed, drawled

យាវ a kind of vine used for string

យាស to cry, call (of animals)

យ៉ាះ /yah!/ ouch!

យី interjection of surprise, annoyance, or admiration (usually accompanied by rising intonation)

យឹត to stretch, draw out

យឹតយោង to help out

យឺត slow; slowly

យុគលពិន្ទុ /yukəleə̆qpɨntuq/ the symbol -:

យុតថ្កា (= យុថ្កា) /yuttkaa/ anchor

យុត្តិធម៌ /yuttethɔə/ justice

យុថ្កា /yuttkaa/ anchor

យុថ្កា a kind of flower

យុទ្ធកថា /yuttheə̆qkəthaa, yuttəkəthaa/ epic, tale, narrative

យុទ្ធនា /yutthəniə/ war (Lit)

យុទ្ធភ័ណ្ឌ /yutthəphŏən/ paraphernalia of war

យុវជន /yuwwəcŭən/ youth, young people

យុវតី /yuwwətəy/ feminine youth, young women

យុវនារី /yuwwəniərii/ young lady (Eleg)

យុវ័ន /yuwan/ youth, young person (usually masculine); boy scout

យុរយារ /yuu-yiə/ sagging, protruding, hanging down

យូរ long (in time), late

យូរឆាប់ sooner or later

យូរណាស់មកហើយ for a long time now

យូរថ្ងៃ many days, a long time

យូរដល់ម្ល៉េះ this long, so long as this

យូរ ៗ ម្ដង once in a while, from time to time

យូរលង់ for an extremely long time

យូរអង្វែង for an extremely long time

យួ (= យួរ) to hold or carry in one hand

យួន Vietnam; Vietnamese (n, adj)

យួនអាណាម Annam

យើ exclamation of astonishment or disapproval (superior to inferior)

យើង we (among intimate friends, or by superior to inferior); I (between intimate friends, or by king to inferior)

យើរ to snatch, grab

យើះយើ interjection of surprise

យៀកកុង Viet Cong

យៀកណាម Vietnam

យ៉ែម-សារុង Yêm Sarong (pers. n.)

យោគ to try, attempt, make an effort to

យោគយល់ to understand

យោង to pull up, pull along

យោជន៍ distance of approx. 1600 meters, a mile

យោធា army, military

យោនយោន hanging all around, suspended all over

យោបល់ idea, opinion

យោបំ wail, lamentation, cry

យោល to swing, cause to swing back and forth

យោល to refer to, base oneself on

យៅវ៌មាណ /yɨw-maan/ youth (Lit)

យំ to cry (humans, birds, animals)

យំសោកចេញកខ្លួនប្រាណ to weep violently

# រ

រក /rɔɔk/; Coll: /rɔɔ/ to search for, look for, seek

រកកលឈ្លោះ find a pretext to quarrel, pick a fight

រកឃើញ to search successfully, to find

រកក្តី to stir up trouble, look for an argument

រកដណ្តឹង to search for (a mate)

រកទទួលទាន to make a living

រកបាន to gain, get, be able to get

រកមិនឃើញ to be unable to find

រករឿង to find fault, provoke; to research, get to the bottom of a matter

រកស៊ី to earn a living

រកអ្វីប្រៀបពុំបាន nothing can compare; incomparably, extremely

រ័ក /rĕəq/ lovely, beloved

រកា a thorny tree

រកាកោង Rokakong (a town on the Mekong)

រ័ក្សរួម (= រួមរ័ក្ស) live a conjugal life

រក្សា /rĕəqsaa/ to take care of

រក្សាព្រះទ័យ to comport oneself (Roy)

រខោក sound of rattling of loose boards or slats

រង second, assistant, under; to undergo, suffer; cushion, pillow

រង to defend, to protect, to ward off, block

រង settled, cleared up

រងកម្មវេទនា /rɔɔŋ kam-weetəniə/ to suffer, undergo suffering

រងការ to ward off (a blow, etc.)

រងគ្រោះ victimized

រងទុក្ខ grieved, subjected to grief

រង់ to wait

រង់ចាំ to wait for, await eagerly

រងា to be cold, unpleasantly cool

រងាវ to crow, cluck

រង៉ូវ to pester, annoy

រងំ droning, rumbling, indistinct

រង្គ /ruə̆ŋ/ war, battle

រង្គសាល theater

រង្គាត់ crisscrossing, doubling back, to and fro; to wander about, wander all over

រង្វង់ frame, shape, facing

រង្វាន់ reward, prize

រង្សី /rĕəŋsəy/ brilliance, sparkle, ray

រចនា /raccənaa/ art, handicraft; to decorate, design, create

រជ្ជកាល /raccəkaal/ reign, dynasty

រញ្ជួយ to shake, tremble (iv)

រដិបរដុប rough, heterogeneous

រដូវ season; menstrual period

រដូវក្តៅ hot season

រដូវទឹកឡើង flood season

រដូវប្រាំង dry season

រដូវភ្លៀង rainy season

រដូវរងា cold season

រដូវរំហើយ cool season

រដូវរាំង drought

រដូវវស្សា rainy season

រដូវស្ទូង rice-planting season

រដែ Rhade (a tribal group)

រដោះ come untied, come loose; be separated

រដ្ឋ /rŏət/ state, country, political entity

រដ្ឋការ /rŏəttəkaa/ government, administration

រដ្ឋធម្មនុញ្ញ /rŏətthaqthŏəmmənuñ/ constitution

រដ្ឋមន្ត្រី /rŏət-muə̆ntrəy/ government minister

រដ្ឋសភា /rŏət-saphiə/ national assembly

រដ្ឋាភិបាល /rŏətthaaphibaal/ government, administration

រដ្ឋាភិបាលចម្រុះ coalition government

រដ្ឋាភិបាលស្រោចស្រង់ជាតិ Government of National Salvation
រណសិរ្សជាតិ /rənaqsei-ciət/ national front
រណសិរ្សជាតិនៃសេរីការ National Liberation Front (of South Vietnam)
រណ្តាប់ provisions, prerequisites (for a ceremony)
រណ្តៅ ditch

រណ្តំ to rattle, bang together (iv)

រណ្តំទាំងធ្មេញ teeth even rattled

រត់ to run

រត់គយ (= រត់ពន្ធ) to smuggle

រត់ចូលគ្នា to run together, combine

រត់ប្រទាត់មក to come running from all directions
រត់ពន្ធ /rŭət-pŭən/ to smuggle

រត់ទេទរា to run haltingly

រតន (= រ័តន) /rŏət/ gem, precious stone
រ័តន /rŏət/ gem, precious stone

រតនគិរី /rattənaqkirii/ Ratanakiri (Province)
រតនា /rŏəttənaa/ precious stone

រត្តិចរ /rŏəttəcɑɑ/ nocturnal

រត្ន /rŏət/ jewel, precious stone

រ័ត្ន (= រត្ន) gem, precious stone; precious, beloved
រថ /rŭət/ car, vehicle

រថភ្លើង train

រថយន្ត /rŭət-yŭən/ car, automobile

រថយាន carriage

រទេះ /rɔteh, rəteh, qatiəh/ cart, vehicle
រទេះកង់ bicycle

រទេះភ្លើង train

រទេះឡាន automobile

រទេះអូស rickshaw, hand-drawn cart

រនាបរនៀល falling down in piles

រនាបរនេល falling down in piles

រនាស់ harrow, rake (n)

រនុក bolt, lock (n)

រន្ទាន់ repeatedly, in rapid succession
រន្ទាល gleaming, sparkling

រន្ទឺ menacingly, threateningly

រន្ទះ lightning

រន្ធ /rŭən/ hole, opening, orifice

រន្ធច្រមុះ /rŭən-crɑmoh/ nostril(s)

រន្ធត់ frightened, shocked, agitated

របក to peel off, come off, fall away
របង fence, hedge

របប method, way, order; conduct

របបគ្រប់គ្រង system of government

របរ trade, profession

របរការ business, affair

របស់ thing; of, belonging to

របស់ទ្រព្យ possessions, wealth

របស់ធាតុ elements

របាត the symbol ៌

របូត to come loose, slip off, loosen
របូតរលូត to slip away, slip free, escape (Coll)
របួស wounded; a wound

របើក to have come open, to have been forced open, burst
របៀប style, way, method

របៀបតែង style of writing

របៀបរបប manner; manners

របៀបរៀបរាង style, organization, form
របៀបសិក្សា system of education

របេះ to come loose, crumble, shed

របេះរបក to fall off, come off, fall away
រញេះ sparse, spaced

រប៉ាត់រប៉ាយ scattered

របាំ dance, dancing

របាំអប្សរា dance of Apsaras

របាំង a screen, shade

រពាក់ a kind of rattan

រពាយ scattering, dispersing

រពួន crowding together and piling up

រពើសរពើង rolling, undulating

រមាស rhinocerous

រមិល to look, see (Lit)

រមួល twisted

រមៀត tumeric

រមែង usually

រមែងតែងតែ inevitably, surely

រមាំង a kind of deer

រមាំងងាប់ place name (lit: dead deer)

រម្ងាប់ to appease, relieve, smother, extinguish

រម្យរ័តន៍ /rum-roə̆t/ pleasant, delightful

រយ hundred

រយៈ /rɔyeə̆q/ duration; period, interval

រយ៉ង់ Rayong (pl. n. in Thailand)

រយេងរយោង sagging, hanging down here and there

រយ៉ី tattered

រលក a wave (of water, wind, etc.); to roll, churn (of water)

រលង់ shiny, glistening

រលត់ to go out, be extinguished

រលត់ស្ងាត់ស្ងៀម completely extinguished

រលាក់ to shake (tv)

រលាយ to melt, dissolve (iv)

រលាស់ to shake off (tv)

រលីក very, extremely (intensifier for black)

រលីង smooth; completely

រលីងរលោង to well up (of tears); to water (of eyes)

រលឹក (= រឭក) to miss, think about

រលុប to be erased, effaced

រលុះ to eat away, spread, consume (as a fire or cancer)

រលូត to slip out

រលូតកូន to have a miscarriage

រលើប shining, glistening, glowing

រលេមរលោង polished, shining

រលំ to fall down

រលំទាំងឈរ to fall down from a standing position; to have been overthrown, wiped out, reduced to nothing (suddenly)

រលះ to hurry away

រលះរលាំង to shuffle hurriedly along, to bustle

រឭក (= រលឹក) to remember, miss, think nostalgically about

រវល់ busy; concerned about, preoccupied with

រវល់តែ preoccupied with

រវាង duration, interval; between, during

រវើរវាយ weak, confused, delirious

រវៀល to hurry, hasten

រវែង oblique, wrong, misguided

រវាត to deviate, stray from

រវាន rocky soil, sedimentary rock

រវិវង្សគោវិទ /reə̆qwiwŭəŋ koowɨt/ R. Kovit (a contemporary author)

រវីមរវាម in crisscrossing helter-skelter lines

រវាំង to be on the lookout; be careful, watch out

រស /rŭəh/ taste, flavor, essence

រសជាតិ /rŭəh-ciət/ taste, flavor

រស់ to live, be alive

រស់នៅ to live, be alive, exist, survive; to live in

រស់រវើក vivid, realistic

រ៉ស់ a kind of fresh-water fish

រសាត់ to float along

រសាត់ចុះឡើង float back and forth

រសាយ to dissipate, slacken; be relaxed, relieved; lax, negligent

រសៀល afternoon, early afternoon

រស្មី /reə̆qsməy ~ reə̆hsməy/ light, brilliance

រហង់ in a docile group, by groups

រហ័ស fast, quick

រហាម destitute, penniless, miserable

រហាម brimming, flowing, drooling

រហិតរហង់ (=រហង់)

រហូត until, up to, as far as

រហូតតែម្តង all the way (without stopping)

រហែក torn, worn out

រហោឋាន isolated, remote

រអារ៉ៃ weary

រអាក់រអួល be confronted with difficulties, have rough going; troubled, anguished

រអិល to slip, slide; slick, slippery

រអូច to move the lips silently (as if calculating half-aloud)

រា to reach out for

រា to hesitate, hold back; to back up

រាថយ to back up, retreat

រារង់ to hesitate, hold back

រារាំង to obstruct

រាក់ shallow

រាក់ a kind of small tree

រាក់ទាក់ intimate, tender, gentle

រាគ passion

រាគតណ្ហា sexual passion

រាគី appealing, seductive

រាង shape, form; seem, give the impression of

រាង to have learned one's lesson, be properly taught

រាងកាយ body, self

រាងចាល to be broken of, to have learned one's lesson, repent

រាងចាលចិត្ត to have a change of heart, mend one's ways

រាងរៅ figure, body

រាជ a large scaleless fish, royal fish

រាជការ /riəccəkaa/ government, civil service

រាជព្រឹក្ស a flowering tree, considered a royal tree

រាជទេយ្យ /riəccətɨy/ royal gift

រាជធានី /riəccəthiənii/ royal capital

រាជនិយម /riəccəniyum/ royalist(adj); monarchism

រាជនិវេសនដ្ឋាន /riəccəniweehsənatthaan/ royal residence

រាជបរិពារ /riəccəbɑɑripiə/ royal entourage

រាជបុត្រី /riəccəbottrəy/ princess, royal daughter

រាជបំរើ royal servants (i.e. any official under the monarchy)

រាជពិភព /riəccəpiphup/ throne, palace

រាជស័ព្ទ /riəccəsap/ royal vocabulary

រាជសម្បត្តិ /riəccəsɑmbat/ throne

រាជរដ្ឋាភិបាល /riəc-rŏətthaaphibaal/ royal government

រាជវ័ត្ត /riəccəwŏət/ fence, railing

រាជសីហ៍ /riəccəsəy/ lion (Lit)

រាជស្ថាន /riəccəthaan/ royal capital

រាជាគណៈ /riəciəkənaq/ Buddhist Council, Council of Priests

រាជាធិបតេយ្យ /riəciəthɨppətay/ monarchy

រាជានុញ្ញាត /riəcianuñaat/ to give permission; permission(Roy)

រាជាធិរាជ king

រាជាភិសេក /riəciəphisaek/ to be crowned as official king; coronation

រាជាមាត្យ /riəciəmaat/ royal servant, royal aide

រាជ្យ reign, kingdom

រាត់រាយ dispersed, disseminated;

all over the place, pell-mell

រាត្រី night, evening (Lit)

រាត្រីសិល្បៈ a cultural evening, soirée artistique

រាន platform, stage, tier

រាន ៧ ថ្នាក់ seven tiers

រានទេវតា altar

រានហាល porch, flat deck

រាប smooth, flat

រាបសា polite, circumspect, proper

រាបស្មើ even, flat

រាប់ to count, consider as

រាប់ជើងរាប់ដៃ to count on the fingers and toes

រាប់ថា...ពុំបាន cannot be considered as...

រាបទាប flat, level

រាប់ពាន់តោន by thousands of tons

រាប់មិនអស់ innumerable

រាប់រក consort with, associate with

រាប់រកយកជាគ្នា to cultivate each other's friendship

រាប់អាន to like, respect

រ៉ាប់រង to guarantee, assure

រ៉ាប់រ៉ាយ (= រ៉ាយរ៉ាប់) to tell, relate

រាពណ៍ (= រាពណា) Rāvana, a demonic giant

រាពណា Rāvana, the 10-headed ogre ruler of Lanka

រាមកេរ្តិ៍ /riəm-kei/ Ream-Kei (Cambodian version of the Rāmāyana)

រាមឥសូរ /riəm-qəysou/ a legendary ogre

រាមាជើងព្រៃ Rama Cheungprey, a 16th century Cambodian king at Lovek

រាមាយណ /riəmiəyanaq/ Rāyāyana

រាមារិទ្ធិ /riəmiərɨt/ Rāmāriddhi (= Barommaraja, King of Cambodia 1566-1576)

រាយ to spread, scatter, distribute; to list, arrange in consecutive order; to relate, tell

រាយដំណើរ to relate the facts

រាយមាយ careless, negligent

រាយរង unimportant, insignificant

រាយរៀង arranged in consecutive order

រ៉ាយរ៉ាប់ to tell, relate, recount

រាល to spread, expand

រាល់ every (in a sequence)

រាល់គ្នា each of us, all tōgether

រាល់តែវេលា every time

រាល់រូញ (= រាល់រូប) every one

រាល់រួច (= រួចរាល់) all done, completely executed

រាវ to feel around for

រារី to harm, cause trouble

រាស់ to rake, harrow

រាស្ត្រ /riəh/ people, populace

រាហ៊ុ /riəhuu/ mythological monster having only the upper half of his body (thought to cause eclipses by swallowing the moon)

រាហូ a king of large fish

រិម_គិន /rɨm-kɨn/ Rim-Kin (author of Sophat)

រិះ to worry, ponder

រិះគិត to think, decide

រិះរក to search for, seek to; to do research

រិទ្ធិអានុភាព /rɨtthii-qaanuphiəp/ power

រី as for, concerning

រីក to expand, bloom, flourish

រីកថ្លាមុខ to have a clear and happy expression

រីកមុខ to take on a happy expression

រីករាយ happy, joyful

រីង dry, dried up; to evaporate

រីងរៃ thin, wasted away

រើរា (=រេរា) to hesitate, hold back

រឹង hard, stiff

រឹង increasingly

រឹងជា increasingly, all the more

រឹងជំហរ stable, in strong condition

រឹងរឹត to insist on

រឹងទទឹង firm, unyielding; obstinate, dogged, stubborn

រឹងប៉ឹង strong, firm, stable

រឹងមាត់ to be stubborn

រឹងរឹតរឹត increasingly

រឹត to tighten, constrict

រឹតរឹត increasingly

រឹតរឹត...ទៀត increasingly...

រឹតរួត to constrict, tighten, contract

រឹតទៀត tighter, worse (of an illness)

រឹទ្ធា (= រឹទ្ធិ)

រឹទ្ធិ (= ឫទ្ធិ) /rɨt/ power, magical force, efficacy

រឹម ៗ (flow) gently

រុករក to search

រុករាន to invade, penetrate, disturb

រុក្ខ /rukkhaq/ trees, vegetation, forest

រុក្ខជាតិ /rukkhəciət/ trees, forest vegetation

រុក្ខទេវតា /rukkhaq-teewədaa/ spirit of the forest

រុក្ខវិថី /rukkhaq-withəy/ avenue

រុង high, excellent, successful, of high status

រុងរឿង high, glorious, excellent; success, increase

រុងរោចន៍ (= រុងរឿង) successful, respectable, well-to-do

រុញ to push

រុញរា to dilly-dally, to delay

រុត to fish with a conical basket

រុល to inch ahead, work one's way forward

រុះ to disassemble; to untie, undo, unfold; to fall, drop, sprinkle down

រុះរើ to tear down, dismantle

រូ (= ដូច) like, as (Arch)

រូមណ្ឌលចក្រ like a circle, like a wheel

រូរស់កបរកើត life-like, as if alive

រូង a hole; to make a hole

រូងរាម hole, nest, crevice (in underwater vegetation)

រ៉ូង rattling noise

រួតរះ to hurry

រូប representation, form, figure; specifier for persons, characters, mediums

រូបឆោម figure, appearance

រូបឆោមឡោម /ruup-chaom-loom/ form, shape, figure

រូបរាង form, appearance

រូបរាងកាយ body, figure

រូបល្ខោន dancing figure(s)

រូបសម្បត្តិ /ruup-sɑmbat/ physique, looks, physical endowments

រូបលោក /ruupəlook/ materials things, visible things, tangible form

រូបិយប័ណ្ណ /ruupəyyəban/ currency, foreign exchange

រូបិយលក្ខណៈ /ruupəy-leə̆qkənaq/ physical characteristics, physiognomy

រូហាន like, similar to (Arch)

រូហាន brilliant; bold, brave

រួច then, and then; completed, already; to complete, get free from, escape; following a verb: can, able

រួចខ្លួន to escape

រួចជាស្រេច finished, completed

រួចជីវិត to survive, save one's life

រួចផុត to escape, avoid, get free

រួចពន្ធនឹងអាករគយ to be exempted from

taxes and customs duties

រួចមក afterward

រួចស្រេច completely, completely finished

រួចហើយ finished, already

រួញ kinky, coiled, curled

រួញខ្លួន to back down, withdraw (lit: to shrink back, to draw oneself up)

រួញរា to be reluctant, hang back, hesitate

រួតរឹត (=រឹតរួត) to constrict, tighten, contract

រួប to squeeze

រួបរឹត tight; to tighten, squeeze

រួបរួម to assemble, unite, put together, combine

រួម to combine, put together

រួមខ្នើយ to share a pillow, sleep together, make love

រួមប្រតិព័ទ្ធ be united in love, love reciprocally

រួមរ័ក to be united in love

រួមរ័កដោយលាក់កំបាំង to have an illicit love affair

រួមសង្វាស to make love

រួមល្បែង to play together

រួមរស to indulge in intimacy

រួមរសស្នេហ៍ស្និទ្ធ to make love

រួមស្ថានដួងជីវិត to be together, live together (of lovers)

រួមស្នេហ៍ស្នង become lovers, have sexual relations

រួស quickly, actively, alertly, vigilantly

រួសរង actively, alertly, vigilantly

រួសរាន់ to hurry, be quick; urgent

រួសរាយ genial and entertaining, expansive

រើ to pick out, to extract; to disarrange, take apart

រើខ្លួន to escape, get free, free oneself

រើស to pick up; to select; to gather

រើសបាន to find

រឿង story, subject, affair

រឿងកូរសមុទ្រទឹកដោះ the story of churning the milk ocean

រឿងដើម the story [from] the beginning, original story

រឿងប្រលោមលោក novel (n)

រឿងព្រេង folktale, traditional story

រឿងរង្សី brilliant, glorious

រឿងរ៉ាវ story, legend, history

រឿណរង្គ /rɨən-ruəŋ/ battlefield

រឿងល្ខោន drama

រឿងហេតុ reason, problem, situation

រឿយ ៗ often, continually

រៀង in order, consecutive

រៀង ៗ ខ្លួន each in turn, each on his own

រៀងទៅ continuously into the future, forever

រៀងមក continuously, up to the present

រៀងរាបដរាបមក continuously, up to the present

រៀងរាយ distributed here and there, spread around

រៀងរាល់ continuously, forever

រៀងរាល់ឆ្នាំ year after year

រៀន to study; to learn, learn how to; try to be

រៀនសូត្រ to study (Coll)

រៀប to arrange, prepare

រៀបការ to have a wedding ceremony, get married

រៀបខ្លួន to get ready

រៀបចំ to put in order, organize

រៀបនឹង nearly, almost, about to

រៀបពេល to set the hour, determine the auspicious time

រៀបមង្គលការ to have a wedding ceremony

រៀបរាប់ to lay out, enumerate, recount

រៀបរៀង to be organized, systematized or coordinated; to prepare

រៀបអាហារ to prepare food, serve food

រៀម elder brother (Lit)

រៀមច្បង eldest brother (Lit)

រៀល riel (Cambodian monetary unit)

រៀវ narrow, slim, slender

រេ to change back and forth, to fluctuate

រេរា to be reluctant, hang back, hang around, loiter

រេរាំ to dance; sway back and forth

រេខា [forming a] design; ornate, superb

រេចរិល /rɨc-rɨl/ worn out, deteriorated

រេល to collapse, to spread out (from a pile)

រេហ៍ពល /ree-pŭəl/ army (Arch)

រេះ to wear away, shave off, chip away

រ៉ែ mineral, ore

រែក to carry on a pole across the shoulder

រែង usually, used to, as a rule, generally; increasing(ly)

រៃកណ្ដឹង a large cicada

រោគ disease

រោគ a vine-like tree used in curing hemorrhoids

រោគា (= រោគ) disease

រោគាព្យាធិ /rookiəpyiəthiq/ illness, disease (Lit)

រោង hall, building; groom's temporary quarters

រោងកិនស្រូវ rice mill

រោងកុន movie-house

រោងចក្រ /rooŋ-caq/ factory

រោងចក្រស្រាប៊ីយែរ brewery

រោងដំរី elephant pavilion (pl. n.)

រោងថែវ hall, gallery

រោងពិធី ceremonial pavilion

រោងពុម្ព printing establishment, press

រោងភ្លើង sacred brazier

រោងមហោស្រព /rooŋ-məhaosrɑɑp/ place of entertainment

រោងរម្យ reception hall (of a palace)

រោងឧស្សាហកម្ម /rooŋ-quhsaahaqkam/ factory

រោច to wane (of the moon)

រោទ៍ to resound (music); to roar (lion); to moo (cow)

រោម body-hair, fur (except human head-hair)

រោម to encircle, to surround

រោយ to fall, drop, shed (petals, chaff, etc.)

រោយក្លិន to give off an odor, spread fragrance

រោល to scorch, singe

រោះរាយ (= រួសរាយ) /rŭəh-riəy/ genial, cordial, expansive

រុំ to wrap, wind, roll

រំងាប់ to destroy, kill

រំងាប់ចេញ to exorcise, destroy

រំចេក a kind of cactus with fragrant blooms

រំជួល to shake, cause to tremble, agitate; agitated, moved

រំជំរំជង to break, crash together (of waves, Poetic)

រំដួល a flowering tree

រំដេង a plant similar to horseradish

រំដោះ to free, liberate, let loose

រំពង tumult; tumultuous

រំពត់ to follow, deviate, bend

រំពឹង to think, reflect

រំពឹងឃើញថា feel that, think that...

រំពឹងរំពៃ to consider, ponder, reflect

រំពេស graceful, lithesome (of gesture)

រំពេច moment, instant; suddenly, instantly

រំពៃ to picture, visualize, imagine; glance sidewise, steal glances

រំភាយ to float, soar

រំភើប excited, moved, impressed

រំភើយ fluttering, floating on the breeze

រំយោល tassel, pompon

រំលង to pass by; across, passing

over

រំលត់ to put out, extinguish; to calm down (tv)
រំលាង to destroy

រំលាយ to melt, dissolve (tv)

រំលឹក (=រំឭក) to remind, commemorate

រំលៀក to transfer (a load); to move away, move over
រំលេច to highlight, put in relief

រំសាយ to loosen, spread, distribute loosely
រំសេវ gunpowder

រំលោង (=រលោង) polished, shining

រំលោភ to violate, usurp

រំភើយ cool; to cool, fan

រំដោះ to free, put at leisure, relieve (of work, duty, etc.)
រំដោះកម្លាំង to assist, relieve, help

រំកិលខ្លួន to slide over, move over

រំឭក to remind, commemorate

រាំ to dance

រាំង dry; to dry up; to stop (of rain)
រាំង to bar, block, obstruct

រាំង small tree with edible leaves

រាំងទ្រោះទ័ព to establish a defense line
រាំងផ្លូវ to obstruct one's way

រាំងរា to prevent, block, stop

រាំងភ្នំ a kind of tree

រះ to appear, come out, shine (of sun or moon); to dawn
រះមុខ the symbol -ះ (Skt. visarga)

ឫកពា /rɨk-piə/ attitude, conduct, character
ឫក្ស /rɨk/ propitious time (Astrology)
ឫទ្ធិ /rɨt, rɨtthiq/ power, magical force, efficacy
ឫទ្ធិតបៈ powerful magic

ឫទ្ធានុភាព /rɨtthiənuphiəp/ power, authority

ឫទ្ធិតបៈតេជះ /rɨttəpaq-dacceăh/ magical power
ឫស /rɨh/ root

ឫសកែវ roots, origin

ឫសី /rɨhsəy/ hermit, holy man, rishi
ឫស្យា /rɨhsyaa/ covetous, begrudging; corrupt
ឫស្សី /rɨhsəy/ bamboo

ឫស្សីកែវ a section of Phnom Penh

ឬ /rɨɨ/ or; final question particle used in either-or questions
ឬក៏ or, or on the other hand

ឬទេ final question particle: or not?
ឬមួយ or, or perhaps, or rather

ឬអ្វី or what?

## ល

ល to try, try out

។ល។ /laq/ et cetera

លក to groove, channel out

លក់ to sell

លក់ to fall asleep

លក់ to fine, penalize

លក់ដាច់ to sell (successfully), to move (of merchandise)
លក់ដូរ to trade, deal in

ល័ក្ខណ៍ /leăq/ virtue, quality, principle
លក្ខណៈ /leăqkənaq/ characteristic, attribute
លក្ខណា (=ល័ក្ខណ៍) quality, virtue

លក្ខន្តិកៈ /leăqkhanteqkaq/ official charter, body of rules
លក្ស្មណ៍ Lakshmana (Rama's younger brother)
ល័ខ /leăq/ gum lac

លង to try, test, experiment with

លង to appear, make an appearance (of ghosts, apparitions, etc.)
លង់ to sink, be submerged

លង់ (= យូរ) long (in time)

លង់ទឹក to sink in the water

លង់លក់ (= លក់លង់) to sleep soundly

លង់លុះ when

លង់លុះព្រឹកព្រាងហើយ when it was light, at daybreak

លង្កា /laŋkaa/ Langka (Ceylon)

លង្វែក Lovek, capital of Cambodia, 16th to 19th centuries

លង្វែក period, interval, age

លទ្ធផល /lattəphɑl/ result, yield (Lit)

លទ្ធិ /latthiq, ləthiq/ belief, faith, precept

លន painted, lacquered

លន់ extremely

លន់_នល់ Lon Nol (leader of 1970 coup d'état)

លន្តែ small plant with fragrant flowers

លន្លង់ desolate, melancholic, sad

លន្លង់លន្លោច lugubrious, solemn

លន្លោច sad, melancholic, plaintive

លប to sneak, creep, steal

លបលាក់ secretly, surreptitiously

លយ to float, set afloat

លលក dove

លលាដ៍ skull

លលើ stupid, dumb, naive

លើល high in the air, towering

លលោលលាំ jumping, leaping (repeatedly)

លស់ to skip, miss; intermittently

លា to say goodby; to take leave

លា to spread out, unfold, unwrap (tv)

លា donkey

លាចាក to leave, abandon

លាចាកស្ថានលោកយើងទៅ to die (Lit)

លាក to leave; to turn away

លាកចិត្ត change one's idea, have a change of heart

លាក់ to hide (tv)

លាក់ញាំងអី [why should I] hide anything?

លាង to wash (hands, dishes, etc.)

លាត to spread out, extend

លាតត្រដាង to spread out; extended

លាតសន្ធឹង to spread out, extend; spread out, extended

លាន million

លាន់ to crack, groan, make a noise (of inanimate objects); with a great hubbub, noisily

លាន់មាត់ to cry out, exclaim (involuntarily)

លាភ luck

លាភជ័យ good luck

លាម translator, interpreter (Arch)

លាមក /liəmŭəq/ excrement (Lit)

លាយ to mix; mixed

លាយឡំ mixed with, mixed together

លាវ Lao; Laos

លាវពោះខ្មៅ Lao of Chiengrai (lit: black-stomach Lao)

លាស់ to sprout, come out (of leaves)

លាស់លូត (= លូតលាស់) to expand, flourish

លិង្គ /lɨŋ/ linga, phallus

លិច to be submerged; to sink

លិច (= លេច) to leak

លិចក្បាល to have the head submerged

លិទ្ធ /lɨt/ to lick, lap up

លីត្រ /liit/ liter

លីលា to go, walk (Lit)

លីលា mentally disturbed

លីលាប់ be careless, negligent, half-hearted; confused, dazed

លឹមៗ barely visible

លុក to invade

លុកលុយ to invade

លុងលុះ until, to the point of

លុត to bend (the knees); to kneel

លុតជង្គង់ to kneel

លុប to erase; to wash (the face)

លុបចោល to take out, extract, excise, cut out (lit: erase out)

លុយ money

លុយ to cross water or mud on foot

លុះ when; until, to the point of; to attain, achieve

លុះដល់ even to the extent of

លុះដោយ... resulting from

លុះតែ only if, only when

លុះត្រាតែ unless, until; when, only when

លុះព្រឹកឡើង the next morning

លុះយូរ ៗ មក much later on

លូក to reach out, reach into

លូកដៃ to reach for

លូត to protrude, extrude, extend

លូតលាស់ to expand, increase, flourish

លូន to crawl (on the stomach, or as snakes)

លួង to soothe, comfort, cajole

លួងលោម to cajole, persuade, entice

លួច to steal; to sneak

លួចគេ to steal [from] others

លួចប្រតិព័ទ្ធ to have secret relations

លួចរត់ to run away, sneak away

លួសលេច to stand out, be sharply defined

លើ on, above

លើក to lift up, raise up (tv); to dispatch, deploy (troops); to give (a daughter in marriage)

លើក time, occasion

លើកករវន្ទាបង្គំ /ləək kɑɑ woəntiə bɑŋkum/ to salute, greet, pay homage

លើកខ្លួនជាកូន claim to be the child of

លើកគ្នា to join forces, cooperate

លើកដាក់ to carry (lit: to lift and put down)

លើកតែ except

លើកទ័ព to raise forces, raise troops; to move forces

លើកទុក to set aside; except

លើកលែងតែ except for, with the exception of

លើស to exceed, go beyond

លើសខ្វះពីគ្នា unequal, out of balance

លើសលន់ exceeding(ly)

លើសលុប to exceed, predominate over; exceedingly, predominantly

លើសលែង exceeding, beyond

លើសលែងនានា above everything else

លើសអំពី beyond, exceeding

លើសអំពីមុនទៀត even more than before

លឿន fast, rapid

លឿនលត់ extremely fast (Coll)

លៀង to fête, give a banquet for

លៀងភា a goat-antelope

លេខ /leik/ number, class

លេខទោ (ៗ) /leik too/ repetition sign

លេខាធិការ /leekhaathikaa/ executive secretary

លេខហារី clerk, messenger

លេង to play; to visit; after a verb: for fun, jokingly

លេងកំសាន្ត to relax, be at leisure

លេងគ្នា to fight (Idiom)

លេងជាល្បែង to make a game out of it

លេងស្រី to chase women

លេងស្រីប្រុស to be promiscuous

លេច to stick up, stand out, appear; exceedingly, surpassingly
លេច to leak

លេប to swallow

លេបទឹកភ្នែក to suffer, to endure (lit: swallow one's tears)
លេបលយ to glide, float

លេលាប់ be negligent, careless

លេស /leh/ pretext, excuse, reason

លែង to leave off, desist from, quit; to divorce
លែង (=ឡើង) to ascend (Arch)

លែងលះ to divorce, separate

លែងសូវហ៊ាន no longer dared, rather unwilling
លែបខាយ to extemporize appealingly and provocatively
លៃ to manage, find a way to, manipulate; to apportion; to figure, calculate, scheme
លៃចែក to divide

លៃលក /lɨy-lɔɔk/ to manage (to), find a way (to)
លោ to leap

លោ but, on the contrary, contrary to expectation
លោដូច as if

លោក polite title for a man: Mr.; respectful 2nd and 3rd person masc. pron.: you, he, they
លោក world

លោកគ្រូ teacher (masc); the venerable...
លោកគ្រូចៅអធិការ head priest of a temple, abbot
លោកគ្រូធំ head priest, abbot

លោកថា they say

លោកធាតុ (=ចក្រវាឡ) sphere, galaxy, unit of the universe
លោកធាតុវិទ្យា cosmology

លោកប្រុស he, the master; my husband (Polite, Formal)
លោកសង្ឃ /look-sɑŋ/ Buddhist monk; the clergy
លោកសង្ឃរាជ /look-sɑŋkəriəc/ chief priest, abbot of the monastery; also use to refer to the head of a sect
លោកសន្និវាស /look-sɑnniwiəh/ peoples of the world
លោកស្រី woman of higher rank, wife of government official
លោកស្រី-អ្នកស្រី higher- and lower-ranking women, women in general
លោកឧកញ៉ាព្រះស្តេច title (of high-ranking official)
លោកអ្នក you readers, you listeners

លោកា (= លោក)

លោកិយ /lookəy/ this world, the temporal world
លោកីយ៍ (= លោកិយ ) this world, the temporal world
លោត to jump

លោត a kind of tree

លោតទឹកសម្លាប់ខ្លួន to drown oneself

លោភ greedy

លោម (= លួងលោម) to cajole, entice

លោហិត /loohət/ blood (Roy)

លោះ to redeem, buy back

លោះ to miss, skip, stop temporarily, suspend (activity)
លោះលាយ happy, contented, blissful

លំចង់ a kind of aquatic flower

លំញង graceful, supple, fluid (of motion)
លំដាប់ order, succession

លំដាប់នោះ at that time

លំដាប់ពីនោះ after that, following that
លំទោន to bow, bend over; to submit

លំនៅ address, residence

លំនៅនៃអាត្មា one's own address

លំនាំ manner, gait, stylized movement, gesture, aspect
លំបាក difficult; difficulty, trouble

លំផាត់ Lomphat (capital of Ratanakiri Province)
លំពង់រាជា Lampong Raja (king of Angkor 1409-1416)
លំហើយ to cool, refresh (of wind)

លំហើយ to relieve, lessen, ease (tv)

លំអ beauty, embellishment

លំអង pollen

លំឱត /lumqaot/ be diligent (in), conscientious (about)

លំអោន to bow, bend over; obedient, submissive, polite

លាំងខឹដ a kind of tree

លាំងសាត a variety of litchi

លះ to leave, abandon

លះបង់ to abandon, reject, discard

លះបង់ចោល to abandon

ល្ខោន theater, drama

ល្ខោនជាតិ National Theater

ល្ខោនបាសាក់ Khmer folk drama

ល្គិកបើ if, whenever (Lit)

ល្ងង់ ignorant, stupid

ល្ងាច late afternoon, evening

ល្បង to test, try, experiment

ល្បងវាសនា to test one's luck, to tempt fate

ល្បប់ silt, alluvium

ល្បាត to patrol

ល្បាស់ tender, green

ល្បិចកិច្ចកល ruse, trick, artifice

ល្បី fame, renown

ល្បីឈ្មោះ fame; to be famous

ល្បីល្បាញ famous, well-known

ល្បើក improvisation, extemporaneous story

ល្បែង game

ល្បែងស៊ីសងល្បងវាសនា gambling

ល្បះ the symbol ៗ

ល្មម enough, adequate; rather, appropriately; just as, at the same time as; it's about time you...

ល្មមចិន្តា acceptable, agreeable

ល្មមតែ just enough to

ល្វៃ soft, pliant, supple

ល្មោភ overindulge in, be greedy for, crave; addicted to (doing something)

ល្មោភស៊ី to be gluttonous

ល្វន់ល្វៃ graceful, supple

ល្វា fig

ល្វាឯម Lovea Em (a village in Kandal Province)

ល្វាសល្វន់ graceful, willowy, supple

លូ-ហ្វីណូ /lwii fiinou/ Louis Finot

ល្វើយល្វេង vague, indistinct (of sound or smell)

ល្វេតល្វត delicate, soft, effeminate

ល្វែង compartment, section

ល្វែងពីរ place name (lit: two sections)

ល្ហាចល្ហឹម spread all over, continuous

ល្ហឹមល្ហែម tender, sweet

ល្ហុង papaya

ល្ហើយ to feel cool and comfortable

ល្ហែ to slack, let up, be at leisure, fritter

ល្ហែង flowing softly

ល្ហៅ glittering, sparkling (?)

ល្អ good, pretty

ល្អ ៗ very beautiful (intensification of /lqαα/)

ល្អល្អាច់ pretty, attractive (Coll)

ល្អិត carefully, properly; pretty, attractive

ល្អសមសួន attractive

ល្អល្អះ pretty, attractive (Coll)

ល្អអស់អង្គ lovely in every detail (lit: the whole body is pretty)

ល្អក់ to be muddy

ល្អង powder, pollen, dust; beautiful

(of complexion)

ល្អាន disturbance, trace, mark

ល្អិត fine, in small pieces

ល្អី a tightly-woven basket

ល្វៀង to deviate, be different, go astray, diverge, equivocate

ឮ /lɨɨ/ to hear; to be heard

## វ

វក year of the monkey (of the 12-year cycle)

វគ្គ /weə̆q/ chapter, part, section, paragraph; stanza (of longer poem)

វគ្គឃ្លា form, arrangement (of speech or writing)

វង់ a circle; around; specifier for rings

វង់ក្រចក parentheses

វង់ធំ the larger circuit

វង់ភក្ត្រ /wuə̆ŋ-pheə̆q/ face, shape of the face (Lit)

វង្វេង to be lost, confused, muddled

វង្វេងបាត់ to get lost

វង្វេងស្មារតី confused, muddled, half-conscious

វង្ស /wuə̆ŋ/ circle; family

វង្សសក្តា /wuə̆ŋsaqkədaa/ lineage, status, pedigree

វង្សា /wuə̆ŋsaa/ family

វចនានុក្រម /waccənaanukrɑm/ dictionary

វដ្តសង្សារ /wŏətdəsɑŋsaa/ cycle of reincarnation

វ័ណ្ឌ /wŏən/ to encircle, tangle, enwrap

វណ្ណៈ /wannaq/ status, position, color, kind, caste

វណ្ណ-មូលីវណ្ណ /wan mouliiwan/ Vann Molyvan (pers. n.)

វណ្ណយុត្តិ /wŏənnəyut/ diacritic

វត្ត /wŏət/ temple, pagoda, temple compound

វត្ត propriety, respect, respectful behavior

វត្តកំពង់ត្រឡាចក្រោម Vat Kompong Tralach Krom

វត្តគោកកាក Vat Kok Kak

វត្តបទុមវត្តី /wŏət bɑtum-watdəy/ Vat Botum Vaddey (a monastery in Phnom Penh)

វត្តប្រតិបត្តិ propriety, respect

វត្តភ្នំ Vat Phnom (a monastery in Phnom Penh)

វត្តលង្កា Vat Langka

វត្តសិទ្ធបូរ /wŏət sətthəbou/ Vat Set Bo

វត្តអារាម wat, pagoda

វត្តឧណ្ណាលោម /wŏət qonaalaom/ Vat Onalaom (seat of the Mahanikay sect)

វត្ថុ /wŏətthoq/ thing, artifact

វត្ថុធាតុដើម /wŏətthoq-thiət-daəm/ raw materials

វឌ្ឍនភាព /wattənaqphiəp/ progress

វន្ទា /wŏəntiə/ to greet with palms joined

វ័ធ (=វាត់) /wŏət/ to slash, swish, lash

វ័ធវៃ to swish, beat, flail

វប្បធម៌ /wappəthɔə/ culture; cultural

វ័យ age (Lit)

វរ /wɔreə̆q/ beautiful, precious, desirable

វរជន /wɔɔrəcuə̆n/ elite, upper class, important figures

វរមិត្រ /wɔɔ-mɨt/ esteemed friend

វរវឌ្ឍិ /wɔreə̆qroə̆t/ excellent

វរលក្ខណ៍ /wɔɔleə̆q/ high virtue

វរសេនីយ៍ទោ /wɔreə̆qsenəy-too/ Lieutenant-Colonel

វរុណ /wərun/ Varuna (a Hindu god)

វល់ to revolve, whirl, eddy; confused, in a fog

វល់គំនិត confused, disoriented

វលាហក /wəliəhakaq/ horse (Lit)

វល្លិ /wɔə/ vine

វស្សា /wuə̆hsaa/ rain; rainy season; year; Buddhist lenten period

វា familiar or derogatory 3rd person pronoun, used to refer to animals, children, persons of low estate, or inanimate objects

វានេះ this person

វាង to go around, by-pass; indirectly
វាងវៃ keen, sharp
វាចា to say; speech (Lit)
វាត to turn a boat by paddling toward oneself
វាត់ to slash, swish, lash; to beat, smack, swat; to wield, brandish
វាតា wind (Lit)
វាទី the speaker, the one who spoke
វាយ /way/ to beat, hit, strike
វាយដំ (=វាយ) to beat, hit (Coll)
វាយបែក to sack, capture, defeat
វាយឫកខ្លា pretend to be ferocious (lit: act like a tiger)
វាយឫក (ដាក់) be affected, put on airs (toward)
វារ to crawl (on hands and knees)
វាល field, plain; cleared off, cleaned away
វាលហាល to be cleared off, cleaned away
វាលភ្នំ plateau
វាលយន្ត parking lot
វាលរាប a plain
វាលវង់ race track
វាលវង់ចាស់ place name (lit: former race track)
វាលស្រឡះ open field, plain
វាលស្រែ ricefield
វាល់ to measure
វាស់ to measure (lineally)
វាស to scribble, make marks; to gesture, wave, sweep
វាស្នា fortune, destiny, fate
វាហើយ unconcerned, nonchalant, detached
វិចិត្រ /wicət/ nice, refined
វិចិត្រសិល្បៈ /wicət-səlləpaq/ fine arts
វិច្ឆិកា /wɨccəkaa/ November
វិជ្ជា /wɨcciə/ subject, study, field of learning
វិជ្ជាជាន់ខ្ពស់ higher education
វិជ្ជាពិសេស special trade, profession
វិជ្ឈមាត្រ /wɨccəmaat/ diameter
វិញ again, on the other hand (contrastive particle)
វិញ្ញាណ /wiqñiən, wiñiən/ consciousness, essence of life, soul, spirit
វិញ្ញាណក្ខន្ធ /wiqñiənnəkhan/ soul, spirit
វិតក្ក /witɑq/ worry, anxiety; to be worried, anxious
វិថី street, way
វិទ្យាស្ថាន /wɨttyiəthaan/ institute
វិទ្យាស្ថានជាតិគរុកោសល្យ National Pedagogical Institute
វិទ្យាល័យ /wɨttyiəlay, wɨttyaalay/ secondary school, lycée
វិទ្យុ /wɨttyuq/ radio
វិទ្យុជាតិ National Radio (Station)
វិធី way, method
វិន័យ /wiqnɨy/ Vinaya (discipline, rules of conduct for Sangha)
វិនាស to ruin, destroy
វិនាសសាបសូន្យ to disappear, become extinct
វិនិច្ឆ័យ /winɨcchay/ to justify, rationalize; to judge
វិបត្តិ /wibat/ crisis (Lit)
វិភាគទាន /wiphiəqkətiən/ contribution
វិមល /wiqmuəl/ pure, clean (Lit)
វិមាន monument, mansion
វិមានរដ្ឋ state guest house
វិមានឯករាជ្យ Independence Monument
វិយោគ sad, desolate, bereaved
វីរបុរស /wireəqborɑh/ hero
វិល to turn around, rotate (iv)
វិលចុះវិលឡើង back and forth, in circles, in flux
វិលត្រឡប់ to return, turn around
វិលវង់ to circle, encircle, orbit

វិលវិញ to return

វិលាស be coy, coquettish; to flirt

វិវឌ្ឍន៍ /wiwoət/ to progress, develop, evolve

វិវេក sad, melancholy

វិសជ្ជនា /wihsaccənie/ to answer (Lit)

វិស័យ /wihsay/ feeling, mood, mind, heart; characteristic; field (of endeavor); chance, fate

វិសាខា (=ពិសាខ) April-May (lunar system)

វិសាល spacious; admirable, meritorious

វិសុទ្ធិ (=ពិសុទ្ធិ) perfect, flawless

វិសេស special, above all

វិស្ណុ /wihsnuq/ Vishnu

វិស្សមកាល /wihsəmaqkaal/ vacation, recess

វិហារ /wihie/ temple

វ៉ី (=វ៉ឺយ)

វីវក់ frantically, violently

វីវរ to be in trouble, have difficulties; to be in the way, get in the way; with a great commotion, with a hue and cry

វីរិយំ /wiiriyaŋ/ diligence, effort

វឹង right away, with a dash

វឹង (=វិញ) again, on the other hand (Arch)

វ៉ឺយ /wəɨy/ exclamation of surprise, or to attract attention (rather arrogant or impolite)

វៀរចាក to be free of, without

វៀច crooked, winding

វៀតណាម Vietnam

វៀរ to avoid, abstain from

វៀរលែងតែ except for, with the exception of

វៀរ (=ពៀរ) retribution

វេច to wrap up

វេទ Veda; magic formula

វេទនា misery, strife; sensation, feeling

វេទនាចិត្ត to suffer (mentally)

វេទិកា /weetikaa/ podium, platform, forum

វេរា predestined misfortune (caused by past actions)

វេរាកម្ម bad deeds, immoral acts

វេរី (=វេរា) trouble, misfortune, negative karma

វេលា time, period; when

វេហាស៍ air, space (Lit)

វេហាស (=វេហាស៍) air, space (Lit)

វេះ /weh/ to slip away, sneak away, avoid

វែកញែក to explain in detail, to detail, analyze

វែង long (space and time)

វែនតា eye glasses

វៃ keen, quick

វៃវាង (=វាងវៃ) sharp, quick

វ៉ៃ (= វាយ) to hit

វៃតរណីទនី /wɨytəraqnəytənii/ Vaitaranidani (hell for deceivers)

វោត (= វគ្គ) stanza, paragraph, clause

វោហារ /woohaa/ eloquence, wit

វាំង /weəŋ/ palace, enclosure, compound; to enclose, obstruct

វាំងចំណារ to fence off, surround with a stake fence

វាំងនន curtain

# ស

ស white

ស៊ក to insert (into a pre-existing groove or hole)

សក់ hair (of the human head)

សក់ស្កូវ grayhaired

ស័ក /saq/ era

សកម្មភាព /saqkamməphiəp/ activities

សក្កវា /saqkəwaa/ title of a palace song

សកុណា /saqkomaa/ male bird (Lit)

សកុណី /saqkənəy/ female bird (Lit)

សក្ការៈ /saqkaaraq/ worship, homage; idol

សក្តិ /saq/ rank, status, grade

សក្តិសម /saq-sɑm/ fitting, appropriate (Lit)

សក្តិសិទ្ធិ /saq-sət/ efficacious

សង to repay, reimburse; back again, in return; to enhance, contribute to

សង two (Thai)

សងខាង the (two) sides, at the sides

សងសារ (=សារសង) to converse, answer reciprocally

សង់ to build

សង់ទីក្រាដ /sɑŋtikraat/ centigrade

សង់ទីម៉ែត្រ /sɑŋtimaet/ centimeter

សង្កត់ to press, to push down

សង្កត់សង្កិន to oppress, suppress

សង្កថា /saŋkəthaa/ a talk, impromptu speech

សង្កា doubt, suspicion; be suspicious, doubtful

សង្កាត់ division, sector, quarter, section

សង្កេត to observe; to consider

សង្កែ a plant whose leaves are used to roll local cigarettes

ស័ង្ខ spiral shell used as a trumpet

សង្ខរណ៍ /sɑŋkəran/ building materials

សង្ខារ /sɑŋkhaa/ life, existence, cycle of rebirth (Lit)

សង្ខាង the sides, at the sides

សង្ខេប /sɑŋkhaep/ to abbreviate; abbreviated

សង្គម /sɑŋkum/ society

សង្គមកិច្ច /sɑŋkumməkəc/ welfare

សង្គមរាស្ត្រនិយម /sɑŋkum-riəh-niyum/ Sangkum Reastr Niyum (the Popular Socialist Community)

សង្កៀតធ្មេញ to grit the teeth, gnash the teeth

សង្គ្រាម war

សង្គ្រាមពិភពលោកលើកទី ២ World War II

សង្គ្រោះ to help, assist, support

សង្ឃ /sɑŋ/ priesthood; the Sangha

សង្ឃកិច្ច /sɑŋkhəkəc/ religious ceremony

សង្ឃ័រ a thorny tree

សង្ឃឹម to hope, expect

សង្ឃឹមយ៉ាងមាំ to hope fervently

សង្រេង to grieve, suffer

សង្រេងសង្រែង to grieve

សង្រែក a truss for carrying a basket

សង្វាត work hard (at), try hard (to), be diligent (in)

សង្វារ chain or sash worn across both shoulders, crossing at the chest and fastened with a pin or brooch

សង្វាស union, relation

សង្វេគ grief, distress; sad, mournful

សង្ស័យ /sɑŋsay/ to doubt, suspect, wonder

សង្សារ reincarnation; Fig: sweetheart, beloved

សច្ចៈ /saccaq/ truth

សច្ចា /saccaa/ to swear, promise

សច្ចាប្រណិធាន oath of allegiance (to the king)

សច្ចំ /saccaŋ/ truth, honesty, goodness

សញ្ជាប់ sad and pensive (of face)

សញ្ជាតិ /sañciət/ nationality, race

សញ្ជឹង to reflect, ponder, daydream

សញ្ជឹងសញ្ជាប់ to daydream, be in a reverie, be preoccupied with one's thoughts

សញ្ញា /saññaa/ sign, symbol; to promise

សញ្ញាបត្រ /saññaabat/ degree; diploma, certificate

សញ្ញាសង្ខារ /saññaa-sɑŋkhaa/ signs of life

សណ្ដ /sɑndɑɑ/ edge, border

សណ្ដាន់ a tree with sour fruit used in cooking

សណ្ដាប់ custom, convention; order, sequence

សណ្ដាយ a kind of scaleless fish

សណ្ដូក to stretch out, lie down

សណ្ដែក bean(s)

សណ្ដែកដី peanut

សណ្ដោង to tow

សណ្ឋាគារ /sɑnthaakiə, sɑnthəkiə/ hotel, guesthouse

សណ្ឋាគារខេត្ត governor's mansion

សណ្ឋាន shape, aspect

សតវត្ស /sattəwoət/ century

សតិ /satteq/ reason, memory, power of thought

សតិសម្បជញ្ញៈ /sətteqsɑmpañcəññeəq/ conscience

សត្តបង្គ័ជ (= សប្បង្គ័ជ) /sattəbaŋkac/ a variety of lotus

សត្បា /sattəbaa/ a kind of tree

សត្យ /sat/ truth; truthful

សត្យា (= ស័ត្យ, សត្យ) /satyaa/ truth

សត្រូវ /sattrəw/ enemy

សត្វ /sat/ animal, being (human or animal)

សត្វកំពួលអាចម៍ dung-beetle

សត្វនរក /sat-nɔrŭəq/ creatures of hell

សត្វនិងព្រៃព្រឹក្សា fauna and flora

សត្វបក្សី /sat-baqsəy/ birds, the bird kingdom

សត្វបំរើ beast of burden, domesticated animal

សត្វពាហន /sat-piəhanaq/ livestock

សត្វរត្តិចរ /sat-rattəcɑɑ/ nocturnal birds

សត្វលោក animal world; animals

សត្វវិស័យ living animal, real animal, living being

សទ្ធា /satthiə/ generosity; religious faith

សទ្ធាសម្បទា the possession of faith

សន្ដាន /sɑndaan/ family, kind, lineage

សន្ដានចិត្ត intention

សន្តិភាព /sɑnteqphiəp/ peace, tranquillity

សន្តិវិធី /sɑnteq-withii/ peaceful means

សន្តោស to support, help out, assist; support, assistance, kindness

សន្ថិត to stay, reside in

សន្ទនា /sɑntəniə/ to converse

សន្ទភាព /sɑnteə̆qphiəp, sɑntəphiəp/ density of population

សន្ទរ (= ពីរោះ) /sontəreə̆q/ euphonious

សន្ទិះ to doubt, suspect, be suspicious

សន្ទុះ boom, leap, increase; burst (of flame)

សន្ទូច fish-hook

សន្ទើ a kind of vine with sour fruit

សន្ទុះទ្រូង sternum, chest

សន្ទប់ to close off, suppress

សន្ធរម៉ុក Santhor Mok (usually considered the author of Tum-Teav)

សន្ធាប់ to shout loudly and menacingly (in order to intimidate or cause panic)

សន្ធិយា (= សាណិយា) /sɑnthiyaa/ curtain

សន្ធឹក many, a large number, in great numbers; thunderous, tumultuous

សន្ធឹកសន្ធើ dejected, weary

សន្ធឹង to spread out, extend (tv)

សន្ធើ (= សន្ធឹងសន្ធើ) to sprawl despondently, be enervated with despair, sulk

សន្ធើសន្ធឹក (= សន្ធឹកសន្ធើ) sprawled despondently, prostrate with dejection

សន្ធៅ fiercely, like an inferno

សន្ធ្យា /sɑntyiə/ dusk, twilight

សន្និសិទ /sɑnnisət/ conference

សន្មត់ /sɑnnəmɑt/ to agree, allow, promise; to presume

សន្យា /sɑnniyaa/ to promise

សន្លប់ to faint, lose consciousness

សន្លឹក specifier for pages, leaves, sheets

សន្លឹកបើកចេញចូល shutter, movable covering

សន្សឹម ៗ slowly, laboriously

សន្សើម dew

សន្សំ to save, accumulate

សន្សំសាងសីលា accumulate merit (i.e.by keeping the precepts)
សប្តាហ៍ /sappdaa/ week (Lit)

សប្បាយ /sapbaay, səbaay/ happy, pleasant, enjoyable
សប្បាយចិត្ត to be happy, content

សប្បុរស /sαpborαh/ kind, friendly; kindness, generosity
សប្បុរសជន /sαpborαh-cŭən/ generous people
សព /sαp/ corpse

សព៌ាង្គ /sarəpiəŋ/ body (Lit)

ស័ព្ទ /sap/ sound, word, speech

សព្វ /sαp/ every

សព្វគ្រប់ all, entirely; every

សព្វគ្រប់ប្រការ in every detail, exhaustive
សព្វថ្ងៃនេះ nowadays, these days

សព្វបើ just, only (disparaging)

សព្វព្រះរាជហឫទ័យ /sαp-preə̆h-rieccəhaqrɨtɨy/ to be willing (to), pleased (to); satisfied, pleased (Roy)
សព្វសាយ spreading all around; everywhere; everything
សព្វសារពើ (=ទាំងអស់) /sαp-saarəpəə/ every, all; everything
សព្វសិទ្ធិ /sαp sət/ Sabvasiddhi (name of one of the fifty apocryphal Jatakas popular in Cambodia, Thailand, and Laos)
សភា /saphiə/ house, parliament, assembly
សភាព /saphiəp/ atmosphere, attitude, aspect
សភាវៈ (=សភាព) /saphiəweə̆q/ condition, state
សភាវបញ្ញត្តិ /saphiəwappaññat/ state of the mind, intellect
សម /sαm/ appropriate, fitting, becoming; to fit, go well with; then, accordingly; undoubtedly, obviously, likely that
សម /sααm/ fork

សមគាត់នឹងរឭកខ្ញុំ she will surely miss me

សមគួរ /sαm-kuə/ appropriate, proper

សមតែ it would be only appropriate that
សមនឹង plus the fact that; go well with, fit

សមបើ surely, undoubtedly

សមភាព /sαmməphiəp/ equality (Lit)

សមរម្យ /sαm-rum/ appropriate

សមសក្តិ /sαm-saq/ appropriate to one's rank
សមសព្វ /sαm-sαp/ comely in every respect
សមសួន /sαm-suən/ proper, appropriate (to), consistent (with)
សមត្ថកិច្ច /samattəkəc/ responsibility

សមត្ថភាព /samattəphiəp/ ability, capability
សម័យ /samay/ period, era; modern, recent; information, matter, circumstance
សម័យថ្ងៃនោះ that day

សម័យថ្ងៃមួយនោះ one day

សម័យថ្មី modern times, recent times

សម័យដំបូង in the beginning, the earliest times
សម័យមុនអង្គរ pre-Angkorian period

សម័យមុនៗ earlier times, in the past

សម័យអង្គរ Angkor period

សម័យអាណាព្យាបាល the colonial period, the (French) protectorate period
សមរភូមិ /samααrəphuum/ battlefield (Lit)
សមាគម /samaakum/ association, union
សមាជជាតិ /samaac-ciət/ National Congress
សមាជិក /samaacɨk/ member (of a club, society, etc.)
សមាទាន concentration, meditation

សមាធិ concentration, meditation

សមិទ្ធិ /samətthiq/ achievements, accomplishments
សមុទ្រ /səmot/ sea, ocean

សម្គម frail, skinny; skinny person

សម្គាល់ to point out, indicate; to understand (that), agree (that); sign, indication, symbol; knowledge, familiarity (with)
សម្ងាត់ secret, confidential

សម្ងំ (= សំងំ ) be still, stay quiet

សម្ដេច /sɑmdac/ royal title: Prince

សម្ដេចចៅហ្វា title for a high-ranking prince

សម្ដេចព្រះបរមរាជារាមាធិបតី title for King Chan Raja

សម្ដេចព្រះបិតុលា royal uncle

សម្ដេចព្រះភាគិនេយ្យា /-pheə̆qkineeyoo/ royal nephew

សម្ដេចព្រះមហាក្សត្រិយានីជាអម្ចាស់ជីវិតលើត្បូង Her Royal Highness the Queen

សម្ដេចលីលា name of a poetic style used in the Ream-kei

សម្ដេចឪ Royal Father (term of affection for Prince Sihanouk)

សម្ដែង to show, demonstrate; to perform, show off, posture; to say, declare

សម្មាយ /sɑmmətiəy/ ordinary, common, general

សម្នាក់ (=សំណាក់)

សម្បក peel, skin, bark

សម្បត្តិ /sɑmbat/ possessions, wealth

សម្បទា /sɑmpatiə/ attribute, natural gift

សម្បុរ /sɑmbao ~ sɑmbol/ complexion, color

សម្បុរសម្បក color, complexion (Coll)

សម្បូរ, សម្បូណ៌, សម្បូរណ៌, សំបូរណ៌ /sɑmbou/ complete, plentiful, full, rich

សម្បូរណ៌សប្បាយ affluent

សម្បូណ៌ាញ្ញាសិទ្ធិរាជ /sɑmbourənaacñaa-sətthiriəc/ absolute monarchy

សម្បើម grand, awesome, impressive

សម្ពង្ស /sɑmpŭəŋ/ formula for predicting conjugal success

សម្ពន្ធ /sɑmpŏən/ tie, relationship, alliance

សម្ពាយ shoulder-bag

សម្ពោធ to dedicate, inaugurate

សម្ភារ /sɑmphiə/ accumulation of merit; to accumulate merit

សម្ភារភ្លឹក /sɑmphiə-plɨk/ magical formula

សម្ភារៈ /sɑmphiəreə̆q/ things, goods, provisions, merchandise

សម្រប to reconcile, to agree

សម្រស់ charm

សម្រាក to rest, relax, take a break

សម្រាន្ត to sleep (Eleg)

សម្រាប់ for the purpose of

សម្រាប់ set, suit

សម្រាយ translated from Pali or Sanskrit, in the vernacular

សម្រាល to lighten, relieve

សម្រាលញានកូនប្រុស to give birth to a boy

សម្រិទ្ធិ (=សំរិទ្ធិ) success, achievement

សម្រឹង to ponder in silence, be pensive

សម្រុះសម្រួល to conciliate, appease, reconcile

សម្រួល to ease, make easy, make comfortable, facilitate

សម្រេច /sɑmrac/ to settle, decide, resolve; to achieve; to finish, fulfill

សម្រេចការ to be over, come to an end, conclude

សម្រេចព្រះនគរ gain accession to the throne (Arch)

សម្រេចសង្ខារ put an end to his life

សម្រែក yell, shout, scream (n)

សម្ល /sɑmlɑɑ/ stew, thick soup

សម្លម្ជូរ pungent stew

សម្លក់ to stare at, scowl at

សម្លប to fold, bring together

សម្លាញ់ friend

សម្លាញ់ beloved

សម្លាប់ to kill

សម្លាប់ខ្លួន to commit suicide

សម្លឹង to stare (at)

សម្លុត to threaten

សម្លៀក clothing worn below the waist

សម្លៀកបំពាក់ clothes, clothing

សម្លេង voice, sound

សម្អាត to clean (tv)

សយនដ្ឋាន /sayyαnnəthaan/ dormitory

សយនា /sayyənaa/ bed, sleeping place (Lit)

សរ /sαα/ arrow (Lit)

សរកាយសិទ្ធិ magical arrow

សរពេជ្ញ /sarəpɨc/ the one who knows all (i.e. the Buddha)

សរសើរ /sαsaə, təsaə/ to praise, flatter

សរសើរហេមន្តមាស 'In Praise of Winter', a romantic poem ascribed to King Sri Dhammaraja

សរសេរ /sαsei, təsei/ to write

សរសៃ /sαsay, təsay/ vein, thread; specifier for threads, strings, slender sticks

សរសៃ (=ត្រសៃ) a kind of turtle

សរសៃឡើង veins stick out, veins protrude

សរិល /saqrəl/ body, oneself (Lit)

សរីរៈ /sərəyreə̆q/ body (Lit)

សល់ to remain, be left over; remains

សល់ many, in abundance, extremely

សល់ at, on, upon

សល់ស្រី exceeding all other women

សល់ទ័ល់ involved, attached (i.e. to this life, to worldly concerns)

សវនា /sawəniə/ to listen; ears (Lit)

សសរ pillar, post, column

សសាត់ (=រសាត់) to float along

សសិត to preen, to trim or dress the feathers with the beak

សសិត a kind of sharp-bladed grass

សសូល (=ត្រសូល) gently rounded

សសៀរ to skirt, go carefully along the edge, sidle along the edge of

សស្ត្រាវុធ /sattraawut/ weapons

សស្រាក់ to be dripping, soaked

សស្រាញ់ vigorously, with abandon

សរស្រាក profusely

សហករណ៍ /sahaqkaa/ cooperative (organization)

សហករណ៍សាខា branch cooperative

សហការី /səhaqkaarəy/ colleague, associate

សហជីវិន /səhaqciiwɨn/ comrade (a general title used especially with members of the Sangkum Reastr Niyum)

សហប្រជាជាតិ /səhaq-prαciəciət/ United Nations

សហប្រតិបត្តិការ /səhaq-prαtebat-kaa/ cooperation, cooperative effort

សហរដ្ឋ /sahaqroə̆t/ union; the United States

សហរដ្ឋអាមេរិក /sahaqroə̆t-qaamerɨc/ United States of America

សហឹស bold, fierce, savage

សហស្សកុមារ /sahahskomaa/ Sahassakumāra, Rāvana's youngest son

សហាយ lover; to have an affair

សា to retrace, redo, recommence, repeat; to tell one's story, recount past misfortunes

សាស័ព្ទ to speak, say (Lit)

សាជាថ្មី anew, again

សាកល្បង to test, try, experiment

សាកសួរ to inquire, ask, interrogate

សាកសួរសុខទុក្ខ to inquire about the wellbeing of

សាកល /saakαl/ universal, general

សាកលលោក /saakαl-look/ the world, universe

សាកលវិទ្យាល័យ /saakαl-wɨttyiəlay/ university

សាកលវិទ្យាល័យភូមិន្ទវិចិត្រសិល្បៈ Royal University of Fine Arts

សាខា spread out, bushy; branch, limb, division

សាគរ ocean, sea (Lit)

សាង to build (Lit)

សាង...ទុកទៅ established, set down, prescribed

សាងវេរី create negative karma

សាច់ flesh, meat; texture; kin

សាច់ក្រក sausage

សាច់គោ beef

សាច់ជ្រូក pork

សាច់ជ្រូកខ្វៃ roast pork

សាច់ឈាម complexion (lit: flesh and blood)

សាច់ឈើ inner flesh, core (of a tree)

សាច់ដុំ muscle

សាច់ទា duck meat

សាច់មាន់ chicken meat

សាច់រឿង facts, plot, subject matter

សាត់ (=រសាត់) to drift off, float away

សាទរ to empathize with, rejoice with

សាធារណ /saathiərənaq/ public

សាធារណការ /saathiərənaqkaa/ public works

សាធារណរដ្ឋ /saathiərənaqroə̆t/ republic

សាធារណរដ្ឋនិយម republicanism

សាធុ /saathuq, saathuup/ fine, so be it, amen (Buddhism)

សាធុការ blessing, good wishes

សាធុជន /saathucuə̆n/ good people

សាន់វ៉ាន់ (=សាន់វ៉ាន់) /san-wan/ to be in the way, to impede

សាន្ត peaceful, tranquil, quiet

ស៊ាន buzzing, humming

សាប to broadcast, spread, sow

សាប bland; fresh (not salty); weak, diluted

សាប sable

សាបព្រោះ to spread, broadcast

សាបសូន្យ to die out, become extinct, disappear, be eliminated

សាប៊ូ soap

សាមគ្គី /saaməkii/ unity, togetherness, affection; to unite

សាមគ្គីសាមគ្គា /saaməkii-saaməkiə/ unity, togetherness, affection; to unite

សាមញ្ញ /saamañ/ common, ordinary

សាមណេរ /saamənei/ novice monk, student monk

សាមសិប thirty

សាមាន្យ (=សាមញ្ញ) low, evil, common

សាមីខ្លួន /saaməy-kluən/ the person in question; himself, herself, themselves

សាមីខ្លួនខាងស្រី bride (lit: female member of the bridal couple)

សាយ to spread, diffuse, suffuse

សារ letter, message (Roy)

សារ /saareə̆q/ cause, basis, reason

សារថី driver (of a carriage)

សារផាត់ /saarəphat/ all kinds, everything

សារពត៌មាន /saa-poədɑmiən/ news, newspaper; the press

សារពើ (=ទាំងអស់) /saarəpəə/ all, everything

សារពើភាពផង the whole scene, panoply

សារពេជ្ញ (=សព្វញ្ញូ) /saarəpɨc/ the enlightened one (Buddha)

សារភាព /saarəphiəp/ to confess

សារសង /saa-sɑɑŋ/ to converse; to answer

សារ-សរ Sar Sor (pers. n.)

សារៈសំខាន់ /saareə̆q-sɑmkhan/ importance, matters of importance

សារាចរ /saraacɑɑ/ circular, memo

សារាយ seaweed

សារិកា blackbird

សាល hall (Fr. salle)

សាលសន្និសីទចតុមុខ Cattomuk Conference Hall

សាលា school, hall, pavilion

សាលាជំនុំ court

សាលាដំបូង provincial supreme court

សាលាទេវរុក្ខ a small square pavilion built for the forest spirit

សាលាព្រះជ័យចេស្តា Preah Chey Chesda School

សាលារៀន school

សាលាវត្ត pagoda-school

សាលាសិក្សាវត្ត pagoda schools

សាលាសំណាក់ resting place; public hall

សាលាស្រុក district office

សាវ young unmarried girl (Lao)

សាវតារ /saawədaa/ history, record

សាវ៉ា irresolute, fickle

សាសន៍ /saah, sah/ nationality, race

សាសនា /sahsnaa/ religion

សាសនាព្រាហ្មណ៍ /sahsnaa-priəm/ Brahmanism

សាសនាឥស្លាម /sahsnaa-qihslaam/ Islam, the Moslem religion

សាស្ត្រា /sahstraa ~ satraa/ palmleaf manuscript (usually religious)

សាស្ត្រាចារ្យ /sahstraacaa/ professor

សាហស /sahah/ wicked, mean

សាហាវ vicious, mean

សាឡាង ferryboat (Fr. chaland)

សិក្ខាបទ /səkkhaabɑt/ precepts (of the Buddha)

សិក្សា to study, do research; education

សិក្សាធិការ /səksaathikaa/ education (administration)

សិង្ហ /səŋ/ lion

សិត to pour out from a jar

សិតសក់ to comb the hair

សិតា /seedaa/ Sita (Rama's mate)

សិទ្ធិ /sətthiq, səthiq/ right, privilege

សិទ្ធិមនុស្ស human rights

សិន first, before (polite hortatory final particle)

សិន(=២០ ព្យាម ) a distance of about 40 meters

ស៊ិនក្យាង /sɨŋkyaaŋ/ Singkiang

សិនេរុរាជ /səneeruriəc/ (Mt.) Meru

សិរ /sei/ head (Roy)

សិរសា (=សិរសី ) /seirəsaa/ head (Roy)

សិរសី /seirəsəy/ head (Roy)

សិរី /serəy/ beauty, charm, power (an element frequently found in place names)

សិរីវឌ្ឍ /seriiwŏət/ Sirivath (pers. n.)

សិរីសួស្តី /serəy-suəsdəy/ blessing, good fortune

សិរីសោភ័ណ /serəy-saophŏən, siisəphon/ Sisophon (a district in Battambang Province)

សិលា /səylaa/ stone, slab

សិលាចារិក /səylaa-caarək/ stone inscription

សិល្ប /səl/ magic, having magic power

សិល្បៈ /səlləpaq/ art, arts

សិល្បករ /səlləpaqkɑɑ/ artist

សិល្បសាស្ត្រ /səl-saah/ science of magic

សិវ /səywĕəq/ Siva

សិវលិង្គ /səywəlɨŋ/ Siva linga

សិស្ស /səh/ student

សិស្សានុសិស្ស /səhsaanusəh/ students

ស៊ី /sii/ to eat (familiar, or of animals); to use, consume

ស៊ី to win (of the dealer in a card game)

ស៊ីការ attend a wedding banquet

ស៊ីផឹក to eat and drink, to feast

ស៊ីសងគ្នា to contest, challenge, compete (with)

ស៊ីកុងទី Sei Kong Ti (pers. n.)

ស៊ីក្លូ cyclo, pedicab

សីតា (=សិតា , សេតា ) Sita, Rama's mate

ស៊ីបេរី /siibeirii/ Siberia

ស៊ីម៉ង់ត៍ cement

សីមា boundary, border

សីរមាន់ /sei-mŏən/ a variety of rambutan

ស៊ីរ៉ូ syrup (Fr. sirop)

ស៊ីវិល /siiwɨl/ civil, civilian (Fr. civil)

សីល /səl/ precept, principle

សីល /səylaq/ virtue, moral excellence

សីលទាន /səl-tiən/ morality (lit: precepts of charity)
សីលប្រាំ the first five principles (of Buddhist disciples)
សីលសិក្ខា /səl-sekkhaa/ pursuit of virtue
ស៊ីសុវត្ថិ /siisowat/ auspicious, felicitous
ស៊ីសុវត្ថិ Sisovath (king of Cambodia 1904-1927)
សីហ /səyhaq/ lion (Lit)
សឹក war, army; military
សឹក to leave the monkhood
សឹង almost, almost all; surely, almost certainly, precisely, just having, being
សឹងក៏មាន is possible, can happen
សឹងចុះចូលច្រើន subjugated in considerable numbers
សឹងតែ almost, on the point of
សឺងង៉ុកថាញ់ /səɨŋ-ŋok-than/ Son Ngoc Than (a politician)
សឹង្ហ (= សីង្ហ) /səŋ/ lion (Lit)
សឹត (= សិត) to pour
សឹម then, and then
សឹម ៗ slowly
ស៊ឹម-វ៉ា Sim Var (a former Prime Minister of Cambodia)
សុ prefix: good, excellent
ស៊ុកគ្រលុក be involved, implicated; disorganized, involved, haphazard
សុកល /sokɑl/ happy, cheerful
សុក្រទិន /sokkrətɨn/ Friday; Venus
សុក្រិតភាព /sokrəttəphiəp/ perfection, flawlessness, ideal appearance
សុខ to be healthy, happy; good health, happiness
សុខចិត្ត to be willing (to), agree (to)
សុខទុក្ខ good [luck] and bad, happiness and sorrow; fate, life
សុខភាព /sokkəphiəp/ health
សុខសប្បាយ to be well and happy
សុខសាន្តត្រាណ peaceful, quiet, at peace
សុខា health, wellbeing
សុខាភិបាល health (administration)
សុខោទ័យ /sokhaotɨy/ Sukhothai
សុគត /sokŭət/ to die (Roy, Clergy)
សុគ្រីព /sukrɨp/ Sugriva, a monkey king
សុចរិត /soccərət/ honest, moral, just
សុជាតា name of one of Indra's wives
សុដន់ breast (Roy)
សុទ្ធ /sot/ pure; all, completely; exactly, just like
សុទ្ធតែ exclusively, all without exception
សុទ្ធសាធ /sot-saat/ pure, unmitigated; really, truly
សុន្ទរ good, excellent, pleasing to the ear
សុន្ទទាន /son-tiən/ willing charity, unbegrudged gift
សុន្ទរកថា /sontərēəqkəthaa/ speech, address
សុបិន dream (n., Lit)
សុបិនកុមារ main character of the story of the same name
សុពណ៌ /sopɔə/ gold (Lit)
សុភមង្គល /sophēəq-mŭəŋkŭəl/ good fortune, prosperity and happiness
សុភា sage, wiseman, magistrate
សុភាទន្សាយ The Wise Hare
សុភាព polite, kind, gentle, good
សុភាពរាបសារ polite, gentle, well-mannered
សុមេរុ (Mt.) Meru
សុរង់ neck (Roy)
សុរភី fragrance, perfume
សុរា liquor
សុរាគារ distillery
សុរិយា /soriyaa/ sun (Lit)
សុរិល (= សរិល) body (Roy)
សុរិលភក្ត្រពិនរេកត extremely fair of face and form
សុរ្យកាន្ត /sourəkaan/ sunstone
សុវណ្ណ /sowan/ gold (Lit)

សុវណ្ណគត /sowannəkŭət/ to die (Roy)

សុវណ្ណបុប្ផ (= ផ្កាមាស) /sowannəbopphaa/ gold flower tribute

សុវណ្ណភូមិ /sowannəphuum/ Suvarnabhumi (Golden Land; ancient name of Indianized Southeast Asia)

សុវណ្ណរេខា one of Preah Chinavong's wives

សុវណ្ណវង្ស /sowannəwŭəŋ/ name of Preah Chinavong's father

សុវណ្ណហង្ស /sowannəhɑŋ/ golden swan

សុវត្ថិភាព /sowattəphiəp/ safety, good health

សុសសព្វសាយ all over, everywhere

សុទ្យាទិព្យ (= សុរាល័យ) heaven, abode of the angels

ស៊ូ to be determined, persistent; would rather, would sooner

ស៊ូស្លាប់ would rather die

សូក to bribe, entice with gifts

សូគ្រីព (= សុគ្រីព) Sugriva, a monkey king

សូត្រ /sout/ to recite; the Sutra (a section of the Tripitaka)

សូត្រ /sout/ silk

សូត្រមន្ត /sout-mŭən/ to say prayers, recite scriptures, recite incantations

សូន to mold, shape

សូន្យ /soun/ zero; absent, lacking

សូន្យសព្ទ (= សព្ទសូន្យ) /sɑp-soun/ to die out, be extinguished, completely silent

សូន្យសុង completely (disappeared), completely (gone out)

សូន្យសោះ (= សោះសូន្យ) to die out

សូផាត /souphaat, sophaat/ Sophat, hero of the novel by the same name, by Rim-Kin

សូភាព (= សុភាព) gentle, polite

សូភាពរាបទាប meek, polite, gentle

សូម polite auxiliary: to beg to; please...

សូមឆុតជូចសច្ចា please answer my prayers, fulfill my request

សូមជំរាប [I] beg to inform..., Dear...

សូមជំរាបមក...សូមទានជ្រាប Dear... (stylized salutation used in formal letters)

សូមជ្រាបថា bear in mind that (lit: please understand that)

សូមទានជ្រាប please be advised

សូមទានមេត្តាប្រោស please be good enough to, do [me] the favor of

សូមទោស to ask forgiveness; I'm sorry, excuse me

សូមទ្រង់ជ្រាប please know, please be advised (to royalty)

សូមទ្រង់ព្រះមេត្តាប្រោស polite formula used in addressing royalty: If it please your Majesty

សូមលា goodby

សូមស្លេះត្រឹមនេះសិន let me digress for a moment

សូម្បី although, even if, if; to the extent of, to the extent that

សូម្បីតែ even

សូយា Soya (Sophat's mother)

សូរ noise, sound

សូរសព្ទ /sou-sap/ noise, sound; to make a noise

សូរសម្លេង voice, noise, sound (of a voice)

សូរង /sourŭəŋ/ neck (Roy)

សូរភី (= សោភី) beautiful

សូរេច /sorac/ to conclude, bring to a close

សូរ្យ /sou, souriyeəq/ Surya (a Hindu god); the sun (Lit)

សូវ rather, it is better to

សូវ...កុំឱ្យ... rather...than...

សូវស្តួចកុំឱ្យដាច់ it's better to have a little than nothing at all

សួ to walk (a rope, wire, branch, etc.)

សួគ៌ /suə/ heaven

សួគ៌នាយ heaven, the world beyond

សួគ៌ា (= សួគ៌) /suəkiə/ heaven

សួគ៌ាល័យ /suəkiəlay/ heaven

សួន garden

សួន Suon (name of Sophat's father)

សួនកុមារ playground, children's park

សួនច្បារ yard, decorative garden

សួនសត្វ /suən-sat/ zoo

សួយ tribute (material)

សួយសារ tribute (material)

សួយសារអាករ financial or material tribute

សួរ to ask, inquire; to visit

សួរដោយរាប់អាន to inquire politely

សួរឈ្លេច to press for an answer

សួរសង to ask again

សួរសៀតសឹក to interrogate, pry into

សួស Suos (pers. n.)

សួស្ដិ៍ (= សួស្ដី) /suə/ blessed, felicitous (having those qualities which produce health, happiness, and prosperity)

សួស្ដី /suə-sdəy/ greetings, salutations (Formal); to prosper, have health, happiness, and prosperity

សើច to laugh

ស៊ើប to investigate

ស៊ើបសួរ to investigate, to inquire around

សើរើ to probe deeply, get to the bottom (of something)

សៀង sound, voice

សៀត to insert, stick in, wedge apart, pry apart

សៀម Thailand; Thai

សៀមរាប Siemreap (Province)

សៀរ to proceed cautiously or stealthily, to skirt quietly

សៀវសៀត slide by, slide around, skirt

សៀវភៅ book(s)

សៀវភៅមើល books to read

សៀវភៅសរសេរ notebook

សេក parrot

សេចក្ដី /səc-kdəy/ subject, affair, composition; matter of, quality of (forms abstract noun compounds with verbs)

សេចក្ដីក្នុងសំបុត្រ contents of the letter

សេចក្ដីគោរពខ្លាច respect, veneration

សេចក្ដីខិតខំ hard work, effort

សេចក្ដីខ្វះខាត lack, need, deficiency

សេចក្ដីគោរព respect, honor

សេចក្ដីចំរើន prosperity, success

សេចក្ដីឈ្នានីស malice, evil intentions, ill-wishing

សេចក្ដីតប revenge, retaliation, response

សេចក្ដីទាល់ក្រ poverty, misery

សេចក្ដីទាស់ objectionable or inappropriate things

សេចក្ដីទុកចិត្ត confidence, consent

សេចក្ដីនាំផ្លូវ guide, manual

សេចក្ដីប្រាថ្នា desire, wish; intention, design

សេចក្ដីពិត truth

សេចក្ដីព្យាយាម effort, endurance, perseverance

សេចក្ដីព្រហើនភ្លើន disrespect, arrogance

សេចក្ដីរាយការណ៍ report (n)

សេចក្ដីរុងរឿង success, prosperity

សេចក្ដីរំភើប emotion, excitement

សេចក្ដីសង្កេត observation, opinion

សេចក្ដីសង្ស័យ doubt, suspicion

សេចក្ដីសុខ peace, tranquillity

សេចក្ដីស្លាប់ death

សេចក្ដីអធិប្បាយ composition, elaboration, development (of theme)

សេចគ្រេច substance, essence, hidden meaning

សេដា (= ស៊ែដា) persimmon tree

សេដ្ឋកិច្ច /saettəkəc/ economics, economy

សេដ្ឋា /setthaa/ extraordinary, great

សេដ្ឋី /saetthəy/ wealthy merchant, mandarin, person of high estate

សេន cent

សេនា commander, officer; army, military

សេនាធិបតី commander (higher than /seinaa/)

សេនាបតីទាំង ៤ សម្រាប់ commander of all four ministries: Army, Navy, Interior, and Justice

សេនាយោធាមាត្យ /seinaayoothiəmiət/

king's commanders and officials

សេនីយ៍ /seinəy/ troops, army

សេពសប្បាយ partake of [carnal] pleasure

សេព /saep/ to partake of, indulge in; associate with

សេពគប់ /saep-kup/ associate with, hang around with

សេពចំណង់ to gratify desire

សេពកាមា to have sex, to fornicate

សេយ្យាសន៍ /sayyiəh/ sleep (n., Roy)

សេរី /seirəy/ free

សេរីការ /seirəykaa/ liberation

សេរីភាព /seirəyphiəp/ freedom

សេសសល់ /saeh-sɑl/ remaining, left-over

សេះ /seh/ horse

សេះចងអាន horse with saddle

សែ patronym, lineage (Chinese)

សែស្រឡាយ lineage

សែក to recite (a magic formula), to incant

សែង to carry between two persons

សែង ray, gleam, light (of the sun) (Lit)

សែន 100,000

សែន extremely, highly

សែន to make a propitiatory offer-in to spirits

សែនព្រេន to make an offering to spirits, to make a propitiatory offering

សែនមនោរម្យ /saen mənoorum/ Sen Monorom (capital of Mondulkiri Province)

ស៊ែម to put a decorative border on, embellish around the edges

សែសិប forty

សៃយ៉ាំ /sayyam/ dancing in time to drum beats

សោក to grieve, mourn

សោកសៅ to grieve

សោកាល័យ (=សោក + អាល័យ ) to grieve bitterly

សោច rationality, sense, reason

សោត whereas, while

សោតសល់ however, to whatever extent

សោតសឹង inevitably

សោភ័ណ /saophŏən/ beautiful; beauty

សោភ័ណភាព /saophŏənnəphiəp/ beauty

សោភា beautiful (Lit)

សោភី beautiful (Lit)

សោមនស្ស /saomənŏəh/ pleased, delighted; pleasure, delight

សោយ to eat (Roy)

សោយរាជ្យ to reign, to rule

សោយសោក to grieve

សោយអារម្មណ៍ /saoy-qaarɑm/ to enjoy feelings, have conscious experiences

សោរ lock (n)

សោរទិន /saorətɨn/ Saturday; Saturn (?)

សោហ៊ុយ money to defray expenses (of travel, etc.)

សោឡស /saolɑh/ sixteen (Lit)

សោះ after negatives: (not) at all

សោះ so as not to have to, to get rid of, obviate the necessity of; finally: not at all

សោះតែខាន minimally, just as a formality

សោះនឹង so not to

សោះសា completely, all over the place

សោះសូន្យ in vain, futile, to no purpose

សោះឡើយ (not) at all (after negatives)

សៅហ្មង /sao-mɑɑŋ/ unclean, impure, offensive

សុំ to ask for, request

សុំខ្លួន to volunteer

សុំតម្លៃ to bargain

សំកាំង to float, glide, soar

សំខាន់ important, crucial

សំខាន់បំផុត the most important; most importantly

សំគម (= សម្គម) frail, skinny; skinny person

សំគាល់ to point out, indicate; to understand (that), agree (that); sign, symbol, indication; knowledge, familiarity (with)

សំងំ be still, stay quiet (neither speaking nor moving)

សំច័យ (= សំចៃ) to save, be frugal

សំចៃ to save, be frugal

សំញែង to show off (one's power, wealth, etc.)

សំដី speech, words

សំដីសំដៅ speech, manner of speech (Coll)

សំដែង to show, demonstrate; to perform, display; to show off, posture; to say, declare

សំដែងគំនិត to express one's ideas

សំដៅ toward, directly toward

សំណង recompense, repayment

សំណាក់ to rest, stay temporarily, stay over; refuge, shelter, place to stay

សំណាក់អាស្រ័យ to stay temporarily

សំណាខម a style of poetic meter used in the Ream-Kei

សំណាង luck, fortune, chance

សំណាញ់ a conical fishing net

សំណាត់ driftwood

សំណើករបើ if, in the event that

សំណើច laughter

សំណេះ to reminisce, exchange fond memories

សំណេះសំណាល to exchange fond memories, reminisce

សំណៅ printer's proofs

សំណុំ small wrapped package

សំទៀរ (= សំទារ) to scream, yell, roar (Arch)

សំទូន model, figure, sculpture

សំនៀង sound, acoustic impression

សំបក bark, skin, peel, shell

សំបុក nest

សំបុត្រ /sɑmbot/ letter, ticket

សំបុត្រសំគាល់ identification card

សំបួងស្រួង to conjure, summon

សំបូរណ៌ (= សម្បូណ៌) /sɑmbou/ complete, plentiful, full, rich

សំប៉ាន sampan, skiff

សំបើម grand, awesome, impressive

សំពង to club, beat with a club

សំពត់ Cambodian-style sarong; cloth, dry goods

សំពត់ចងក្បិន sarong caught up in a roll at the back

សំពត់ផាមួង plain (unpatterned) silk sarong

សំពត់ហូល a variegated silk sarong

សំពៅ sailing vessel (sea-going)

សំពះ to greet, salute with palms together

សំពះព្រះខែ Salutation to the Moon (a ceremony)

សំពះលា to bow out, bow and take leave

សំពះសួរ to greet (with palms joined)

សំយុង hang down, point down; downward

សំយ៉ែ name of a former province

សំយោគសញ្ញា /sɑnyook-saññaa/ the symbol ័

សំរាក (= សម្រាក) to rest, relax, take a break

សំរាកកំលាំង to rest, recuperate

សំរាន្ត (= សម្រាន្ត) to sleep (Eleg)

សំរុក to thrust

សំរើប to excite sexually (tv)

សំរេច (= សម្រេច) /sɑmrac/ to settle, decide, resolve; to succeed, achieve; complete

សំរែ Samré (a tribal group)

សំរែក (= សម្រែក) cry, shout, scream (n)

សំរោងទង a former province

សំលៀក (=សម្លៀក) clothing worn below the waist
សំលៀកបំពាក់ clothing

សំស្ក្រឹត /sɑŋskrət/ Sanskrit

សំឡក់ (=សម្លក់) to look sternly at, sccwl at
សំឡាញ់ (=សម្លាញ់) friend

សំឡាប់ (=សម្លាប់) to kill

សំឡឹង (=សម្លឹង) to stare

សំឡុត (=សម្លុត) to threaten

សំឡេង (=សម្លេង) sound, voice

សំអាង to decorate, adorn; embellishment, decoration
សំអាង to rely on, count on, depend on; model, proof, evidence
សំអាត to clean (tv)

សាំ riddled with marks, slashes, or cuts
ស៊ាំៗ over and over, repeatedly
ស៊ាសួរ to nag, ask repeatedly
សះ to heal, recover (iv)

សះស្បើយ to heal, get better, recover

ស្កក stunted, underdeveloped

ស្កន្ធ /skan/ Skanda (a Hindu god)

ស្កប់ satiated, content (with food or sleep); to have slept well, be well-rested
ស្កប់ស្កល់ satiated, content; prosperous, having enough of everything

ស្ករ sugar

ស្ករក្រហម brown sugar

ស្ករគ្រាប់ candies

ស្ករស white sugar, processed sugar

ស្កល់ satiated, content, satisfied

ស្កា a kind of chess game

ស្កាត់ to intercept

ស្កាត់មុខ across the path of, cutting off the advance of
ស្កឹមស្កៃ (=ស្គឹមស្គៃ) huge, immense

ស្កុងស្កល់ bright, white

ស្កូវ to be gray (of hair)

ស្កាំ to be satisfied, sated, fulfilled
ស្គន់ a kind of waterlily

ស្គម thin, slender, skinny

ស្គាល់ to know, be acquainted with, recognize
ស្គុះ a kind of waterlily

ស្គោក pithy, dried out, dessicated

ស្គាំងស្គម thin, emaciated

ស្ងប់ calm, becalmed

ស្ងាច intensifier for white

ស្ងាត់ quiet, calm; isolated, lonely (because no one around to make noise)
ស្ងួត dry (of a surface not normally wet)
ស្ងួន to pamper, treat tenderly, caress; pampered, innocent; My Beloved, My Innocent One
ស្ងួន parsimonious, stingy

ស្ងួនភ្ងា to pamper, indulge, adulate

ស្ងួនវិវរល័ក្ខណ៍ My Innocent One

ស្ងើច to wonder at, admire, be impressed by
ស្ងៀម quiet (of both sound and motion)

ស្ងោរ to boil (usually with meat); boiled (meat) soup
ស្ញប់ស្ញែង astonished, awed

ស្ញាញ bared, exposed, gleaming

ស្ញិញ with lips drawn back showing the teeth
ស្ញិញស្ញាញ grimacing with the teeth bared
ស្ញេញ /sñəñ/ to grimace, draw the lips back
ស្ញែង to fear, stand in awe of, dread

ស្ដម្ភ /sdɑm/ pillar (Lit)

ស្ដាប់ to listen, obey

ស្ដាប់ការ to scout, spy, eavesdrop

ស្ដាយ to regret, be sorry for

ស្ដាយក្រោយ to regret afterwards

ស្ដាយជីវិត regret the loss of life

ស្ដាយតែ [I] especially regret [that]

ស្ដី to say, to speak; to blame, criticize, scold
ស្ដី a kind of large tree

ស្ដីបន្ទោស to scold, blame

ស្ដីទី acting, temporary

ស្ដីលើ to blame, criticize

ស្ដីឱ្យ to scold, blame

ស្ដឹងស្ដូក (= ស្ដូកស្ដឹង) to lie motionless

ស្ដុកស្ដម /sdok-sdɑm/ impressive, grand

ស្ដុកស្ដុរ /sdok-sdao/ a kind of large tree
ស្ដូក extended, stretched out

ស្ដួច thin; worn, tattered

ស្ដួចស្ដើង minute, very little, insignificant
ស្ដើង thin, slight

ស្ដេច /sdac/ king; frequently precedes verbs describing royal action, in which use it is not clear whether it is an auxiliary or a royal pronoun
ស្ដេចកន a usurper, king of Cambodia 1512-1525
ស្ដេចស្រី queen (Coll)

ស្ដែង clearly; clear; real, essential, important; power
ស្ដែងស្ដេច the king, the person of the king, the king himself
ស្ដៅ a tree with edible leaves

ស្ត្រី /sətrəy/ lady (Eleg)

ស្ថាន /sthaan, thaan/ place, stage

ស្ថាននរក /thaan-nɔrŭəq/ hell

ស្ថានភាព /sthaan-phiəp/ situation

ស្ថានលោក this world, the temporal world
ស្ថានសួគ៌ /thaan-suə/ heaven, paradise

ស្ថានីយ /sthaanii/ station

ស្ថាបនា /sthaapənaa/ to build, establish

ស្ថាពរ /sthaapɔɔ/ solid, firm, permanent
ស្ថិត /sthət, thət/ to place; be situated; to last, stay, endure
ស្ថិតស្ថេរ /thət-thei/ stable, durable, lasting
ស្ថិតស្ថេរចិរកាល permanent, stable, lasting
ស្ទក់ swollen and lifeless

ស្ទា to sidle back and forth evasively, dodge back and forth
ស្ទាស្ទប់ to crouch and move from side to side in anticipation of an attack
ស្ទាក់ to intercept, interrupt

ស្ទាក់ស្ទើរ barely, almost, not quite, semi-
ស្ទាញស្ទុះ (= ស្ទុះ) to jump up, bound

ស្ទាត់ skilled (at)

ស្ទាប to touch, caress

ស្ទឹង river, tributary, stream

ស្ទុះ to jump up

ស្ទុះលេចលរ to leap and feint

ស្ទុយ everted, pouting, turned outward

ស្ទូង to transplant, set out (rice)

ស្ទូច to fish (with a hook and line)

ស្ទួយ to hold aloft on the palm of the hand
ស្ទើត curved upward, protruding upward, up-thrust, thrusting upward (of breasts, buttucks, etc.)
ស្ទើរ insufficient, incomplete, not quite enough
ស្ទើរ (= ស្ទើរស្ទាក់) to hesitate

ស្ទើរតែ on the point of, almost

ស្ទើរតែនឹងស្លាប់ on the point of dying

ស្ទៀង Stieng (name of a tribal group)

ស្ទះ to block, obstruct, close off

ស្នង replacement, succession; replacing, in place of
ស្នង back, reciprocally, in reply

ស្នា crossbow

ស្នាក់ to stay, stop over

ស្នាច a hollowed-out log or bamboo, used for scooping water, feeding pigs, etc.

ស្នាដៃ work, product, accomplishment (of a given person)

ស្នាព្រះហស្ត /snaa-preə̆h-hŏəh/ royal work, royal achievement

ស្នាម trace, mark, print

ស្នាលស្និទ្ធ (=ស្និទ្ធស្នាល)

ស្និទ្ធស្នាល /snət-snaal/ close, intimate

ស្នឹង tether-stake

ស្នូក turtle-shell

ស្នូល axle

ស្នៀត trick, strategem; wedge, insert

ស្នេហ៍ /snae/ love

ស្នេហ៍ស្នង be deeply in love

ស្នេហ៍ស្នាល to love (Poetic)

ស្នេហ៍ស្និទ្ធ to be deeply in love

ស្នេហា /snaehaa/ to love; love

ស្នែង horn (of an animal); wind instrument made of animal horn

ស្នែង a carrying pole for two people

ស្នំ concubine, female royal attendant

ស្នំឯក ranking concubine

ស្បង់ monk's robes

ស្បង្កើច /sbaŋkac/ an aquatic plant

ស្បថ /sbat/ to swear, promise

ស្បាត់ clearly, obviously, plainly (usually occurs as an intensifier)

ស្បិត care to, concerned with, take an interest in

ស្បូវ thatching grass

ស្បើម to be amazed at, impressed by, stand in awe of, intimidated by

ស្បើយ to abate, slacken, subside, diminish

ស្បៀង provisions, food, stores

ស្បៃ loosely-woven cloth, diaphanous cloth, muslin

ស្បែក skin; leather

ស្បែកជើង shoes

ស្ពាន bridge

ស្ពានមេត្រី to form an alliance, ally with

ស្ពានយមរាជ /spiən-yumməriəc/ name of a bridge

ស្ពាយ to carry suspended from the shoulder

ស្ម័គ្រ /smaq/ to be devoted or attach-ed (to); to volunteer

ស្ម័គ្រចិត្ត to volunteer

ស្ម័គ្របក្សពួក /smaq-paq-puəq/ supporter, partisan

ស្ម័គ្រស្មាន willingly, voluntarily

ស្ម័គ្រស្មោះ sincere, devoted; to love, accept, be amenable to

ស្មសាន jungle, deep forest

ស្មា shoulder

ស្មាច់ a tree whose resin is used for torches

ស្មាន to guess, assume, consider

ស្មាន់ a kind of deer

ស្មារតី /smaarədəy/ attention, consciousness, presence of mind

ស្មី a kind of tree with edible leaves

ស្មឹង hermit; spiritual medium

ស្មុគស្មាញ complex, confused

ស្មូត្រ to chant, sing (religious texts)

ស្មូម beggar

ស្មើ to be equal, even

ស្មៀន clerk, secretary

ស្មោញ a kind of fishing bird

ស្មែ a tree whose roots attract sea-crabs

ស្មោះ honest, sincere

ស្មោះចំពោះ directly, implicitly; faithfully

ស្មោះត្រង់ honest, sincere, faithful

ស្មោះស្ម័គ្រ sincere, heartfelt

ស្មោះសរ sincere pleasure, genuine cordiality; sincerely, genuinely

ស្មោះស្មាន ready, willing, agreeable (to)

ស្មៅ grass, hay

ស្មៅព្រៅ a kind of grass

សៀមប្រទេស Siam

ស្រះ /sraq/ vowel

ស្រក to recede (of water)

ស្រក់ to drip

ស្រក់ទឹកភ្នែកប្រេចាក to burst into tears

ស្រកា scales (of a fish); to scale (a fish)

ស្រកី gill

ស្រគំ a tree with edible fruit

ស្រគាំ dark brown

ស្រង់ to taste, hear, smell, partake of; to take out, extract; to bathe (Roy, Clergy)

ស្រងាក supine, motionless, in suspended animation

ស្រងាត់ quiet, tranquil; deep, rich (of color)

ស្រងូត sad, solemn

ស្រងូតស្រងាត់ sad, solemn, melancholic

ស្រដី (=ស្ដី) to say, speak (Lit)

ស្រដី (=ស្រដីឲ្យ, ស្ដីឲ្យ ) to blame, to scold

ស្រដីដើម (=និយាយដើម) to talk about (critically), to ridicule

ស្រដីឲ្យស្រួលស្រេច speak moderately, be soft-spoken, reserved in one's speech

ស្រដៀងនឹង just like

ស្រណុក comfortable, convenient, easy

ស្រណោះ to miss, remember nostalgically

ស្រណោះពេកណាស់ how amusing!, how interesting!(Idiom)

ស្រទប bark (of the banana tree)

ស្រទាង to stretch out, extend, spread

ស្រទាប់ petal; layer, stratum

ស្រទំ dark, overcast

ស្រប parallel (with), in agreement (with)

ស្រប់ to soak

ស្រប់ (=ស្រព) to sprinkle or splash water on the body

ស្របក់ moment, instant

ស្រញាល same, equal (with regard to time or age)

ស្រញាលគ្នានឹង same age as

ស្រញ៉ប flat, prostrate

ស្រពោន wilted, withered

ស្រមុក to snore

ស្រមូវ bushy

ស្រមេះៗ dejected, resigned

ស្រមៃ to recall to mind, visualize a previous experience

ស្រមៃឃើញ to see as in a dream, see a mirage, have a hallucination

ស្រមោច (small red) ant

ស្រមោល shadow

ស្រយង់ to be numb, asleep (of a limb)

ស្រយាល late; distant, remote

ស្រយុត to sag, droop, collapse, feel enervated

ស្រល់ pine tree, conifer

ស្រលូត slim, slender

ស្រលៀង cross-eyed

ស្រវឹង drunk, dizzy, intoxicated

ស្រវឹងមួន really drunk

ស្រស់ fresh; charming, attractive

ស្រស់ស្រូប to eat something, have a snack

ស្រស់ស្រី beautiful

ស្រឡប់ (=សន្លប់) to faint

ស្រឡប់ dusk, twilight

ស្រឡាញ់ to love, to like

ស្រឡាញ់ស្ងួនភ្ងា to cherish, love tenderly

ស្រឡិត dwarf fig tree

ស្រឡី a kind of tree

ស្រឡៀង cross-eyed

ស្រឡៅ a hardwood tree

ស្រឡះ clear, cleared up; completely

ស្រា whisky, alcohol, alcoholic beverage

ស្រាតំណើបខ្មៅ black-rice whisky

ស្រាទឹកត្នោត palm-sugar beer

ស្រាក to slacken, slow down, lessen, abate

ស្រាកស្រាន្ត to be abated, relieved

ស្រាង opaque

ស្រាងសុរិយា to be just light, light as at pre-dawn

ស្រាត to take off the clothes

ស្រាន្ត to get better, improve

ស្រាប់ /srap/ is a final adverbial whose translation, depending on context, is 'obviously, already, as a matter of fact, since the foregoing is true'; all its meanings include an element of 'obviousness'

ស្រាប់ provisions, accessories

ស្រាប់តែ suddenly, unexpectedly, just

ស្រាយ to untie, unwrap, undo

ស្រាល to be light (in weight, intensity, or seriousness)

ស្រាវ to pull up, draw up

ស្រាស់ to patch, cover, block (with branches

ស្រី woman; feminine, female

ស្រី ៗ girls, women

ស្រីកំដរ bridesmaid

ស្រីក្រមុំ young girl, virgin

ស្រីទេពអប្សរ /srəy-teep-qapsαα/ Apsara, heavenly maiden

ស្រីធម្មរាជា Sri Dhammaraja, king of Cambodia 1627-30

ស្រីបម្រើ female servant

ស្រីពិរាស្ត្រ (Kingdom of) Srībirāstra

ស្រីសុគន្ធបទ /srəy sokŭənthəbαt/ Srey Sokonthor Bat (king of Cambodia 1504-1508)

ស្រីសួស្តី /srəy-suəsdəy/ wellbeing

ស្រុក country, district, village; headword in compounds referring to countries or districts

ស្រុកកំណើត hometown, native village

ស្រុកខ្មែរ Cambodia

ស្រុកស្រែ the country, rural area

ស្រុត to descend, fall from heaven (both morally and physically)

ស្រុប to take cover, go under a tree (of elephants)

ស្រ៊ុប descriptive of a sudden slump

ស្រុះស្រួល to agree

ស្រូត to hurry (Coll)

ស្រូតរូត to hurry (Coll)

ស្រូប to absorb, suck

ស្រូវ paddy, unhusked rice

ស្រូវប្រាំង dry-season rice

ស្រូវវស្សា rainy-season rice

ស្រូវសាលី wheat

ស្រូវសំណាប rice sprouts, seedlings

ស្រួច pointed, sharp

ស្រួយស្រិប crisp, well-articulated

ស្រួល easy, pleasant, comfortable; well (physically)

ស្រួលខ្លួន to be well, feel well

ស្រួលបួល comfortable, pleasant

ស្រើប to become sexually excited, to lust, desire

ស្រៀប pleasing, comely, prepossessing

ស្រៀវ to fill a chill of fear, to shiver

ស្រេក to be thirsty, to thirst for

ស្រេច /srac/ to finish, complete

ស្រែ ricefield

ស្រែចំការ land, farmland

ស្រែក to yell, shout

ស្រែកទា to cry out for, clamor for

ស្រែកយកជ័យ to exhort to victory

ស្រែកហៅ to call out loud

ស្រែកអំពាវនាវលក់ to shout one's wares, peddle by shouting

ស្រែង a skin disease

ស្រោង straight, erect, pointing straight up

ស្រោច to water, sprinkle

ស្រោចស្រង់ to save, salvage

ស្រោប to enclose, envelop

ស្រោម sheath, envelop (n)

ស្រះ man-made pond, moat

ស្រះកែវ Glass Pond

ស្ល to cook, stew, boil (usually meat and/or vegetables)

ស្លកកូរ to make a kind of vegetable soup

ស្លស្លុក to cook, stew

ស្លក់ to be pale

ស្លន់ to panic, be terrified

ស្លា areca-nut

ស្លាពាន areca bowl

ស្លាកស្នាម trace, mark, scar (n)

ស្លាក់ to choke on something, have something caught in the throat

ស្លាត a flat fish used in making fish-balls

ស្លាប wing

ស្លាបច្រវ៉ា an aquatic plant (lit: oar blades)

ស្លាបទា an aquatic plant (lit: duck feathers)

ស្លាបប៉ាកកា fountain pen

ស្លាបព្រា spoon

ស្លាប់ to die

ស្លាប់ចោលឆ្អឹង to die in exile (lit: to die and have one's bones discarded)

ស្លឹក leaf

ស្លឹកគ្រៃ lemon grass, citronella

ស្លឹករឹត palm-leaf manuscript, palm leaves

ស្លឹង an old coin worth about 25 cents

ស្លឹង wide-eyed, staring

ស្លុង fully, completely, wholeheartedly; speedily

ស្លុត stunned, shocked, terrified

ស្លូត good, polite, gentle

ស្លូតបូត modest, polite, proper

ស្លៀក to put on, to wear below the waist

ស្លៀកពាក់ to wear; to dress

ស្លេះ to digress, change the subject

ស្លេះទំខាន for a change, as a change of routine, take a rest

ស្លោម to fold, retract (the wings); dense, crowded together

ស្លាំង pale, drained of blood

ស្លាំងកាំង stupified, stunned

ស្វ័យភាព /swayyəphiəp/ autonomy

ស្វា monkey

ស្វាង cleared up (of weather or drowsiness)

ស្វាញស្វិត (= ស្វិតស្វាញ) stingy, miserly

ស្វាត a thorny vine

ស្វាមី husband (Eleg)

ស្វាមីភក្តិ loyalty

ស្វាយ mango; purple; venereal disease

ស្វាយរៀង Svay Rieng (Province)

ស្វាល male sexual organ (Lit)

ស្វែង to seek after, search for

ស្វែងសម្បត្តិ /swaeŋ sɑmbat/ to seek after the rewards, attainments (of the Path to Nirvana)

ស្វះស្វែង to seek, search diligently

ស្អប់ to hate, detest, despise

ស្អាង to decorate, embellish

ស្អាង to do, commit

ស្អាត clean; attractive, pretty

ស្អាត ៗ very neat and attractive (intensification of /sqaat/)
ស្អាតបាត clean, neat, attractive

ស្អាតស្អំ clean

ស្អារ to irritate, bother (the throat)
ស្អិត sticky, adhesive; Fig: addictive, capable of ensnaring, pernicious

ស្អិតស្អាង to beautify, decorate

ស្អី what?, whatever

ស្អី (= ធ្វើស្អី) what?; what are you doing?
ស្អីឡើង whatever comes up, in every case, invariably
ស្អុយ foul-smelling, stinking, rotten

ស្អូច Saoch (a tribal group)

ស្អែក tomorrow

ស្អំ to apply a heating pad or warm cloth to the skin

# ហ

ហក់ to jump at, to lunge

ហង្ស /haŋ/ Hamsa, a mythological swan (Brahma's mount)
ហង្សយន្ត /haŋ yŭən/ Mechanized Swan (lit: motorized Hamsa)
ហត់ to be exhausted

ហត្ថ /hat/ cubit (distance from elbow to fingertips); hand (Lit)
ហត្ថកម្ម /hattəkam/ manual labor

ហត្ថករ /hattəkɑɑ/worker, laborer (Lit)
ហត្ថលេខា /hatthəleikhaa/ signature

ហត្ថី /hatthəy/ bull elephant

ហ៊ិន-ហ៊េវ Hon-Hew (pers. n.)

ហនុមាន /haqnumaan/ Hanumān (chief of the monkey army)
ហប to puff, pant with the mouth open
ហប់ stuffy (of air); suffocated

ហរិរាជរតនីក្រៃកែវហ្វា /haqririəc-roə̆ttənɨy-kray-kaew-waa/ title

ហឫទ័យ /haqrɨtɨy/ heart, mind (Clergy, Roy, Lit)

ហា to open (the mouth)

ហាក់ as if; almost; perhaps

ហាក់កាន់តែ increasingly

ហាក់ដូចជា as if, perhaps

ហាក់ដូចស្រួល become pleasant, act agreeable
ហាក់នឹង as if to

ហាក់បី (= ហាក់ដូច)

ហាង shop, store

ហាងជំនួញ store, business office, commercial firm
ហាងបាយ restaurant

ហាងលក់ដូរ shops, stores

ហ៊ាន to dare (to); be brave

ហាណូយ Hanoi

ហាប unit of weight and volume: approx. 60 kg.
ហាប់ firm

ហាម to prohibit

ហាម brim (of a hat)

ហាមប្រាម to prohibit, forbid

ហាល to expose to the sun

ហាលថ្ងៃ exposed to the sun, in the sun
ហាស to laugh; laughter (Arch)

ហាសិប fifty

ហិកតា /həctaa/ hectare (10,000 square meters)
ហិកតូលីត្រ /həctouliit/ hectoliter

ហិង្សា to harm, bother, mistreat

ហិចហើរ (=ហើរ) to fly (Poetic)

ហិចហែល to swim (Poetic)

ហិត to sniff, smell, inhale

ហិនហោច ruined, destroyed, obliterated, in ruins
ហិប box, chest, trunk

ហិបសង្គមកិច្ច welfare fund

ហិមគិរិ golden mountain (Lit)

ហិមពាន្ត (=ហេមពាន្ត) the Himalayas

ហិរញ្ញវត្ថុ /heqraññəwoə̆tthoq/ finance (n)

ហិរិ /heqreq/ (feeling of) guilt

ហិល dull, blunt

ហ៊ឹង (= ហ៊ុង) a kind of toad

ហីនយាន /hənnəyiən, hɨnnəyiən/ Hinayāna (Buddhism)

ហឹរ /haə, həl/ hot (spicy)

ហ៊ឺះ /hɨh/ interjection of frustration, sigh of relief

ហ៊ឺហា ostentatious, extravagant (Coll)

ហុកសិប sixty

ហុងកុង Hongkong

ហុច to hand, pass

ហុត to sip noisily (from a bowl)

ហុយ to rise, puff (of smoke, steam, etc.)

ហូត withdraw, pull out, extract (from a sheath, socket, etc.)

ហូតជីវិត to kill (Eleg)

ហូបបាយ to eat, have a meal (Rural)

ហូរ to flow

ហូរធ្លាក់ទឹកភ្នែក to shed tears

ហូរហែ continually, in a continuous stream

ហូល patterned silk

ហូលជរ an embroidered silk sarong

ហួត to evaporate

ហួស to surpass, exceed, go beyond

ហួសខ្លួន excessive, exaggerated

ហួសពី beyond, exceeding

ហួសសម័យ outdated, obsolete

ហើប to open; to be slightly open, ajar

ហើម swollen

ហើយ and, and then, then; perfective particle: already, finished; to finish

ហើយនឹង and

ហើយឬនៅ yet?, yet or not?

ហើរ /haə/ to fly

ហៀបតែនឹង just about to

ហៀបនឹង just about to, almost, nearly

ហៀរហោះ to fly (Poetic)

ហេ Hey! (interjection to attract attention or express surprise)

ហេតុ /haet/ reason, cause, motive

ហេតុដូច្នេះហើយ for this reason, therefore

ហេតុដ្បិត since, because

ហេតុតែ since, because

ហេតុនេះហើយបានជា this is the reason that...

ហេតុផល /haet-phɑl/ reason, cause, justification

ហេតុហ្នឹងហើយបានជា this is the reason why...

ហេតុអ្វីបានជា why is it that...?

ហេមន្តមាស /heimɑn-miəh/ winter months, cool season (Lit)

ហេមពាន្ត /haeməpiən/ the Himalayas

ហេមស្រិង្គស /haemsrəŋkeeh/ name of a Brahman devata

ហេរញ្ញិក (=ហិរញ្ញិក) /heiraññək/ treasurer

ហេវហោះ (=ហោះ) to fly, soar (Poetic)

ហែ to parade, accompany in procession; in succession, one after the other

ហែហម to follow along in procession

ហែក to tear open, tear a hole in

ហែង parched

ហែល to swim

ហែលចុះហែលឡើង swim back and forth

ហែលភ្នាល់ to race

ហៃ hortatory particle: Hey!, hey there!, now listen!, now hear this!

ហ៊ោ to yell, cheer

ហ៊ោហា to shout, roar, cheer

ហោង /hɑɑŋ/ euphonic final particle widely used in verse

ហោច scarce, minimum

ហោជាង eaves, lintel

ហោតិល /haotəl/ hotel

ហោប៉ៅ /hao-paw/ pocket

ហោរ fortune-teller, astrologer

ហោរា (= ហោរ) /haoraa/ astrologer

ហោរាធិបតី /haoraathɨppədəy/ chief astrologer

ហោរាសាស្ត្រ /haoraasaah/ astrology

ហោះ /hɑh/ to fly (by mechanical or supernatural means)

ហៅ to call, to name, to invite; called, named; before a verb: really, extremely

ហៅថា be called, is called; be considered as

ហៅពេញជាមានលាភ this is what you call luck

ហៅយក to order, have brought

ហៅក្លាហាន really brave

ហោះ /hɑh/ to fly (by mechanical or supernatural means)

ហ៎ះ /qəh/ Coll. final question particle

ហ្ន៎ /nɔɔ!, nɑɑ!/ there!, look there!

ហ្ន៎ /nah, nəh/ hortatory final particle soliciting agreement or compliance

ហ្ន៎ះ /nah!, nəh!/ hortatory final particle

ហ្នឹង /nɨŋ, nəŋ/ right now, right there, there

ហ្នឹងហើយ that's right, you've got it

ហ្នឹងឯង that same thing, that same one

ហ្មង trouble, blemish, disgrace, compromise

ហ្មងសៅ (= សៅហ្មង) unclean, impure, offensive

ហ្មត់ /mɑt/ fine, powdered

ហ្មត់ចត់ thorough(ly), careful(ly)

ហ្មបហ្វាយ to prostrate oneself in an attitude of obeisance

ហ្មឺន /məɨn/ 10,000; the lowest title of nobility

ហ្មឺនភក្តីអក្សរ /məɨn-pheə̆qkdəy-qaqsɑɑ/ royal title for a scholar

ហ្លួង /luəŋ/ king; royal; a royal or conferred title

ហ្វង់ /wɑŋ/ extremely (clear, bright, fragrant)

ហ្វីលីពីន /fiilipiin/ the Philippines

ហ្វីស៊ិក /fiizik/ physics

ហ្វឹកហ្វឺន /wək-wəɨn/ to train, drill, discipline

ហ្វូង /wouŋ/ flock, herd, group

ហ្វូងហ្វាយ flock, herd

ហ្សឺណែវ /zəɨnaew/ Geneva (Fr. Genève)

ហ្អែង (= ឯង) you (Pej)

# ឡ

ឡូ loud, clear, sharp (of a shout or cry)

ឡូក to dance and posture playfully, to clown

ឡាន car, cart, vehicle

ឡានសម្រាប់ស្ទូច tow-truck

ឡានរ៉េស្លូក name of a theater

ឡាវី Lavi (Saphay's daughter)

ឡឺនឡង់ wide-eyed (with fear or surprise)

ឡឺរេស៊ីដង់ /ləɨ-reiziidɑŋ/ governor (Fr. le résident)

ឡូឡា loudly, noisily

ឡើង to ascend, go up, come up; after av: increasingly, more

ឡើងក្រហម to flush, blush, become red

ឡើងថ្នាក់ to be promoted, to advance one grade

ឡើងយសស័ក្តិ to advance in rank, be promoted

ឡើងស្ដាប់បង្គាប់ come under the control (of)

ឡើយ always; after a negative:(not) at all

ឡៅ to carve, cut designs on

ឡៅ balcony

ឡៅ (= ឡៅតឿ) second floor, upper floor

ឡាំង crate (n)

# អ

អក to eat (dry food) by handfuls

អកប្បិយ /qaqkappəy/ improper, impure, inappropriate (in a religious sense)
អកុសល /qaqkosɑl/ past mideeds, negative merit, misfortune
អកោធនៈ /qaqkaothəneə̆q/ consideration, thoughtfulness
អក្ខរា /qaqkəraa/ letter, missive

អក្សរ /qaqsɑɑ/ letters, writing

អក្សរខម a style of Cambodian script

អក្សរជ្រៀង slanted letters, oblique script
អក្សរឈរ standing letters, vertical script
អក្សរមូល round script (decorative style of script used for names, titles, and religious texts)
អក្សរសាស្ត្រ /qaqsɑɑsaah/ literature; the study of letters
អក្សរសាស្ត្រខ្មែរ Khmer literature

អគារ building (Lit)

អគ្គនាយក /qaqkeə̆q-niəyuə̆q/ managing director
អគ្គមគ្គុទ្ទេសក៍ /qaqkeə̆q-meə̆qkutteeh/ guide, leader
អគ្គមហាសេនា /qaqkeə̆q-məhaa-seinaa/ very high-ranking military officer (higher than /seinaapədəy/)
អគ្គមហេសី /qaqkeə̆q-məhaesəy/ first queen
អគ្គរាជទូត /qaqkeə̆q-riəccətuut/ ambassador (of a kingdom)
អគ្គសាវ័ក /qaqkeə̆qsaawaq/ first disciple
អគ្គិសនី /qaqkihsənii/ electricity; electric
អគ្គី /qaqkii/ fire (Lit)

អគ្គិភ័យ fire (Lit)

អគ្នេយ៍ (= អាគ្នេយ៍) southeast (Lit)

អឃោសៈ /qaqkhoosaq/ voiceless; the 1st series of Khmer consonants
អង់គ្លេស /qɑŋkleeh, qɑŋglee/ English; England
អង់អាច determined, persistent; courageous, valorous
អង្ករ uncooked rice

អង្កាញ់ a large tree with bitter fruit

អង្កាល់ when? (in the future); whenever
អង្កោល a large thorny tree

អង្កាំ beads

អង្គ /qɑŋ/ body (Lit., complimentary); specifier for sacred persons and Buddhist images

អង្គការ /qɑŋ-kaa/ organization

អង្គការសហប្រជាជាតិ United Nations Organization
អង្គការឥណទាន credit organization

អង្គចន្ទ្រ /qɑŋ-can/ moon (Lit)

អង្គឌួង /qɑŋ-duəŋ/ Ang Duong (King of Cambodia 1841-1860)
អង្គប្រជុំ quorum; meeting, assembly

អង្គព្រះចក្រី the king

អង្គសេចក្ដី topic, theme

អង្គអញ /qɑŋ qañ/ I, myself, oneself (Roy, Lit)
អង្គរ /qɑŋkɔɔ/ Angkor

អង្គរធំ Angkor Thom

អង្គរវត្ត /qɑŋkɔɔ-wŏət/ Angkor Wat

អង្គា (= អង្គ)

អង្គា themselves (P. pl.)

អង្គី so that not... (Arch)

អង្គុយ to sit

អង្គុយក្រទោមក្បាលជង្គង់ to sit and hug one's knees in an attitude of dejection
អង្គុយបត់ជើង to sit with legs folded to one side
អង្គ្រង a vine-like tree

អង្រឹង /qɑŋrɨŋ/ hammock

អង្រឹងស្នែង a hammock suspended from a carrying pole
អង្រុត /qɑŋrut/ a conical fishing basket
អង្រួន to shake, rock

អង្វរ /qɑŋwɑɑ/ to beg, plead, implore

អង្វរចិត្ត to plead (with)

អង្សា degree (of temperature)

អង្អែល to caress

អច្ឆរិយៈ /qacchariyeə̆q/ supernatural

អចិន្ត្រៃយ៍ /qaccəntray/ permanent

អជនេយ្យ (= អាជនេយ្យ) /qacənɨy/ horse (Lit)

អញ /qañ/ I (first person pronoun used among intimates, or by a superior to an inferior)

អញខ្ញុំ (= ខ្ញុំ; អញ was once more deferential than it is today)

អញដឹងឯណា how do I know?

អញស្មានមកថា I had assumed that

អញអំពល់អី why should I bother?, what do I care?

អញ្ចាញ a plant with edible fruit

អញ្ចាញធ្មេញ gums (of the mouth)

អញ្ចឹង /qαñcəŋ, ñcəŋ/ in that case, then, therefore

អញ្ចឹងឬ is that so?, really?

អញ្ជលី (= អញ្ជុលី) the joined palms

អញ្ជាល (= ម្ជុល) needle

អញ្ជើញ to invite, invoke, summon; to take, carry; before a verb: please, go ahead and... (word of polite invitation)

អដ្ឋស័ក /qattəsaq/ 8th year (of the 10-year cycle)

អដ្ឋា (= អដ្ឋ) /qatthaq/ eight (Skt)

អណ្តាត tongue; wick

អណ្តូង a well, mine

អណ្តូងរ៉ែ a mine, ore mine

អណ្តើក turtle

អណ្តែង walking catfish

អណ្តែត to float (iv)

អណ្តែតត្រសែត to float

អត់ to withstand, resist, bear; to do without, be without, lack

អត់ឃ្លាន to be hungry, be without food

អត់បង្ហាន់ល្ងាច to fast in the afternoon

អត់ដង្ហើម to hold one's breath

អត់ទោស to excuse, forgive; pardon me, I'm sorry

អត់ទ្រាំ to withstand, endure, hold up

អត់ធន់ to endure, withstand

អត់ពី without

អត់មិនបាន unable to resist

អត់អាហារ to fast, refuse food; without food

អត់ឱ្យម្តង I'll forget it this time

អតិត /qadɨt/ formerly, in the past

អតិបរមា /qateq-parəmaa/ extreme, maximum, highest degree

អតិផរណា /qateq-phaqrənaa/ inflation

អតិរេក /qateqraek/ supreme, extreme

អតីត /qaqtəytaq, qadɨt/ past, the past

អតីតកាល /qadɨttəkaal/ the past

អតីតជាតិ /qadɨttəciət/ former life, former incarnation

អត្តៈ /qattaq/ magical mathematical formula

អត្តឃាតកម្ម /qattaqkhiətəkam/ suicide (Lit)

អត្ថ /qatthaq/ meaning, significance, value

អត្ថន័យ /qatthənɨy/ meaning, significance

អត្ថបទ /qattəbαt/ article, composition, text

អត្ថប្រយោជន៍ /qatthaq-prαyaoc/ usefulness

អត្ថាធិប្បាយ /qatthaathibaay/ commentary, explanation; to explain, describe

អទស្សនភាព invisibility

អធិក great, extreme, many

អធិកអធម /qathɨk-qathɔɔm/ grand, festive, gay

អធិការ /qathikaa/ supervisor, head, one in authority

អធិការកិច្ច administration, direction

អធិដ្ឋាន /qathithaan/ recite, invoke, swear by

អធិបតីភាព /qathɨppədəy-phiəp/ power, authority; presidency, leadership, direction

អធិបតីសេនា /qathɨppədəy-seinaa/ high-ranking official

អធិបតេយ្យ /qathɨppətay/ power

អធិប្បាយ /qathibaay/ to explain, describe

អធិស្ឋាន (=អធិដ្ឋាន) to swear by, invoke, recite

អធ្យាស្រ័យ /qattyiəsray/ tolerance, lenience

អធ្យោគ /qaqtyook/ to persevere

អធ្រាត្រ /qatriət/ midnight (Lit)

អធ្រាត្រដាស់ទុំ in the depth of night

អធ្វា /qaqtwiə/ way, road; forest, woods (Lit)

អន់ to be disappointed, downcast; mediocre

អន់ចិត្ត to have hurt feelings

អន់អៀន shy, bashful, embarrassed

អនាគត /qanaakŭət/ future (n)

អនាថា derelict, vagabond, destitute (adj)

អនិច្ចកម្ម /qanɨccəkam/ death; to die (Eleg)

អនិច្ចា /qanɨccaa/ to pity, be compassionate toward

អនីតិភាព /qanəytephiəp/ minority (of legal age)

អន្ធ (=អន្ធ /qαntheə̆q/) blind (with passion, desire, etc.)

អនុគណស្រុក /qanuqkŭən-srok/ ecclesiastical head of a district

អនុជ /qanoc/ younger sibling (Roy)

អនុញ្ញាត /qaqnuññaat/ to permit; permission

អនុពាល unenlightened, worldly, wicked (from the standpoint of Buddhist ethics); worldliness, wickedness

អនុម័ត /qaqnumat/ to approve, adopt, agree to

អនុលោម /qanulaom/ to conform, go along with

អនុវត្ត /qanuwŏət/ to comply with, accord with, conform to; practical, applied

អនុវិទ្យាល័យ /qanuq-wɨttyiəlay/ junior high school, academy

អនុស្សាវរីយ /qanuhsaawərii/souvenir, remembrance

អនេក /qanaek/ extremely, especially

អនេកអនន្ត /qanaek-qanαn/ great, extreme

អនេកអនន្តគណនា indescribable, boggles the mind

អន្តរជាតិ /qαntəraq-ciət/ international

អន្តរាយ /qαntəraay/ danger; dangerous

អន្ទង់ eel

អន្ទាក់ a trap, a snare

អន្ទោល to follow (through transmigration)

អន្ទះអន្ទែង restless, impatient, agitated

អន្ធពាល /qαntəpiəl/ foolhardy, foolish

អន្លើ /qαnləə/ place, location; phase, stage (of a journey, etc.)

អន្សម rice-cake

អប់ to perfume, imbue with fragrance

អប់រំ to train, discipline, educate

អបុញ្ញាភិសង្ខារ /qaqpoññaaphiqsαŋkhaa/ accumulation of negative karma, demerit

អបាយមុខ /qabaayəmuk/ vice

អប្បភាគ /qappəphiəq/ minority (in number or size)

អប្រិយ /qaprəy/ morally bad, disgusting, shameful, despicable (Lit)

អប្សរា /qapsaraa/ Apsara, heavenly maiden

អផ្សុក /qαpsok/ to be bored; boredom

អ័ព្ទនភី /qap nəphii/ darkening the sky, producing a fog, air heavy (with noise)

អព្យាក្រិត /qapyiəkrət/ neutral; neutrality

អភ័ព្វ /qaqphŏəp/ unlucky, unfortunate

អភ័យ /qaqphɨy/ fearless

អភ័យទោស to forgive; forgive [me]

អភិបាល /qaphibaal/ administrator; to administer, govern, regulate

អភិបាលខេត្ត governor (of a province)

អភិបាលស្រុក district-chief

អភិប្រាយ to talk, converse (Lit)

អភិធម្ម /qaphiqthɔə/ Abhidhamma (metaphysics, highest law of Buddhism, in the form of questions and answers)

អភិរូឍិ /qaqphiruu/ advancement, improvement, benefit

អភិវន្ទន៍ /qaqphiwŏən/ respect, veneration; to venerate

អភិសេក /qaqphisaek/ to anoint, confer, consecrate; to crown (a king)
អម to flank, accompany, surround
អមនុស្ស /qaqmənuh/ supernatural
អមរ /qamaraq/ god, angel; holy, sacred
អមោក្យ sad, disconsolate
អម្ចាស់ /qamməcah/ lord, master, ruler
អម្ចាស់ផែនដី the king (lit: owner of the land)
អម្មេញ /qammənɨñ/ to suffer (mental anguish)
អម្បាញ់មិញ a moment ago, just now
អម្បាល degree, extent, amount
អម្បូរ lineage, family, origin
អម្ពរ /qampɔɔ/ space, air, sky (Lit)
អម្ពរ cloth, clothing
អម្រស់អម្រ occupation, trade
អម្រាម (= ម្រាម) finger (Arch)
អម្រឹក (= ម្រឹគ) fourfooted wild animal (Lit)
អង្រែក a shoulder-pole with two suspended baskets
អម្លុង period of time, lapse of time
អយស្ម័យយាន /qayeə̆hsmaayiən/ train (Lit)
អរ /qαα/ happy
អរគុណ to thank; in isolation: thank you
អរិន្ទ /qaqrɨn/ principal enemy
អរុណ /qaqrun/ dawn (Lit)
អរូបព្រហ្មស្ថាន /qaqruuppəprumməthaan/ intangible realm of Brahma
អលង្ការ /qalaŋkaa/ jewelry, regalia
អវលោកិតេស្វរៈ /qawəlookəteeswaraq/ Avalokitesvara
អវសាន /qawəsaan/ last, final
អវសានកាល /qawəsaanəkaal/ end, conclusion
អវៈយវៈ /qaweə̆q-yəweə̆q/ limbs, appendages (Lit)
អវិចី /qawəcəy/ hell of ceaseless fire

អវិរោធៈ /qaqwirootheə̆q/ respect for the law
អវិហិំសា /qaqwihəŋsaa/ nonviolence, kindness
អវីចិ /qawəcəy/ Avīcī (hell for wealthy sinners)
អវីតិក្កមីយភាព /qawəyteqkəməyyəphiəp/ inviolability, integrity
អវុធា (=អាវុធ) weapon (Lit)
អស់ /qαh/ to use up; entirely, all of
អស់កម្លាំង tired, exhausted
អស់កាលជាយូរអង្វែង for an extremely long time
អស់ចិត្ត to be satisfied
អស់ចិត្តពី to get over, forget about
អស់តម្លៃ at a cost of
អស់ទិសា in every direction, all around (Poetic)
អស់ទាំងក្មេង all the children
អស់ទាំងខ្លួន all over the body
អស់បើគិត perplexed, nonplussed, bewildered
អស់មិនសល់ all of it, every bit of it
អស់មួយយប់មួយថ្ងៃ for a full 24 hours
អស់មួយរាជ្យ throughout the reign (of)
អស់លោកអ្នកស្រុក all you villagers
អស់សំណើច to break out in laughter
អស់អង្គស្រេច all over the body, the whole body (Lit)
អស់អម្បាល entirely, all, to any extent
អស់អ្នករាល់គ្នា all of you, every one of you
អស់អាយុ to come to the end of one's days, to die
អសារ uselessly, needlessly, futilely
អសារបង់ futile, useless
អសារឥតការ needlessly, uselessly, in vain
អសុរ /qasoraq/ ogre, giant, demon (Lit)
អសុរកាយ /qasoraqkaay/ demon, ogre, inhabitants of hell
អសុរា (= អសុរ) demon, giant
អសុរី (= អសុរ) ogre

អសុរោះ crude, rude, nasty

អសោចិ៍ /qasaoc/ to smell bad, stinking, disgusting

អសោជ (=អសោច) stinking, disgusting

អសោចិ៍កេរ្តិ៍ to be compromised, have a damaged reputation

អស្ចារ្យ /qαhcaa/ extraordinary, marvelous; the marvelous, the supernatural (n)

អស្តង្គត /qαhsdαŋkŭət/ dusk, twilight, sunset; to set (of the sun, Lit)

អស្ថិភង្គ /qahstiphŭəŋ/ Asthibhanga (hell for those who destroy the property of others)

អស្មិមានះ /qahsmeqmiəneəh/ conceit

អស្រិកប្បូណ៌ហ្រទ /qasreqkəbourənahrəteəq/ Asrikpūrnahrada (hell for adulterers)

អស្សុជ /qasoc/ September-October (lunar system)

អស្សតរ /qahsədαα/ horse (Lit)

អស្សពាហ៍ /qahsəpiə/ horse (Lit)

អស្សពាហន៍ (= អស្សពាហ៍) horse (Lit)

អស្សា /qahsaa/ horse (Lit)

អា derogatory or diminutive prefix; nominalizing prefix: the one which; you (Pej. before man's name, affectionate before girl's)

អាក្មេង kid (disrespectful)

អាខ្វាក់ the blind one, a blind person

អាខ្វិន the lame one, a lame person

អាចំកួតហ្លួង you idiot, that idiot (lit: that crazy king)

អាជ័យ that (rascal) Chey

អាដែង Pej. term of address or reference: you there; that bastard; those guys; you guys

អានាង my boy, my dear young fellow (condescending)

អាមុខខៀវ the green-faced one (some ogres are traditionally thought to have green skin)

អាម្នាក់ one (of them)

អាសុខ Asok (pers. n. with diminutive prefix)

អាឡេវ /qaaleiw, qaleiw/ Alev (name of the principle character of a famous Cambodian folktale)

អាអន្តរធាន /qaa-qαndαα-thiən/ you idiot!, damn you! (lit: may you be ruined)

អាឯង you (disrespectful, condescending)

អាក់ខាន to fail (to do something), not fulfill (an intention or promise)

អាក់អន់ downhearted, disappointed

អាក់អន់ចិត្ត to have hurt feelings, be displeased, disappointed

អាក់អួល to stammer, stutter

អាកប្បកិរិយា /qaakappəkeriyaa/ characteristic, behavior, conduct

អាករ duty, tax, tariff

អាការ action, situation, condition

អាកាស air; atmosphere

អាកាសចរ /qaakahsəcαα/ air travel; airline

អាកាសចរភូមិនកម្ពុជា /qaakahsəcαα phuumɨn kampucciə/ Royal Cambodian Airways

អាកាសយាន /qaakahsəyiən/ airplane (Lit)

អាក្រក់ bad, wicked, dirty

អាក្រាត naked

អាក្រាតសំពត់ divested of clothing, naked

អាក្រោស to revile, repudiate aloud; coarse, crude, loud

អាគម /qaakum/ magical formula, incantation, magic

អាគមវិជ្ជាការ /qaakum-wɨcciəkaa/ science of magic

អាគ្នេយ៍ /qaqknee/ southeast (Lit)

អាឃ៏ /qaakheəq/ valuable, precious

អាង to depend on, rely on, refer to (as a basis or proof)

អាង wide stone basin

អាងថា rely on the fact that

អាងអួត (=អួតអាង) to boast, brag, be arrogant

អាច to be able to, likely to, might; dare to, have the courage to

អាចក្តី I, me, my (Clergy)

អាចម៍ /qac/ excrement, dung; secretion

អាចម៍ច្រមុះ nasal secretion; speck

អាចម៍ត្រចៀក ear wax

អាចម៍ភ្នែក eye secretion, sand (of the eyes)

អាចម៍រុយ freckles (lit: fly-specks)

អាចរិយា (= អចរិយ = អាចារ្យ) /qaacaqriyaa/ teacher, master

អាចារ្យ៍ (= អាចារ្យ) /qaacaa/ teacher, sage (Religious); head layman of a pagoda

អាចារ្យលាក់ leader of an Anti-French movement

អាចារ្យហែម-ចៀវ name of a monk, scholar, and politician who died in exile on the island of Puolo Condore

អាជានេយ្យ /qaacənɨy/ horse (Lit)

អាជីវៈ /qaaciweə̆q/ livelihood, profession, occupation

អាជ្ញា /qaac-ñaa/ order, command

អាណត្តិ /qaanat/ mandate

អាណានិគម /qaanaanikum/ colony

អាណានិគមកិច្ច colonization

អាណានិគមនិយម colonialism

អាណាព្យាបាល /qanaapyiəbaal/ protector; protectorate

អាណាម Annam

អាណិត to pity, take pity on

អាណោចអាធ័ម sad, pathetic, pitiable; feel great compassion for

អាត្មា self, I (Clergy)

អាត្មានិយម /qaatmaaniyum/ selfishness

អាថ៌ /qaat/ hidden meaning, subtlety; substance; beginning; to begin

អាទិត្យ /qaatɨt/ week; Sunday; sun

អាទិត្យក្រោយ next week, the following week

អាទិត្យមុន last week, the week before

អាទិត្យវង្សា /qaatɨt-wŭəŋsaa/ name of a mythological king

អាទិទេព /qaatiteep/ god (Lit)

អាន saddle

អាន to read, to pronounce

អានិសង្ស blessing, benefit

អានុភាព /qaanuphiəp/ power, force, influence

អាប់ to dim, tarnish, compromise; foggy, dense, dim

អាប់ឱន to degrade, compromise

អាប្រិយ (= អប្រិយ) /qaaprəy/ morally bad, disgusting, shameful, despicable (Lit)

អាពាហ៍ពិពាហ៍ /qapiə-pipiə/ marriage, wedding

អាពុក (= ឪពុក) father (Coll)

អាព្យាក្រឹត /qaapyiəkrət/ neutralism; neutralist

អាមាត្យ companion (Roy)

អាម៉ាស់មុខ to be ashamed, lose face

អាមេរិក /qaamerɨc/ America

អាមេរិកាំង /qaamerikaŋ/ American (n, adj)

អាយ nearby

អាយនាយ here and there

អាយ័ត to give strict orders to, to instruct

អាយុ /qaayuq/ age; to have the age of

អាយុជីវិត vital, a matter of life or death

អាយ៉ៃ a kind of folk music involving a musical dialogue between a man and a woman

អារ to saw (wood, etc.)

អារក្ខ /qaareə̆q/ capricious spirit, demon

អារម្មណ៍ /qaarɑm/ cause, condition (esp. of life); senses, feelings; mood, attitude

អារាម /qaaraam/ wat, pagoda

អារ្យធម៌ /qaarəyeə̆qthɔə/ culture, civilization

អារីក្សត្រ a village across the Mekong from Phnom Penh

អាលក្ស /qaalaq/ Palace officials in charge of inventory and royal treasury

អាល័យ to miss, think affectionately of

អាល័យរ៉ែត preoccupied with (Coll)

អាឡោះអាល័យ to grieve for, to miss desperately

អាល្លឺម៉ង់ /qaaləmɑŋ/ German; Germany (Fr. Allemand)
អាវ shirt, coat
អាវកក្រត់ straight-collared jacket
អាវងូតទឹក bathing suit
អាវដៃខ្លី short-sleeve shirt
អាវដៃវែង long-sleeve shirt
អាវភ្លៀង raincoat
អាវរងា sweater, heavy coat
អាវុធ /qaawut/ weapon (Lit)
អាវុធយុទ្ធភណ្ឌ /qaawut-yuttəphŏən/ weapons and paraphernalia of war
អាស shameless
អាសន្ន /qaasɑn/ trouble, problem
អាសាឍ (=អាសាធ) /qaasaat/ June-July (lunar system)
អាសិរ /qaasei/ fangs
អាសិរពិស /qaaseirəpɨh/ poison fangs
អាស៊ី /qaasii, qaazii/ Asia
អាស៊ីប៉ែកអាគ្នេយ៍ Southeast Asia
អាសូរ have compassion for
អាសៅ to degrade, to smear, tarnish
អាស្រម /qaasrɑm/ hermitage, forest retreat
អាស្រ័យ to eat (Polite, Rural); to take shelter, depend on
អាស្រូវ blemished, tarnished, compromised, diminished, ruined (reputation, character, etc.)
អាហារ food
អាហារូបករណ៍ /qahaaruupəkaa/ scholarship, subvention
អាហារភោជន /qahaa-phoocuŏn/ food (Lit)
អាឡោះអាល័យ to grieve for, miss desperately
ឥដ្ឋ /qət/ brick
ឥណទាន /qənnətiən/ credit
ឥណ្ឌូចិន /qəndoucən/ Indochina
ឥណ្ឌៀ /qəndiə/ India; Indian

ឥត negative auxiliary: not; to be without, to lack
ឥតការ futile, to no specific purpose
ឥតគណនា /qət kŭənnəniə/ infinite(ly)
ឥតគេសម nobody will be sympathetic
ឥតឃ្លើស flawless
ឥតត្រាប្រណី mercilessly
ឥតនឹងថ្លឹងថ្លាថ្លែង inestimable, immeasurable
ឥតបើ (= ឥត) without
ឥតបើ (= ឥតបើឧបមា) extremely
ឥតបើគិត heedlessly, thoughtlessly
ឥតផ្ទឹម with no equal, without equalling
ឥតពី (= អត់ពី) without
ឥតមានរួញរា without delay, immediately
ឥតល្ហើយ relentlessly, without respite, unrelievedly
ឥតសំចៃដៃ vigorously, with all one's force (lit: without sparing the hands)
ឥតស្មើ beyond compare, extremely
ឥតឧបមា incomparably
ឥតឯគណនា immeasurable, inestimable
ឥតឯមានទាស់ nothing detracts from; unmarred, flawless
ឥតឯមានហ្មង nothing detracts from; perfect, flawless
ឥតអំពើ needless(ly), useless(ly), pointless(ly)
ឥទ្ធិពល /qətthipŭəl/ influence
ឥន្ទ /qən/ In (a famous Khmer author and scholar)
ឥន្ទធនូ /qəntənuu/ rainbow (Indra's crossbow)
ឥន្ទ្រជិត /qəntrəcɨt/ Indrajita, Rāvana's eldest son
ឥន្ទ្រាធិរាជ /qəntriəthiriəc/ Indra
ឥន្ទ្រី mythological eagle, Indra's bird
ឥន្ទ្រីយ /qəntrii/ self, body (Lit)
ឥន្ទ្រាទ្រិ /qəntriət/ Indra's mountain
ឥរិយាបថ /qəqriyaabɑt/ attitude, demeanor, conduct
ឥសី /qəysəy/ hermit, sage

ឥសូរ /qəysəw/ Siva; top, highest, foremost
ឥសូរមិថិលា King Mithila

ឥស្លាម /qihslaam, qehslaam/ Islam, Moslem
ឥស្សរៈ /qihsəraq, qehsəraq/ independent
ឥស្សរជន /qehsəraqcuǝ̆n/ dignitary, high official
ឥស្សរភាព /qehsəraqphiəp/ freedom

ឥស្សរ៉ូ /qehsarou/ Essaro (pers. n.)

ឥស្សរា /qehsəraa/ free; omnipotent

ឥស្សរាពង្ស Siva

ឥឡូវ /qəyləw/ now

ឥឡូវនេះ now; nowadays

ឥឡូវហ្នឹង right this minute

អី what?; anything (Coll. variant of /qwəy/)
អីក៏...ម្ល៉េះ why so...?

អីចឹង (= អញ្ចឹង) therefore, like that (Coll)
អីចេះ (= ដូច្នេះ) therefore, like that (Coll)
អីយ៉ូយ exclamation of pain or despair

អីវ៉ាន់ things, baggage, merchandise

អ៊ី, អ៊ី /qii!/ interjection of surprise

ឦសាន /qəysaan/ northeast (Lit)

ឦសូរ /qəysou/ Siva

អឹកធឹក /qɨkkəthɨk/ grandiose, festive

អឹមសុខ Im Sok (pers. n.)

អឺ /qəɨ/ hey!; yes, right (Impolite, condescending)
អឺងកង tumultuous

អឺងអាប់ tumultuously, clamorously

អ៊ឺ /qɨɨ/ yes, right (Impolite, condescending)
អឺរ៉ុប /qəɨrop/ Europe; European

អុកឡុក confused, mixed up

ឧកញ៉ា /qokñaa/ title for official of ministerial rank
ឧកញ៉ាកោសាធិបតីកៅ Oknha Kosadhipati Kao, author of the story King Subhamitra

ឧកញ៉ាក្រឡាហោម title, Minister of the Navy and of Water Transport
ឧកញ៉ាចក្រី Minister of the Army and of Land Transport
ឧកញ៉ាជ័យយោធាសង្គ្រាម title

ឧកញ៉ាតេជោ /qokñaa-daĉcoo/ title

ឧកញ៉ាធម្មាតេជោ /qokñaa-thŏəmmədaccoo/ title
ឧកញ៉ាបវរនាយក /qokñaa-bɑwɔɔniəyuə̆q/ title
ឧកញ៉ាពិភក្តិទិព្វរាជ /-pipheə̆qkdəy-tɨppəriəc/ title
ឧកញ៉ាពិស្ណុលោក /-pihsnulook/ title

ឧកញ៉ារាជាមេត្រី title

ឧកញ៉ាវង្សាអគ្គរាជ title

ឧកញ៉ាវិបុលរាជ title

ឧកញ៉ាវាំងវរវៀងជ័យ title

ឧកញ៉ាសុត្តន្តប្រីជា /qokñaa-sottɑn-prəyciə/ title
ឧកញ៉ាស្រីនគរបាល title

ឧកញ៉ាអរជូន title

ឧកញ៉ាអាទិច្ចគាមវ័នសេនា /-qaatɨccəkiəmmə-wɔ̆ən-seinaa/ title
ឧកញ៉ាឥស្សរៈអក្ខរា /-qehsəraq-qaqkhəraa/ title
ឧកញ៉ាឥស្សរាពាណិជ title

ឧក្រិដ្ឋ /qokrət/ criminal

អុង basin similar to /qaaŋ/

អុង-ស៊ីម Ong Sim (pers. n.)

ឧច្ចាស /quccəwaasaq/ Ucchvāsa (hell for murderers and those who eat impure meat)
អុជ to ignite, to light

ឧណ្ហា (= ឧណ្ហ) /qunnəhaq/ heat; to heat; hot (Lit)
ឧតុនិយម /qotoq-niyum/ natural law of the physical universe; physical elements
ឧត្តម /qotdɑm, qutdɑm/ high, excellent

ឧត្តមគតិ /qutdɑmkəteq/ ideal, principle

ឧត្តមសេនីយ /qutdɑm-seinəy/ General (military rank)

ឧត្តរ /qutdαα/ north (Lit)

ឧត្តរា (= ឧត្តរ ) north (Lit)

ឧត្តុង្គ /qutdoŋ/ Oudong (capital of Cambodia 1620-1867)

ឧត្តុង្គមានជ័យ Oudong the Victorious

ឧត្តុង្គឧត្តម /qutdoŋ-qutdαm/ high, glorious, excellent, illustrious

ឧត្បាត /qottəbaat/ harmful influence

ឧទរ /quttɔɔ/ stomach (Roy)

ឧទារ awesome, huge

ឧទាហរណ៍ /quttiəhαα/ example

ឧទ្ទិស /quttɨh/ to dedicate, devote

ឧទ្យាន /qutyiən/ park, garden (Lit)

ឧបការ to provide assistance, render a service to (Lit)

ឧបត្ថម្ភ /qoppəthαm/ to assist

ឧបទូត deputy ambassador

ឧបនាយករដ្ឋមន្ត្រីទី ២ /qoppaq-niəyŭəq-rŏət-mŭəntrəy tii-pii/ second vice-prime minister

ឧបបាតិកៈ /quppəbaatekaq/ spontaneous rebirth, self-generation

ឧបភោគ /quppəphook/ to use, consume (Lit)

ឧបមា /quppəmaa, qoppəmaa/ to compare with, draw an analogy between; example; like, such as

ឧបមាដូចជា like, as if, such as

ឧបមេយ្យ /quppəmay/ comparison, simile

ឧបរាជ /qupperaac/ vice-king

ឧបសគ្គ /quppəsaq, qoppəsaq/ obstacle, impediment, problem

ឧបាយ trick, stratagem, device

ឧបាយកល /qobaayyəkαl, qobaay-kαl/ trick, devious strategy

ឧបាសក /qobaasαq, qaobaasαq/ Buddhist layman; the laity

ឧបាសិកា /qobaasikaa/ female members of the laity

ឧរា /qaoraa/ chest, breast (Roy)

ឧរី /qaorii/ chest, breast (Roy)

ឧរូ /qaoruu/ chest, breast (Roy)

ឧស (= អុស ) /qoh/ logs, firewood

អុស firewood

ឧសភ /quhsəphĕəq/ bull (Siva's mount)

ឧសភរាជ /quhsəphĕəq-riəc/ royal ox(en)

ឧសភា /quhsəphiə/ May

ឧស្សាហ៍ /quhsaa/ diligent, industrious; often

ឧស្សាហកម្ម /quhsaahaqkam/ industry

ឧឡារិក /qolaarɨk/ gay, splendid, grandiose, boisterous

អុ៎ះ ! interjection of surprise

ឪ /qəw/ father (familiar or affectionate term)

ឪម៉ៅ name of a former province

ឪពុក /qəwpuk/ father (Formal)

ឪពុកក្មេក father-in-law

ឪពុកចិញ្ចឹម foster father

ឪពុកធម៌ foster father

ឪពុកធំ uncle (older brother of either parent)

ឪពុកមា uncle (younger brother of either parent)

ឪពុកម្ដាយ father and mother, parents

ឪពុកម្ដាយចិញ្ចឹម foster parents

អូ oh! (interjection)

អូន I (wife to husband, or younger to older sibling); you (husband to wife, or older to younger sibling or friend)

អូរ seasonal stream; marshy pond

អូរក្រងលាយ name of a village

អូររំដេង place name (lit: horse-radish pond)

អូរសេកពង O Sek Pong (place name; lit: swamp [where] the parrot laid an egg)

អ៊ូរី /quurii/ Uri (pers. n.)

អ៊ូរអរ noisy, boisterous

អូស to drag; to take back, reclaim

ឩន /quun/ deficient

អួត to brag, to boast; to draw oneself up
អួតខ្លួន to brag, to boast

អួល to choke, have something stuck in the throat
អួលអាក់ to have a lump in one's throat (from fear or grief)
អើ /qaə/ (Coll. or informal response particle indicating agreement)
អើត to crane the neck

អើយ Oh! (emphatic particle)

អ៊ើយ (conciliatory final particle)

អៀងសាយ Ieng Say (pers. n.)

អៀន embarrassed, ashamed, shy

អៀនប្រៀន shy, timid

អៀនប្រៀន to be bashful, embarrassed
អៀនអន់ក្នុងចិត្ត ashamed, embarrassed

អៀវកើស Iev Koeus (famous Cambodian politician)
អេត្យូពី /qeityoupii/ Ethiopia

អេងសុត Eng Sot (pers. n.; editor of a Cambodian chronicle)
អេះ (final hortatory particle; Coll. equivalent of /rɨɨ/)
ឯ /qae/ at; as for, regarding

ឯណា where?; somewhere, anywhere

ឯណាបាន where can one...?

ឯទៀត other, different

ឯទៀតៗ various other

ឯ...វិញ as for...on the other hand

ឯក /qaek/ one, first, alone

ឯកធីតា the only daughter

ឯកស័ក /qaekkəsaq/ first year (of the 10-year cycle)
ឯកសណ្ឋាន uniform (n); to be uniform

ឯកសារ /qaekkəsaa/ document, chronicle
ឯកា /qaekaa/ alone

ឯករាជ្យ /qaekkəriəc/ independent; independence
ឯកអគ្គរាជទូត /qaek-qakeəq-riəccətuut/ ambassador plenipotentiary

ឯកឧត្តម /qaek-qutdɑm/ His Excellency

ឯង /qaeŋ/ reflexive pronoun: yourself, oneself, itself; familiar 2nd person pronoun
ឯងនេះ you (condescending)

ឯប /qaep/ to stay close to, get alongside
អ៊ែម Ahem!

ឯ.ឧ. (=ឯកឧត្តម) His Excellency

ឰ /qay/ in, at (Lit)

ឰដ៏ (=ឯ) at (Lit)

ឰយុធ្យា /qayyutyiə/ Ayuthia

ឰរាវ័ណ /qayrəwoən/ Erawan, the tricephalic elephant (Indra's mount)
ឱ /qao!/ interjection of surprise or excitement
ឱកាស /qaokaah, qokaah/ chance, opportunity, occasion
ឱកាសល្អហុចឲ្យ a good opportunity was presented
ឱដ្ឋ /qot/ intelligence, facility of speech
ឱត្តប្បៈ /qaotəpaq/ fear of evil

ឱទ្យាន (=ឧទ្យាន) park, garden

ឱន to bend, bow

ឱនអង្គ to bow the body; Fig: humble

អោប (=ឱប) to hug, embrace

ឱប /qaop/ to hug, embrace

ឱបបាទជើង to embrace the feet (of)

ឱភាស light, bright (Lit)

ឱយ (=ឲ្យ)

ឲ្យ /qaoy/ to give; to let, allow, cause; following a verb: for, on behalf of
ឲ្យខាងតែ to insure that

ឲ្យខ្ជាប់ tenaciously, firmly

ឲ្យឆេះឯណាបាន how can it burn?

ឲ្យដឹងថ្វីដៃ to show one's power, let [them] know who's boss
ឲ្យតែ just for; provided that

ឲ្យតែច្រើន just so it's a lot

ឲ្យទាន as a favor

ឲ្យជាប់ទាក់ in order to involve [others]

ឲ្យឆាប់រួសរាន់ quickly, immediately

ឲ្យពរ to bless

ឲ្យរុងរឿង to enhance, elevate, brighten

ឲ្យល្អមើល really make a spectacle (Idiom)

ឲ្យសំគាល់នឹងថា indicating that

ឲ្យអន្តរាយ to violate, transgress, do violence to, harm

ឲ្យអស់ដៃ with all one's strength

ឲ្យអស់សង្ស័យ to dispel one's doubts

ឲ្យអស់សេចក្ដី thoroughly, completely

ឱរ /qao/ to rain hard

ឱរស /qorŭəh/ child, offspring (Lit)

ឱរា (= ឧរា) chest, breast (Roy)

ឱរ៉ៃ gold

ឱវាទ /qaowiət/ advice, instruction, admonition

ឱសថ /qaosot/ medicine, cure, solution

ឱស្សាហ៍ (= ឧស្សាហ៍) diligent, conscientious; often

ឱះឱ /qah-qao/ Oh! (Lit. interjection)

ឱះឱអនិច្ចា Oh, woe is me!

អុំ to paddle with a loose oar

អ៊ំ uncle, aunt (older sister or brother of either parent)

អំណត់ endurance, patience

អំណរ happiness, gratitude

អំណរគុណ gratitude, show of gratitude

អំណាច power, control

អំណាចផ្ដាច់ការ absolute power, dictatorial power

អំនួត a boast

អំណោយ gift

អំបាយ (=អម្បាយ) so, such, to such an extent; extremely (Arch)

អំបាល among

អំបែងថ្ម a kind of tree

អំបោះ cotton, cotton thread

អំបោះដេរ thread

អំពល់ to trouble, bother; to concern oneself with, go to the trouble

អំពាវ to call out, summon

អំពាវនាវ to plead, beseech, appeal

អំពិល tamarind tree

អំពី of, about, from

អំពីថ្ងៃនេះទៅ from this day on

អំពើ conduct, actions

អំពៅ sugarcane

អាំង to roast, barbecue

អាំងភ្លើង to warm in front of a fire

អះ (interjection of surprise)

អះអញ (= អញ)

អះអាង to guarantee; to claim

អ្នក /neə̆q/ person; headword in compounds referring to persons

អ្នក /neə̆q/ you (between intimates, or superior to inferior); he, she, they (definite)

អ្នកកាច់ចង្កូត pilot, navigator

អ្នកក្រុង urbanite, city-dweller

អ្នកខ្ពស់ upperclass person, member of the elite

អ្នកគ្រប់គ្រង overseer, supervisor

អ្នកគ្រូ teacher (fem)

អ្នកចេះដឹង learned person, scholar

អ្នកចៅ term of address for one's grandchildren, or children of one's grandchildren's generation (Polite)

អ្នកចំណូល newcomer

អ្នកជម្ងឺ patient, sick person

អ្នកជា respectable people, free men (as opposed to slaves)

អ្នកជាតិនិយម nationalist (n, adj)

អ្នកជិតខាង neighbor

អ្នកជំនាញ expert

អ្នកជំនួញ businessman, merchant

អ្នកដទៃ other people, stranger(s)

អ្នកដើមចោទ plaintiff

អ្នកដំណើរ traveler, passenger

អ្នកតា guardian spirit

អ្នកតែងខ្លួន dressing-maid, bride's dressing assistant

អ្នកថ្មើរជើង pedestrian

អ្នកថ្លៃ My Dear One

អ្នកទូក river people, boatmen

អ្នកទេសចរ /neə̆q-teehsəcαα/ tourist, sightseer

អ្នកទោស prisoner

អ្នកធំ important person(s)

អ្នកធ្វើចំការ gardener

អ្នកធ្វើម្ហូប cook, chef

អ្នកធ្វើស្រែ rice-farmer

អ្នកនគរ townspeople

អ្នកនិពន្ធ /neə̆q-nipŭən/ writer, author

អ្នកនិរុត្តិសាស្ត្រ /neə̆q-niruttisaah/ philologist

អ្នកនេសាទ fisherman

អ្នកនាំផ្លូវ guide, leader

អ្នកបង you (respectful title, wife to husband or younger to older sibling or friend)

អ្នកបំរើ servant, waiter

អ្នកប្រាជ្ញ sage, wiseman

អ្នកប្រុស respectful 2nd or 3rd pers. masc. pron.: you, he, him; man, young man

អ្នកផង people, others, the public

អ្នកផ្លូវ female go-between in a marriage negotiation

អ្នកផ្សារ townspeople

អ្នកភ្នំពេញ resident of Phnom Penh

អ្នកម៉ាក់ Mother (snobbish, rare)

អ្នកមាន wealthy person

អ្នកមានគុណ benefactor (i.e. parents or teachers)

អ្នកមានពូជ person of good breeding, from a good family

អ្នកមីង Aunt (Polite); title of respect for women of one's parents' generation

អ្នកមនាង (= អ្នកម្នាង) concubine or unofficial wife

អ្នកម៉ែ /neə̆q-mae/ Mother (respectful, rare)

អ្នកមុំ young lady (sarcastic)

អ្នកម្ដាយ Mother (respectful)

អ្នកយាយកោមលធិរាជ /-kaomŭəl-thiriəc/ title for palace women

អ្នកយាយចិត្តាភិសេក /-cəttaaphisaek/ title for palace women

អ្នកយាយទេពយុរយារ /-teepəyuurəyiə/ title for palace women

អ្នកយាយឯកអគ្គវង្សា /-qaek-qakeə̆q-wŭəŋsaa/ title for palace women

អ្នករត់កាសែត paperboy

អ្នករាជការ civil servant, government employee

អ្នករាំ dancer

អ្នកលក់ salesman, merchant

អ្នកលក់ទំនិញ salesman, merchant

អ្នកសីល wiseman, sage

អ្នកសីលធម៌និយម moralist, preceptor

អ្នកលើ uplander, highlander, hill people

អ្នកលេង gambler, playboy, rogue

អ្នកស្ដេច the king

អ្នកស្រី title or term of address for women of ordinary rank

អ្នកស្រុក rural people; inhabitants

អ្នកស្រុកស្រីប្រុស the villagers, both men and women

អ្នកស្រុកអាយ local residents

អ្នកស្រែ rice-farmer

អ្នកស្រែចំការ farmer

អ្នកអក title for older women in the palace

អ្នកអកមង្គលនារី /-mŭəŋkŭəl-niərii/ title

អ្នកអកវររាជវង្សា /-wɔreə̆q-riəc-wŭəŋsaa/ title

អ្នកអកស្រឹង្គានុរក្ស /-srəŋkiənureə̆q/ title

អ្នកអកអង្គអគ្គកញ្ញា /-qɑŋ-qakeə̆q-kaññaa/ title for women

អ្នកអង្គម្ចាស់ /neə̆q-qɑŋ-mcah/ title for offspring of a prince and a non-royal wife

អ្នកអង្គម្ចាស់ក្សត្រី /-ksatrəy/ Princess (daughter of a Prince and a non-royal wife)

អ្នកអើយ you, you there (Coll)

អ្នកឯង you (familiar or condescending)

អ្វី /qwəy/ what?; something, anything; whatever

អ្វីខ្លះ what? (pl.), what (specific) things?

អ្វីនោះទៅហ្ន៎! what's that?

+អ្ហះ /hah!/ derisive final particle

+អ្ហា /qaa!/ really?